Primary Source
Fluency Activities
WORLD CULTURES
THROUGH TIME

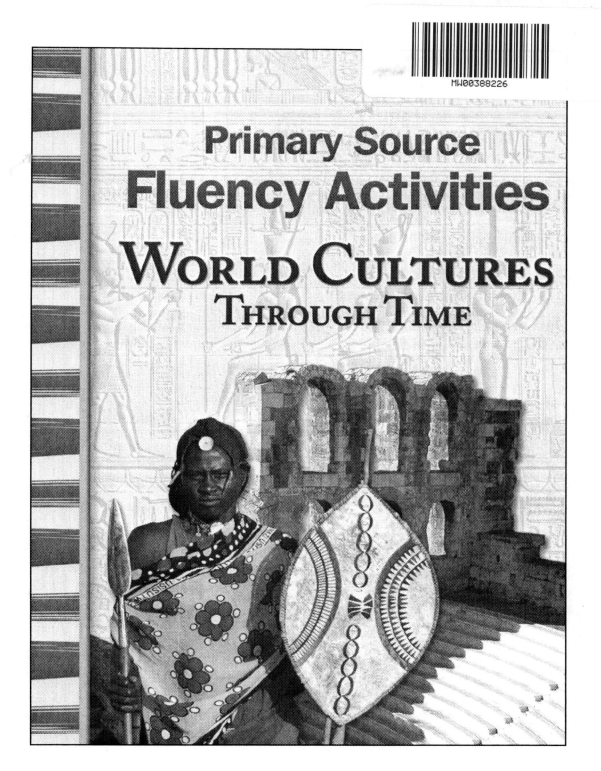

Author

Kathleen Knoblock

SHELL EDUCATION

Editor
Conni Medina

Editorial Assistant
Kathryn Kiley

Editorial Director
Emily R. Smith, M.A.Ed.

Editor-in-Chief
Sharon Coan, M.S.Ed.

Editorial Manager
Gisela Lee, M.A.

Creative Director
Lee Aucoin

Cover Designer
Lesley Palmer

Illustration Manager/Designer
Timothy J. Bradley

Imaging
Phil Garcia
Don Tran

Publisher
Corinne Burton, M.A.Ed.

Shell Education
5301 Oceanus Drive
Huntington Beach, CA 92649-1030
http://www.shelleducation.com
ISBN 978-1-4258-0102-1
© 2007 Shell Education

Table of Contents

Table of Contents *(cont.)*

Introduction to Teaching Fluency

By Dr. Timothy Rasinski
Kent State University

Why This Book?

This book was developed in response to the need we have heard from teachers for good texts for teaching reading fluency within the content areas. Within the past several years, reading fluency has become recognized as an essential element in elementary and middle grade reading programs (National Reading Panel, 2001). Readers who are fluent are better able to comprehend what they read—they decode words so effortlessly that they can devote their cognitive resources to the all-important task of comprehension instead of bogging themselves down in working to decode words they confront in their reading. They can also construct meaning (comprehension) by reading with appropriate expression and phrasing.

Readers develop fluency through guided practice and repeated readings—reading a text selection several times to the point where it can be expressed meaningfully—with appropriate expression and phrasing. Readers who engage in regular repeated readings, under the guidance and assistance of a teacher or other coach, improve their word recognition, reading rate, comprehension, and overall reading proficiency.

Students will find the texts in this book interesting and sometimes challenging. Students will especially want to practice the texts if you provide regular opportunities for them to perform the texts for their classmates, parents, and other audiences.

So, have fun with these passages. Read them with your students and read them again. Be assured that if you regularly have your students read and perform the texts in this book, you will go a long way to develop fluent readers who are able to decode words effortlessly and construct meaning through their interpretations of texts.

How to Use This Book

The texts in this book are meant to be read, reread, and performed. If students do this, they will develop as fluent readers, improving their ability to recognize words accurately and effortlessly, and reading with meaningful expression and phrasing. However, you, the teachers, are the most important part in developing instruction that uses these texts. In this section, we recommend ways in which you can use the texts with your students.

Introduction to Teaching Fluency (cont.)
By Dr. Timothy Rasinski

Scheduling and Practice

The texts should be read repeatedly over several days. We recommend that you introduce one text at a time and practice it over the next three, four, or five days, depending on how quickly your students develop mastery over them. Write the text you are going to read on chart paper or put it on an overhead transparency.

Have the students read the text several times each day. They should read it a few times at the beginning of each day, read it several times during various breaks in the day, and read it multiple times at the end of each day.

Make two copies of the text for each student. Have students keep one copy at school in their "fluency folders." The other copy can be sent home for students to continue practicing with their families. Communicate to families the importance of children continuing to practice the text at home with their parents and other family members.

Coaching Your Students

A key ingredient to repeated reading is the coaching that comes from a teacher. As your students practice reading the target text each week—alone, in small groups, or as an entire class—be sure to provide positive feedback about their reading. Help them develop a sense for reading the text in such a way that it conveys the meaning that the author attempts to convey or the meaning that the reader may wish to convey. Through oral interpretation of a text, readers can express joy, sadness, anger, surprise, or any of a variety of emotions. Help students learn to use their reading to convey this level of meaning.

Teachers do this by listening from time to time as students read, and coaching them in the various aspects of oral interpretation. You may wish to suggest that students emphasize certain words, insert dramatic pauses, read a bit faster in one place, or slow down in other parts of the text. And, of course, lavish praise on students' best efforts to convey a sense of meaning through their reading. Although it may take a while for students to learn to develop this sense of "voice" in their reading, in the long run, it will lead to more engaged and fluent reading and higher levels of comprehension.

Introduction to Teaching Fluency (cont.)
By Dr. Timothy Rasinski

Word Study

Although the goal of the passages in this book is to develop fluent and meaningful oral reading, the practicing of passages should also provide opportunities to develop students' vocabulary and word decoding skills. Students may practice a passage repeatedly to the point where it is largely memorized. At this point, students may not be looking closely at the words in the text. By continually drawing attention to interesting and important words in the text, you can help students maintain their focus and develop an ongoing fascination with words.

After reading a passage several times through, ask students to choose words from the passage that they think are interesting or important. Put these words on a word wall, or ask students to add them to their personal word banks. Talk about the words—their meanings and spellings. Help students develop a deepened appreciation for these words. Encourage students to use these words in their oral and written language. You might, for example, ask students to use some of the words in their daily journal entries.

Once a list of words has been added to a classroom word wall or students' word banks, play various games with the words. One of our favorites is "word bingo." Here, students are given a card containing a 3 x 3, 4 x 4, or 5 x 5 grid. In each box, students randomly write words from the word wall or bank. The teacher then calls out words or sentences that contain the target words or definitions of the target words. Students find the words on their cards and cover them with markers. Once a horizontal, vertical, or diagonal line of words is covered, a student calls "Bingo" and wins the game.

Have students sort the chosen words along a variety of dimensions—by syllable; part of speech; presence of a certain phonics feature, such as long vowel sound or a consonant blend; or by meaning (e.g., words that express how a person can feel and words that don't). Through sorting-and-categorizing activities, students get repeated exposure to words, examining the words differently with each sort.

No matter how you do it, make examining selected words from the passages part of your regular instructional routine for these fluency texts. The time spent in word study will most definitely improve students' overall fluency.

Introduction to Teaching Fluency (cont.)
By Dr. Timothy Rasinski

Performance

After several days of practice, arrange a special time for the students to perform the text, as well as other ones practiced from previous days. This performance time can range from 5 minutes to 30 minutes. Find a special person (such as the principal) to listen to your students perform. You may also want to invite a neighboring class, parents, or community members. Have the students perform the targeted text as a group. Later you can have individuals or groups of students perform the text again, as well as other texts that have been practiced previously.

As an alternative to having your students perform for a group that comes to your room, you may also want to send your students to visit other adults and students on campus and perform for them. Principals, school secretaries, custodians, playground aides, and visitors to the campus are usually great audiences for students' readings. Tape recording and video taping your students' readings is another way to create a performance opportunity.

Regardless of how you do it, it is important that you create the opportunity for your students to perform for an audience. The magic of the performance will give students the motivation to want to practice their assigned texts.

Performance Not Memorization

Remember that the key to developing fluency is guided oral and silent reading practice. Students become more fluent when they read the texts repeatedly. Reading requires students to actually see the words in the texts. Thus, it is important that you do not require students to memorize the texts they are practicing and performing. Memorization leads students away from visually examining the words. Although students may want to try to memorize the texts, the instructional emphasis needs to be on reading with expression so that an audience will enjoy the students' oral renderings of the texts. Keep students' eyes on the texts whenever possible.

One of the most important things we can do to promote proficient and fluent reading is to have students practice reading meaningful passages with a purpose—to perform them. This program provides students with just those opportunities to create meaning with their voices as well as the wonderful words in these primary sources.

How to Use This Product

General Information

This book contains reader's theater scripts, proverbs, poems, stories, fables, book excerpts, and songs. Activities for each lesson teach important fluency strategies as well as an understanding of world cultures through time. Some lessons also contain primary source photographs. These photographs help students understand the changes and developments that have occurred over time.

Depending on the reading levels of your students, you may find some of these pieces too difficult to use at the beginning of the year. Instead, focus on the pieces that have a lower reading level. This book is set up to help your students be successful and fluent readers. Instead of just reading the text once and moving on, the students practice and reread the pieces in preparation for authentic presentations. That way, not only does their fluency grow through careful repetition, but as the class discusses the pieces, the students' comprehension improves as well.

Side Trips

In addition to the regular fluency lessons, scattered throughout this book are optional Side Trips—opportunities for students to read more, learn more, or apply a variety of thinking skills to tasks related to the topics. These are intended to supplement and extend the lessons.

Presentations

One of the most important aspects of these lessons are the presentation pieces. The author and editors of this book have tried to provide you with plenty of ideas. If the idea suggested for a certain piece will not work for your classroom situation, flip through the book and look for other suggestions that might be suitable. The key is that you have the students practice reading the pieces for authentic reasons. If the end presentations are always just to their own classes, students will quickly lose interest. Once they have lost interest in the performance, they will not work as hard at perfecting their fluency. You will not see much growth in your students if they feel that all their practice is for nothing.

Instead, be creative and fun as you plan these presentations. Invite different guests, such as parents or administrators in to watch the presentations. Performing for other classes will give students the experiences that they need. Other classes make great audiences if the content is something they are also studying.

How to Use This Product *(cont.)*

Presentations *(cont.)*

If you have a hard time finding people to whom your class can present, try to tie the presentations into celebrations or holidays. Some possible times to hold presentations might include Presidents' Day, the beginning of spring, Memorial Day, Flag Day, the first day of summer, Father's Day, Labor Day, the beginning of autumn, Thanksgiving, and the first day of winter. Do not forget about celebrations that take place over whole months. Some of these include Black History Month, American Indian Heritage Month, Hispanic Heritage Month, and Women's History Month.

Finally, try to tie your presentations into schoolwide events. For example, you could have your students add to the school's morning announcements. Or, you could present one of the selections as part of a multicultural celebration, literacy day, or arts festival. Consider teaming with other teachers or grade levels to hold a Poetry Celebration or Storytellers Celebration. Remember, your students' fluency will only improve if you make the performances important and authentic.

Reader's Theater

Throughout the lessons in this book, you will find numerous reader's theater scripts. This is an exciting and easy method of providing students with the opportunity to practice fluency leading to a performance. Because reader's theater minimizes the use of props, sets, costumes, and memorization, it is an easy way to present a play in the classroom. Students read from a book or prepared script using their voices to bring text to life. Reader's theater has the following characteristics:

1. The script is always read and never memorized.
2. Readers may be characters or narrators, or they may switch back and forth.
3. The readers may sit, stand, or do both, but they do not have to perform any other actions.
4. Readers use only eye contact, facial expressions, and vocal expression to express emotion.
5. Scripts may be from books, songs, poems, letters, etc. They can be performed directly from the original material or adapted specifically for the reader's theater performance.
6. Musical accompaniment or soundtracks may be used but are not necessary.
7. Very simple props may be used, especially with younger children, to help the audience identify the roles played by the readers.
8. Practice for the reader's theater should consist of coached repeated readings that lead to a smooth, fluent presentation.

How to Use This Product (cont.)

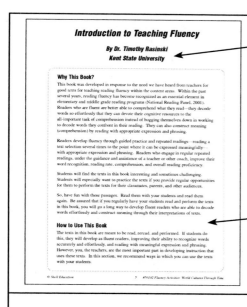

Introduction Written by Dr. Timothy Rasinski

- In a survey conducted by the National Reading Panel, fluency was determined to be one of the five research-based components of reading. Dr. Timothy Rasinski from Kent State University is an expert on teaching students to become fluent readers. His book *The Fluent Reader* is an excellent resource of oral reading strategies for building word recognition, fluency, and comprehension.

How to Use This Book

- Dr. Rasinski's introduction contains important information and ideas of how to use this book with your readers.

Objective

- A fluency objective is included for each lesson. This objective tells you which fluency strategy will be practiced within the lesson. See pages 13–14 for descriptions of the fluency strategies used within this book.

Fluency Suggestions and Activities

- These steps in the lesson plan describe how to introduce the piece to your students. Suggestions for ways to practice and perform the piece are also provided for your use. Remember that authentic performances are very important to ensure successful fluency for your readers.

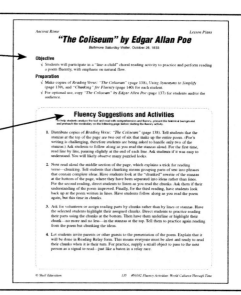

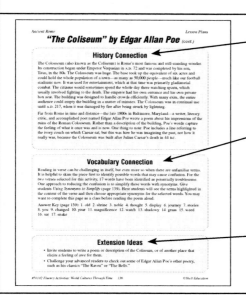

History Connection

- Each text in this book relates to world cultures. Information in each lesson gives you the historical context of the people and places of the time period.

Vocabulary Connection

- Vocabulary words have been chosen and defined for your use. Introduce the words to your students and have them define the words or simply record the definitions on the board for student reference.

Extension Ideas

- Extension ideas are given for each lesson. These ideas are usually fun, challenging, and interesting.

How to Use This Product (cont.)

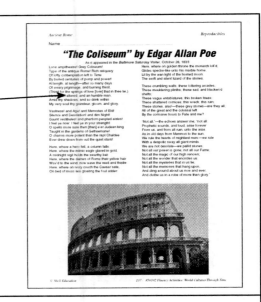

Primary Sources

- For each lesson, a copy of at least one primary source is provided. These texts are ideal for developing an understanding of world cultures through time. The teacher can make copies of this page, or use it to create an overhead transparency.

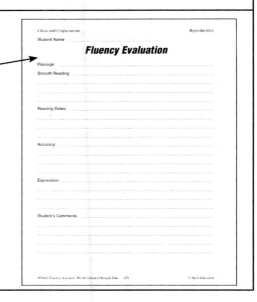

Fluency Texts

- The fluency texts provided are designed to be read and reread to promote fluency. The texts differ in strategy, but most are designed for students to work together in small groups or as a whole class. There are also reader's theater scripts for the students to perform.

Fluency Evaluations

- At the end of some lessons, there are Fluency Evaluations. Students can listen to a tape-recording of their performance and complete the forms. This is a great way for students to evaluate their own fluency.

Fluency Strategy Descriptions

Below are brief descriptions of the fluency strategies taught through the lessons in this book. These descriptions provide teachers with basic information about the strategies before beginning the lessons.

Antiphonal Reading/Divided Reading

In this version of choral reading, the text is divided, and assigned sections are read by students or groups of students.

Call and Response/Refrain

Call and response is a type of choral reading. One student reads a portion, and then the class or a group responds by reading the next portion in unison. When the response portion is repetition of the same text, it is called a refrain.

Choral Reading

In choral reading, groups of students read the same text aloud together, rather than single students reading while the others just listen. This engages students in the reading and increases reading time by all students.

Cumulative Choral Reading

In this strategy, a single student begins reading. Then others join in along the way, so that by the end everyone is reading in unison. This can also be done in reverse.

General Oral Reading/Supported Reading

Here, the focus is just on engaging students to read aloud, with or without extra support.

Oral Preview

Oral preview involves having students hear how the text should sound when reading fluently, before they attempt to read it themselves. This strategy is especially helpful for students who are English Language Learners or who need more support. It is used in conjunction with other strategies.

Paired Reading/Dialogue

These strategies involve two readers sharing the presentation of the text. In paired reading, this can be two students, a student and an adult, a student and an older student, or a student and teacher. In its pure form, this strategy involves pairing a more proficient reader with a less proficient one, so that the stronger one can support the other.

Poem for Two Voices

A poem, verse, or song is divided to be read orally by two voices. Those voices can be individuals or groups. Some lines or parts may be read in unison.

Radio Reading

The twist in this strategy is to have students read orally as if on the radio. Providing props, such as microphones, increases the students' awareness of their tone, diction, volume, etc. Radio reading can be done by individuals, pairs, or groups.

Reader's Theater

With this method, the text is read in the form of a script. It is like a play, but with some important differences. Although the students practice for the performance, they read their lines, instead of memorizing them. There may be simple props, but there are no costumes, sets, or action. The script may have a few parts, many parts, and even parts read by all participants.

Repeated Reading

Rather than being called upon to orally read unfamiliar text, repeated reading gives students chance to get to know the text before being asked to perform it. The opportunity to practice increases both willingness and proficiency with regard to oral reading. This method is incorporated into all of the lessons in this book.

Fluency Strategy Chart

Lesson Title	Choral Reading					General Oral Reading/ Supported Reading	Reader's Theater	Repeated Reading
	Call and Response/ Cumulative Reading	Antiphonal and Divided Reading/ Refrain	Radio Reading/ Oral Preview	Poem for Two or More Voices	Paired Reading/ Dialogue			
Mesopotamia/Babylonia								
A Sumerian Poem		X						X
A Description of Mesopotamia					X			X
The Code of Hammurabi	X				X	X		X
Ten Babylonian Proverbs						X		X
Side Trip: Seven Wonders of the Ancient World			X					X
Ancient Egypt								
The Shipwrecked Sailor							X	X
Hymn to the Nile	X							X
Side Trip: History of Plumbing in Egypt						X		X
Herodotus's Description of Mummification						X		X
Exodus from Egypt	X							X
Ancient Greece								
Ancient Greek Olympics							X	X
Aesop's Fables						X		X
Plato and Socrates					X			X
Alexander the Great							X	X
Side Trip: Homer and the *Odyssey*				X				X
India, Hinduism, and Buddhism								
Arrian's Description of India			X			X		X
Side Trip: Reflection on Society					X			X
One Law There Is	X							X
Buddha and His Teachings		X						X
Tales from Ancient India						X		X

Fluency Strategy Chart (cont.)

Material for Student Reading	Choral Reading					General Oral Reading/ Supported Reading	Reader's Theater	Repeated Reading
	Call and Response/ Cumulative Reading	Antiphonal and Divided Reading/ Refrain	Radio Reading/ Oral Preview	Poem for Two or More Voices	Paired Reading/ Dialogue			
China and Confucianism								
San Zi Jing (Three Character Classic)								X
Side Trip: Lun Yu—The Analects of Confucius						X		X
Marco Polo's City of Heaven		X			X			X
An Old Chinese Poem				X				X
Side Trip: When I Went to School in China						X		X
Side Trip: Try Your Hand at Chinese								
Ancient Rome								
Julius Caesar	X	X						X
"The Coliseum" by Edgar Allan Poe				X				X
The Last Day of Pompeii							X	X
Sub-Saharan Africa								
Ibn Battuta's Travels to Mali			X					X
I Was Taken from My Village and Sold!						X		X
The Magic Flyswatter: A Hero Tale of the Congo							X	X
The Mayas, Incas, and Aztecs								
The Mystery of the Mayas					X	X		X
Side Trip: The Mayan Numeral System								
The Incas of Peru		X						X
Sacred Songs of the Aztec	X			X				
Side Trip 1: Legends of Foundation of Mexico								
Side Trip 2: Before and After the Conquest								X

A Sumerian Poem

Objective

√ Students will participate in a cooperative choral reading activity that focuses on mood and tone in order to enhance expressive reading skills.

Preparation

√ Makes copies of the world map (pages 188–189) for each student.

√ Make a transparency of *A Sumerian Poem for Divided Reading* (page 19).

√ Copy *A Sumerian Poem for Divided Reading* (page 19) and *Checking Out* (page 20) for each student.

Fluency Suggestions and Activities

To help students analyze the text and read with comprehension and fluency, present the historical background and preteach the vocabulary on the following page before starting the fluency activity.

1. Ask students to locate Iraq on their maps. Tell them to help each other until everyone finds it. Next, have students find the location of Mesopotamia, and then specifically Sumer.

2. Project the transparency of the poem. Use a blank sheet of paper to block out all but the first stanza. Ask students to follow along as you read aloud. Be sure to read the poem with appropriate expression and fluency. Follow by asking students to comment on the mood and content of the text. Ask what clues the author gives about the cause of his feelings and which words set the tone. Continue in this same manner, demonstrating fluent reading and discussing the remaining stanzas.

3. When the entire poem has been read once and appears in its entirety on the screen, ask a volunteer to reread aloud the first stanza, but make it sound happy. Ask another student to read the second stanza as if a robot were reciting it. Continue through in this manner with each stanza being read in a different style.

4. Have the poem read aloud a third time with volunteers using the correct expression and pausing. Finally, for the fourth reading ask students to reread the whole poem in "silent voice," which means hearing themselves read it aloud in their heads.

5. Distribute copies of *Checking Out* (page 20). Have students complete it to self-check their comprehension of the poem. Note: If they answer all the questions correctly, students will get the answer, "The dude was dying."

6. Distribute copies of *A Sumerian Poem for Divided Reading* (page 19). Divide the class into six groups and assign each group a stanza. Then direct students to practice reading their stanzas until they can read them aloud fluently. Tell them to prepare for a presentation in which they read their stanzas in unison or take turns reading one line each.

7. On presentation day, ask one of your students to act out the role of the writer and pantomime the feelings and emotions expressed as the stanzas are read. If you like, invite the student to be wrapped in a white sheet and reclining while the poem is read.

A Sumerian Poem (cont.)

History Connection

Mesopotamia is a term used to describe a large area of fertile valleys lying between the Tigris and the Euphrates rivers. Here, "between the rivers," sprang up some of the earliest civilizations. Today it is the country of Iraq. In the south of this region, in what is now parts of Kuwait and northern Saudi Arabia, a unique group of people thrived for more than 1,000 years. They lived in city-states. They had organized government and laws. They had human monarchs (kings) and spiritual deities (gods and goddesses). The area was called Sumer and the people, Sumerians. Perhaps most interesting of all, Sumerians developed a language unlike any other known to modern historians. Today the Sumerian language is preserved only on clay tablets written in cuneiform, which is a system of wedge-like strokes made with a reed. It resembles Egyptian hieroglyphics, but it is more abstract than picture writing. When the Assyrians and Babylonians later dominated the region, an alphabet based on syllables was developed. Cuneiform became extinct.

"Ludlul Bêl Nimeqi" was written on clay tablets in cuneiform in 1700 B.C. The poem contained at least 64 stanzas by an official of Nippur, the religious capital of Sumer. The author's Sumerian name is Laluralim. He may have been one of the early kings of the region. Though 3,700 years old, the poem's subject is one that is just as relevant and emotional today—the fear and helplessness of knowing one's death is imminent.

Vocabulary Connection

Discuss unfamiliar vocabulary encountered in the text. Begin with these and then add any others you feel need to be reviewed or introduced. Discuss the words' meanings and how they are used specifically in the context of the source.

- **uprightness**—moral and honorable behavior
- **oracle**—message believed to come from a god; prophecy
- **libation**—liquid, such as oil or wine, poured as a religious offering
- **seer, diviner**—someone who is able to see or predict the future
- **necromancer**—someone who communicates with the dead to influence the future
- **conjurer**—one who practices magic
- **transfixed**—immobilized by shock; pierced through with a weapon or object
- **asunder**—into parts or pieces

Extension Ideas

- Have students work individually or in pairs to rewrite one of the poem's stanzas in simpler, modern language. Example: (Line 1) *I advanced in life, I attained to the allotted span:* I got old and was running out of time . . .
- The poem is untitled. Ask students to come up with a good title for it.

Name_____

A Sumerian Poem for Divided Reading

Excerpts from "Ludlul Bêl Nimeqi" (1700 B.C.)
By an official of Nippur who may have been an early king of Sumer

R1: I advanced in life, I attained to the allotted span
Wherever I turned there was evil, evil—
Oppression is increased, uprightness I see not.
I cried unto god, but he showed not his face.

R2: I prayed to my goddess, but she raised not her head.
The seer by his oracle did not discern the future
Nor did the enchanter with a libation illuminate my case
I consulted the necromancer, but he opened not my understanding.
The conjurer with his charms did not remove my ban.

R3: How deeds are reversed in the world!
I look behind, oppression encloses me
Like one who the sacrifice to god did not bring
And at meal-time did not invoke the goddess
Did not bow down his face, his offering was not seen;

R4: What in one's heart is contemptible, to one's god is good!
Who can understand the thoughts of the gods in heaven?
The counsel of god is full of destruction; who can understand?
Where may human beings learn the ways of God?
He who lives at evening is dead in the morning;

R5: With a whip he has beaten me; there is no protection;
With a staff he has transfixed me; the stench was terrible!
All day long the pursuer pursues me,
In the night watches he lets me breathe not a moment
Through torture my joints are torn asunder;

R6: The diviner has not improved the condition of my sickness—
The duration of my illness the seer could not state;
The god helped me not, my hand he took not;
The goddess pitied me not, she came not to my side
The coffin yawned; my heirs took my possessions.

Name_____

Checking Out

Directions: You have read a poem written by a Sumerian in 1700 B.C. Read each statement below, and follow the directions based on your answer.

1. In the first stanza, the author is disgusted with the behavior of the people around him. If this statement is true, write **D** on blank 1. If it is false, write **S**.

2. In the second stanza, the author says that the oracle predicted his future and thus, his fate. If this statement is true, write **A** on blank 2. If it is false, write **U**.

3. In the same stanza, the author thought that giving an offering to the goddess would get her attention. If this statement is true, write **D** on blank 3. If it is false, write **N**.

4. The author believed that the living could contact the dead. If this statement is true, write **E** on blank 4. If it is false, write **I**.

5. In the third stanza, the author admits that he didn't always give sacrifices, praise the gods, or bow down to them. If this statement is true, write **L** on blank 5. If it is false, write **W**.

6. In the third stanza, the author thinks that he deserves a better fate than what he faces. If this statement is true, write **A** on blank 6. If it is false, write **P**.

7. In the fourth stanza, the author is getting angry because he doesn't understand why the gods aren't doing something about his condition. If this statement is true, write **S** on blank 7. If it is false, write **G**.

8. In the same stanza, the author asks God to take him now rather than let him die in his sleep. If this statement is true, write **N** on blank 8. If it is false, write **D**.

9. In the fifth stanza, the author changes from feeling rage at others to feeling helpless to defend himself. If this statement is true, write **Y** on blank 9. If it is false, write **H**.

10. In the fifth stanza, the author states that he is pursued day and night—by a man who beats and tortures him. If this statement is true, write **B** on blank 10. If it is false, write **I**.

11. Also in the fifth stanza, the author implies that he cannot run away or escape from what tortures him—fear. If this statement is true, write **N** on blank 11. If it is false, write **E**.

12. Finally, in the sixth stanza, the author is complaining that no one has helped him, and to add insult to injury, even though he is not yet gone, his heirs are acting as if he is already dead. If this statement is true, write **G** on blank 12. If it is false, write **E**.

The author of this poem was angry, frustrated, disappointed, old, sick, and scared—all because he was having trouble accepting something. What was it?

T H E ___ ___ ___ ___ ___ ___ ___ ___ ___ ___ ___ ___ !
        1 2 3 4   5 6 7   8 9 10 11 12

A Description of Mesopotamia

Objective

√ Students will deliver a group choral reading presentation and read passages fluently after practicing with repeated readings.

Preparation

√ Ask students to have their copies of the world map (pages 188–189) from the previous lesson.

√ Copy *Pliny Describes Mesopotamia: Presentation in Two Voices* (pages 24–25) for each student.

Fluency Suggestions and Activities

To help students analyze the text and read with comprehension and fluency, present the historical background and preteach the vocabulary on the following page before starting the fluency activity.

1. Ask students to locate Mesopotamia on their maps (pages 188–189). Remind students that Mesopotamia was an area in which civilizations developed and thrived 2,000 years before Christ. By the first century A.D., knowledge about the area and cultures was ancient history. Explain that they will be reading a description of Mesopotamia by a Roman author, Pliny the Elder, written in A.D. 23–79 as history!

2. Distribute copies of *Pliny Describes Mesopotamia: Presentation in Two Voices* (pages 24–25). The full excerpt is provided on page 23. For the first reading, tell students that you will read the part of Pliny, and ask for a volunteer to read the part of the Student. (Choose someone who will be able to read the commentary text fluently without rehearsal.) Ask students to follow along as the two of you read aloud. For the second reading, choose a different student to take the part of the Student. This time have the student read the commentary in hushed tones, as though he or she were giving the audience a whispered account of what is happening.

3. Read the script at least two more times—right then, or perhaps as the first activity each of the next few mornings. First switch to you reading the part of the Student, and two new volunteers reading the part of Pliny together. This way they can support each other as they read. The next time, choose another pair of students to read the part of Pliny and a new volunteer to read the part of the Student so that the students have taken over the reading.

4. By this point, students should be reasonably familiar with the text. Explain to students that the word *voice* can mean a single voice or a group reading in unison. Divide the class into three or four performance troupes. Then divide each troupe into the two voice parts. You can assign one person to perform the part of the Student and the rest to perform the part of Pliny, divide the group equally, or devise any combination you feel works best.

5. Give each troupe time to reread and rehearse. Hold a dress rehearsal, or final run-through, in class to iron out any wrinkles. Then send each troupe to a prearranged performance for a social studies, history, literature, drama, or general-education class in your school.

A Description of Mesopotamia *(cont.)*

History Connection

By the time that the years were passing from B.C. into A.D., the Roman Empire was well established. It was the center of power and culture for much of the known world for hundreds of years. A well-educated Roman named Gaius Plinius Secundus, who lived in the first century A.D., became impassioned with writing about the knowledge of his time. His nephew later described his zeal for his work: "In the country it was only the time when he was actually in his bath that was exempted from study. When traveling, as though freed from every other care, he devoted himself to study alone. In short, he deemed all time wasted that was not employed in study."* The older man is known as Pliny the Elder; his nephew, Pliny the Younger.

Pliny the Elder produced an enormous amount of writings—from recording events of his time and grand biographical and historical accounts, to describing plants and the mundane concerns of grammar and rhetoric. Only one of Pliny the Elder's works survives. In the extensive *Naturalis Historia (The Natural History),* Pliny created an encyclopedia of the vast knowledge he gathered from his own and others' experiences. Pliny's description of Mesopotamia, from this work written in the first century, gives those of us living in the twenty-first century an eye-opening perspective on history.

*From *The Letters of Pliny the Younger,* translated by William Melmoth, 1710–1799
Provided by Project Gutenberg Literary Archive Foundation

Vocabulary Connection

Discuss unfamiliar vocabulary encountered in the text. Begin with these and then add any others you feel need to be reviewed or introduced. Discuss the words' meanings and how they are used specifically in the context of the material.

- **reckoning**—counting or calculating
- **quay**—waterside platform where boats are loaded and unloaded
- **channel**—a passage of water, especially one that has been deepened by dredging
- **transverse**—lying or extending crosswise

You may also want to introduce new names and places presented in the text to familiarize students with their pronunciations: Pliny (PLIH-nee), Babylon (BAB-uh-lawn), Chaldaea (kawl-DEE-uh), Assyria (uh-SEER-ee-uh), Nearchus (NEER-kuhs), Onesicritus (own-es-IK-ri-toos), and Seleucia (suh-LOO-she-uh).

Extension Idea

- Present this challenge and offer a prize or an award such as "The Pliny." Obviously, Pliny had no computer or typewriter. In fact, the printing press wouldn't be invented by Johannes Gutenberg for another 1,400 years. So, how did Pliny do his writing, and how were his volumes of books produced? Challenge students to be the first to find out! Remind them to consider themselves lucky—unlike Pliny, they have the World Wide Web of information at their fingertips.

Name_____

Pliny Describes Mesopotamia

Excerpt from Pliny the Elder's *The Natural History*

Babylon, the capital of the nations of Chaldæa, long enjoyed the greatest celebrity of all cities throughout the whole world: and it is from this place that the remaining parts of Mesopotamia and Assyria received the name of Babylonia. The circuit of its walls, which were two hundred feet in height, was sixty miles. These walls were also fifty feet in breadth, reckoning to every foot three fingers' breadth beyond the ordinary measure of our foot. The river Euphrates flowed through the city, with quays of marvelous workmanship erected on either side. The temple there—of Jupiter Belus is still in existence; he was the first inventor of the science of Astronomy. In all other respects it has been reduced to a desert, having been drained of its population in consequence of its vicinity to Seleucia, founded for that purpose by Nicator, at a distance of ninety miles, on the confluence of the Tigris and the canal that leads from the Euphrates. Seleucia, however, still bears the surname of Babylonia: it is a free and independent city, and retains the features of the Macedonian manners.

It is said that the population of this city amounts to six hundred thousand, and that the outline of its walls resembles an eagle with expanded wings: its territory, they say, is the most fertile in all the East. The Parthi again, in its turn, founded Ctesiphon, for the purpose of drawing away the population of Seleucia, at a distance of nearly three miles, and in the district of Chalonitis; Ctesiphon is now the capital of all the Parthian kingdoms. Finding, however, that this city did not answer the intended purpose, king Vologesus has of late years founded another city in its vicinity, Vologesocerta by name.

Besides the above, there are still the following towns in Mesopotamia: Hipparenum, rendered famous, like Babylon, by the learning of the Chaldæi, and situated near the river Narraga, which falls into the Narroga, from which a city so called has taken its name. The Persæ destroyed the walls of Hipparenum. Orchenus also, a third place of learning of the Chaldæi, is situated in the same district, towards the south; after which come the Notitæ, the Orothophanitæ, and the Grecichartæ. From Nearchus and Onesicritus we learn that the distance by water from the Persian Sea to Babylon, up the Euphrates, is four hundred and twelve miles; other authors, however, who have written since their time, say that the distance to Seleucia is four hundred and forty miles: and Juba says that the distance from Babylon to Charax is one hundred and seventy-five. Some writers state that the Euphrates continues to flow with an undivided channel for a distance of eighty-seven miles beyond Babylon, before its waters are diverted from their channel for the purposes of irrigation; and that the whole length of its course is not less than twelve hundred miles. The circumstance that so many different authors have treated of this subject, accounts for all these variations, seeing that even the Persian writers themselves do not agree as to what is the length of their schœni and para-sangœ, each assigning to them a different length.

Name_____

Pliny Describes Mesopotamia: Presentation in Two Voices

Adaptation of an excerpt from Pliny the Elder's *The Natural History*

First Voice: Pliny the Elder, reading from his text *The Natural History*, in A.D. 75

Second Voice: Modern student, commenting on Pliny's text in the twenty-first century

Pliny: *Babylon, the capital of the nations of Chaldaea, long enjoyed the greatest celebrity of all cities throughout the whole world: and it is from this place that the remaining parts of Mesopotamia and Assyria received the name of Babylonia.*

Student: Chaldaea was the name given to the ancient region of Mesopotamia between the Euphrates River and the Persian Gulf, in modern-day southern Iraq.

Pliny: *The circuit of its walls, which were 200 feet in height, was 60 miles. These walls were also 50 feet in breadth, reckoning to every foot three fingers' breadth beyond the ordinary measure of our foot.*

Student: Pliny is saying that the city of Babylon was surrounded by a wall 200 feet high and 60 miles long. He also says that the wall was 50 feet thick.

Pliny: *The river Euphrates flowed through the city, with quays of marvelous workmanship erected on either side. The temple there—of Jupiter Belus—is still in existence; he was the first inventor of the science of astronomy.*

Student: Pliny says there is a temple in Babylon devoted to the god Jupiter Belus. Although Belus is a name applied to various gods in Babylonian religion, the word Belus in Latin can signify the title "Lord" or "Master." Rather than it being a name, Pliny was likely using it as a title of respect for the Roman god Jupiter.

Pliny: *From Nearchus and Onesicritus we learn that the distance by water from the Persian Sea to Babylon, up the Euphrates, is 412 miles.*

Student: Nearchus was an officer in Alexander the Great's army. His travels in the fourth century B.C. took him as far as the Euphrates River. Onesicritus was a writer who used considerable liberty in his accounts of history and in his biography of Alexander the Great.

Pliny Describes Mesopotamia: Presentation in Two Voices (cont.)

Pliny: *Other authors, however, who have written say that the distance to Seleucia is 440 miles . . . Some writers state that the Euphrates continues to flow with an undivided channel for a distance of 87 miles beyond Babylon, before its waters are diverted from their channel for the purposes of irrigation; and that the whole length of its course is not less than 1,200 miles.*

Student: Seleucia refers to a city on the Tigris a little south of what is now Baghdad, Iraq. The Tigris River originates in Turkey, the Euphrates in Syria. Both rivers transverse the entirety of Iraq on their way to Persian Gulf.

Pliny: *The fact that so many different authors have written about this subject accounts for all these variations, seeing that even the Persian writers themselves do not agree as to what is the length.*

Student: Considering that the calculations were made 1,500 years before Columbus set sail, we might question the accuracy of any of these ancient geographers' accounts of distances. After all, their modes of travel were limited to boat, beast, or their own two feet. But, when we compare our modern measurements against theirs, they are amazingly close. So, without the even the thought of the possibility of human flight, let alone the aid of satellite photos, the ancient geographers were only a few miles off in their computations!

The Code of Hammurabi

Objective
√ Students will participate in a call-and-response choral-reading activity to practice and perform reading fluently in a whole-group presentation.

Preparation
√ Copy *Selected Laws from Hammurabi's Code* (pages 28–30) for each student.

√ Prior to the lesson, choose an appropriate part (there are 32 individual parts) for each of your students to perform and jot down the names on your own copy. For example, you could assign the one-line parts to students who have limited English or would be intimidated by longer passages.

√ For optional use, copy *Abridged Prologue and Epilogue* (page 31) for selected students.

Fluency Suggestions and Activities

To help students analyze the text and read with comprehension and fluency, present the historical background and preteach the vocabulary on the following page before starting the fluency activity.

1. Distribute copies of *Selected Laws from Hammurabi's Code* (pages 28–30). Tell students that this list represents only a fraction of the 282 rules in the complete document, and that the selected laws have been renumbered and broken into parts. The first part states the action or behavior addressed in the law, and the second part gives the consequence.

2. Present the following example: "If a sister of god open a tavern, or enter a tavern to drink, then shall this woman be burned to death." (Law 110) The first part—the "if" statement—is the action or behavior. The second part—the "then" statement—tells the consequence.

3. Explain to students that they will present these laws as a group. Each student will be assigned at least one rule. They will read the first part—the action—aloud on their own. Then everyone will join in to read the second part—the result.

4. Announce the preselected assignment of parts. Have each student write the number(s) of the law(s) he or she was given at the top of the first page. Then direct students to practice reading their assigned rule alone, with a partner, and at home, until they can read it fluently. Remind students that *fluently* means "smoothly," that is, without stumbling on words, chopping the text to bits, or sounding like a robot.

5. Next, direct students to follow along as you model reading the laws. Remind them to focus on how you read in phrases, respond to punctuation, and use your voice expressively.

6. The *Abridged Prologue and Epilogue* (page 31) is included as an option. If you have a few students who are especially interested in this topic and can read these passages independently, have them add these parts to the beginning and end of the performance.

7. Finally, invite your principal or other school administrator to your class to hear what your group has learned about how it was "in the good old days." Have your guest sit in the middle of the room, while your students form a circle around the perimeter, arranged in order of their speaking parts.

The Code of Hammurabi (cont.)

History Connection

As the ruler of Babylon from 1792 to 1750 B.C., Hammurabi expanded and united the Mesopotamia region to form the Babylonian Empire. He is best known today for his code of laws, 282 rules that cover everything from general behavior to specific business dealings. Hammurabi's Code was engraved on a *stele* (STEE-lee), a carved stone slab put on public display. The code begins with a lengthy explanation by Hammurabi about why he is qualified to make the rules, and ends with a proclamation that his decisions were made through his own exceptional wisdom and that his words should be followed "through all coming generations."

There is much modern speculation as to how these fit into the everyday lives of the largely illiterate people of the time. Was it really a list of functioning laws of the land or a just an ego-driven ruler's musings about morals and values? Either way, Hammurabi's Code is one of the earliest attempts to codify and establish law and order in society.

Today, most people consider Hammurabi's rules harsh and even cruel. But, the fact that many people are familiar with some of his rules almost 4,000 years later shows how his ideas—just or not—have influenced history. Who hasn't heard of "an eye for eye, a tooth for a tooth" as an argument for justice?

Vocabulary Connection

The translation of Hammurabi's Code is in comprehensible English, and the laws selected here are among the most straightforward. Discuss unfamiliar vocabulary encountered in the text. If students have difficulty with antiquated phrasing, offer this further clarification:

- **shall**—will
- **receive into**—bring in
- **cast his eye upon**—to look at or intend to steal
- **sustenance**—anything valuable (food, possessions, etc.)
- **hewn**—cut or chopped

Extension Idea

- Divide the class into cooperative learning groups of 5–6 students. Direct them to compose ten "If . . . then" statements that they think, if made into laws, would reduce crime today. Tell them to make their statements specific and reasonably fair so that a majority of citizens would have no difficulty accepting them as a code of conduct. After recording their final ten statements on a chart, ask groups to share their results with the class.

Name_____

Selected Laws from Hammurabi's Code

R1: If any one ensnare another, putting a ban upon him, but he can not prove it,

All: **then he that ensnared him shall be put to death.**

R2: If any one take a male or female slave of the court, or a male or female slave of a freed man, outside the city gates,

All: **he shall be put to death.**

R3: If any one receive into his house a runaway male or female slave of the court, or of a freedman, and does not bring it out at the public proclamation . . .

All: **the master of the house shall be put to death.**

R4: If any one find runaway male or female slaves in the open country and bring them to their masters,

All: **the master of the slaves shall pay him two shekels of silver.**

R5: If any one is committing a robbery and is caught,

All: **then he shall be put to death.**

R6: If fire break out in a house, and some one who comes to put it out cast his eye upon the property of the owner of the house, and take the property of the master of the house,

All: **he shall be thrown into that self-same fire.**

R7: If a chieftain or a man, who has been ordered to go upon the king's highway for war does not go, but hires a mercenary, if he withholds the compensation,

All: **then shall this officer or man be put to death, and he who represented him shall take possession of his house.**

R8: If a merchant entrust money to an agent for some investment, and the broker suffer a loss in the place to which he goes,

All: **he shall make good the capital to the merchant.**

R9: If the agent accept money from the merchant, but have a quarrel with the merchant (denying the receipt),

All: **then shall the merchant swear before God and witnesses that he has given this money to the agent, and the agent shall pay him three times the sum.**

R10: If any one be on a journey and entrust silver, gold, precious stones, or any movable property to another, and wish to recover it from him; if the latter do not bring all of the property to the appointed place, but appropriate it to his own use,

Selected Laws from Hammurabi's Code *(cont.)*

All: **then shall this man, who did not bring the property to hand it over, be convicted, and he shall pay fivefold for all that had been entrusted to him.**

R11: If any one fail to meet a claim for debt, and sell himself, his wife, his son, and daughter for money or give them away to forced labor:

All: **they shall work for three years in the house of the man who bought them, or the proprietor, and in the fourth year they shall be set free.**

R12: If he [the debtor] gave a male or female slave away for forced labor, and the merchant sublease them, or sell them for money,

All: **no objection can be raised.**

R13: If a man is taken prisoner in war, and there is a sustenance in his house, but his wife leave house and court, and go to another house: because this wife did not keep her court, and went to another house,

All: **she shall be judicially condemned and thrown into the water.**

R14: If a man take a wife, and she be seized by disease, if he then desire to take a second wife he shall not put away his wife, who has been attacked by disease,

All: **he shall keep her in the house which he has built and support her so long as she lives.**

R15: If after the woman had entered the man's house, both contracted a debt,

All: **both must pay the merchant.**

R16: If a State slave or the slave of a freed man marry the daughter of a free man, and children are born,

All: **the master of the slave shall have no right to enslave the children of the free.**

R17: If a son strike his father,

All: **his hands shall be hewn off.**

R18: If a man put out the eye of another man,

All: **his eye shall be put out.**

R19: If he break another man's bone,

All: **his bone shall be broken.**

R20: If he put out the eye of a freed man, or break the bone of a freed man,

All: **he shall pay one gold mina.**

R21: If he put out the eye of a man's slave, or break the bone of a man's slave,

All: **he shall pay one-half of its value.**

R22: If a man knock out the teeth of an equal,

All: **his teeth shall be knocked out.**

Selected Laws from Hammurabi's Code (cont.)

R23: If anyone strike the body of a man higher in rank than he,

All: **he shall receive 60 blows with an ox-whip in public.**

R24: If during a quarrel one man strike another and wound him,

All: **then he shall swear, "I did not injure him wittingly," and pay the physicians.**

R25: If a man strike a free-born woman so that she lose her unborn child,

All: **he shall pay ten shekels for her loss.**

R25: If the woman die,

All: **[the man's] daughter shall be put to death.**

R26: If a physician make a large incision with the operating knife, and kill [a patient] . . .

All: **his hands shall be cut off.**

R26: If a physician make a large incision in the slave of a freed man, and kill him,

All: **he shall replace the slave with another slave.**

R27: If a barber, without the knowledge of his master, cut the sign of a slave on a slave not to be sold,

All: **the hands of the barber shall be cut off.**

R28: If any one deceive a barber, and have him mark a slave not for sale with the sign of slave,

All: **he shall be put to death and buried in his house.**

R29: If a builder build a house for someone, and does not construct it properly, and the house which he built fall in and kill its owner,

All: **then the builder shall be put to death.**

R30: If a builder build a house for someone, even though he has not yet completed it, if then the walls start toppling,

All: **the builder must make the wall solid from his own means.**

R31: If any one agree with another to tend his field, give him seed, entrust a yoke of oxen to him, and bind him to cultivate the field, if he steal the corn or plants, and take them for himself,

All: **his hands shall be hewn off.**

R32: If a slave say to his master, "You are not my master," if they convict him,

All: **his master shall cut off his ear.**

Name_____

Abridged Prologue and Epilogue

Hammurabi's Prologue

When Anu the Sublime and Bel, the lord of Heaven and earth, called by name me, Hammurabi, the exalted prince, who feared God, to bring about the rule of righteousness in the land, to destroy the wicked and the evil-doers; so that the strong should not harm the weak; so that I should rule, and enlighten the land, to further the well-being of mankind.

Hammurabi, the prince, called of Bel am I, who conquered the four quarters of the world, made great the name of Babylon, who brought plenteous water to [the] inhabitants, reunited the scattered inhabitants of Isin; the divine king of the city; the Wise; the Mighty, the lord to whom come scepter and crown, with which he clothes himself; the pure prince, who cared for [the] inhabitants in their need, provided a portion for them in Babylon in peace; the shepherd of the oppressed and of the slaves; who recognizes the right, who rules by law; who humbles himself before the great gods; the royal scion of Eternity; the mighty monarch, the sun of Babylon, whose rays shed light over the land of Sumer and Akkad; the king, obeyed by the four quarters of the world; Beloved of Ninni, am I.

Hammurabi's Epilogue

Hammurabi, the protecting king am I. I have not withdrawn myself from the men, I was not negligent, but I made them a peaceful abiding-place. I expounded all great difficulties, I made the light shine upon them. With the mighty weapons entrusted to me, with the keen vision with which Ea endowed me, with the wisdom that Marduk gave me, I have uprooted the enemy, subdued the earth, brought prosperity to the land, guaranteed security to the inhabitants in their homes; a disturber was not permitted. The great gods have called me, I am the salvation-bearing shepherd, whose staff is straight, the good shadow that is spread over my city; on my breast I cherish the inhabitants of the land of Sumer and Akkad; in my shelter I have let them repose in peace; in my deep wisdom have I enclosed them. That the strong might not injure the weak, in order to protect the widows and orphans, in order to bespeak justice in the land, to settle all disputes, and heal all injuries, set up these my precious words, written upon my memorial stone, before the image of me, as king of righteousness.

The king who ruleth among the kings of the cities am I. My words are well considered; there is no wisdom like unto mine. In future time, through all coming generations, let the king who may be in the land, observe the words of righteousness which I have written on my monument. Let him not alter the law of the land which I have given. The decisions which I have made will this inscription show him; let him rule his subjects accordingly, speak justice to them, give right decisions, root out the miscreants and criminals from this land, and grant prosperity to his subjects.

Ten Babylonian Proverbs (1600 B.C.)

Objective

√ Students will analyze text for word groupings that affect comprehension, and then apply appropriate phrasing, or chunking, to practice reading orally with fluency.

Preparation

√ Copy *Chunking Babylonian Proverbs* (page 34) and *Ten Babylonian Proverbs to Read Aloud* (page 35) for each student.

√ For the optional Side Trip, make a transparency of *The Seven Wonders of the Ancient World* (page 34) and one copy of *The Seven Wonders of the Ancient World: Sign-up Sheet* (page 37).

Fluency Suggestions and Activities

To help students analyze the text and read with comprehension and fluency, present the historical background and preteach the vocabulary on the following page before starting the fluency activity.

1. In his book *The Fluent Reader* (page 32), Dr. Timothy Rasinski stresses the importance of phrasing, or chunking, to achieve comprehension in reading. Demonstrate this concept to students by writing the following sentence on the board: *The strong wind through the forest*. Ask students to read it silently and then raise their hands if they think this doesn't make sense. The explanation is that, as readers, we learn to look at text in chunks. Our minds automatically group certain words together, especially if they often appear together. Most readers will group "the strong wind" as a chunk, and "through the forest" as a chunk. If we do that in this case, the sentence doesn't make sense. Only when we chunk "the strong" (as the subject) and "wind through the forest" (as the predicate) can we comprehend the intended meaning of the sentence.

2. Distribute copies of *Chunking Babylonian Proverbs* (page 34). Explain that these ten proverbs, written in 1600 B.C., appear without internal punctuation. Students will try to decipher their meanings by breaking them into meaningful phrases, or chunks. Before they begin, have students listen (with pencils down) as you read the proverbs with natural fluency. Then challenge students to draw vertical lines between the words to show where they would separate chunks. If you like, give them this added information: Each proverb may have one or more chunks.

3. Review the completed page together. Have volunteers read aloud the proverbs, applying their chunking. Ask the rest of the students if they agree or disagree with how the reader chunked the proverb. Then reread it yourself aloud and invite students to change any divisions they think should be revised on their page.

4. Distribute copies of *Ten Babylonian Proverbs to Read Aloud* (page 35). Explain that these ten proverbs appear as they were written. Have students pair up to practice reading the proverbs aloud with appropriate chunking. Point out that punctuation marks offer clues, but students may need to do further chunking for the sentence to read smoothly.

5. Finally, have each pair of students listen to each other read the list of proverbs and complete the fluency evaluation at the bottom of the page.

Ten Babylonian Proverbs *(cont.)*

History Connection

Along with strict codes of conduct, such as Hammurabi's Code, the Babylonians also had common bits of wisdom known as proverbs. What is a proverb? A proverb (from the Latin *proverbium*) is a brief but important saying that gains acceptance from popular use. Most proverbs express some basic truth or practical advice. A proverb that describes a basic rule of conduct may also be known as a *maxim*.

These wise little sayings began to be popular about as soon as people had a written language with which to record them. Proverbs have been the study of such great thinkers as Aristotle and Plato, and not only survive in the modern age, but often address the same issues even when they come from different cultures and time periods. This is one way we know that people across time and distance have wrestled with similar thoughts about human nature.

Vocabulary Connection

Discuss unfamiliar vocabulary encountered in the text. Begin with these and then add any others you feel need to be reviewed or introduced. Discuss the words' meanings and how they are used specifically in the context of the selection.

- **vengeance**—revenge or punishment in return for a wrong
- **husk**—the outer covering of some nuts and grains (such as corn)
- **reeds**—tall, slender grass that grows in marshes and wet areas
- **course**—the actions one has decided to take; direction or route
- **prosperity**—success; wealth
- **servitude**—in the service of someone else; being ruled by another; slavery

Extension Ideas

- Have students choose five of the ten proverbs to paraphrase in modern wording.

- Challenge students to write a short story to which one of the proverbs serves as the story's lesson or moral. Then ask students to read their stories to a friend or family member.

- **Side Trip:** Use this optional activity to engage students in further study and give them practice using the 5W's + H to summarize information. Read *The Seven Wonders of the Ancient World* (page 36). Then review the directions and post *The Seven Wonders of the Ancient World: Sign-up Sheet* (page 37) as a sign-up sheet for researching one of the topics (independently or with partners). After students have completed the writing process and are ready to orally read their summaries, have them present their findings as a "radio reading." Make an "on the air" sign, set up a microphone, and invite students to read as if they were on the radio.

Name_____

Chunking Babylonian Proverbs

Directions: Below are ten Babylonian proverbs selected from the Library of Ashurbanipal (1600 B.C.). The proverbs are presented without punctuation, except for the final period or question mark. Your job is to mark how they should broken into meaningful phrases, or chunks, in order to be read aloud smoothly. The first one is done for you as an example:

- **A hostile act you shall not perform**   **that fear of vengeance shall not consume you.**

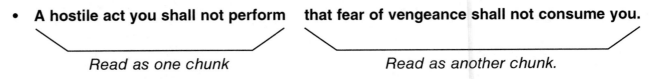

       Read as one chunk   *Read as another chunk.*

- If I put anything down it is snatched away.

- If I do more than expected who will repay me?

- The strong live by their own wages the weak by the wages of their children.

- If the husk is not right the kernel is not right and it will not produce seed.

- Does a marsh receive the price of its reeds or the fields the price of its vegetation?

- If you go and take the field of an enemy the enemy will come and take your field.

- Friendship in days of prosperity is servitude forever.

- He has dug a well where no water is.

- My knees go my feet are unwearied but a fool has cut into my course.

Name_____

Ten Babylonian Proverbs to Read Aloud

Part 1 Directions: Practice reading the Babylonian proverbs. Use phrasing, or chunking, to group words so that their meaning is clear. Read each chunk of words together so that the phrase is a thought rather than individual words. Practice until you think you can read the proverbs aloud fluently.

- A hostile act you shall not perform, that fear of vengeance shall not consume you.
- If I put anything down, it is snatched away.
- If I do more than expected, who will repay me?
- The strong live by their own wages; the weak by the wages of their children.
- If the husk is not right, the kernel is not right, and it will not produce seed.
- Does a marsh receive the price of its reeds, or the fields the price of its vegetation?
- If you go and take the field of an enemy, the enemy will come and take your field.
- Friendship in days of prosperity is servitude forever.
- He has dug a well where no water is.
- My knees go, my feet are unwearied; but a fool has cut into my course.

Part 2 Directions: Join with a partner. Take turns being reader and listener. The reader's job is to read aloud the proverbs as fluently as possible. The listener's job is to attend closely to how the reader reads and then give the reader feedback by filling out and signing the following evaluation.

Reader: _____ Listener: _____

Date read: _____ Number of times practiced prior to this: _____

The reading was	very smooth	somewhat smooth	choppy
The reading speed was	just right	too fast	too slow
The reader's volume was	just right	too loud	too soft
The words were pronounced	clearly	somewhat clearly	not clearly
The reader hesitated	never	a couple of times	many times
The reader used chunking	always	sometimes	not really

The best thing about this reading was _____

_____

This reader could use more practice or help with _____

_____

The Seven Wonders of the Ancient World

If asked to define "the world," you would probably say it is the planet Earth, including all its land, water, and inhabitants. This seems obvious, until you look at it from a perspective other than your own. For example, what is the world to an ant, a whale, or even a person who has never seen a book and who knows nothing beyond the village in which he lives? As you study history, it is important to remember the context—what was known and believed to be true in a particular time and place. With this in mind, think about how knowledgeable people in 500 B.C. might have confidently defined "the world." It was the limits of the known territory at the time—whether that was the jungle between two rivers in Central America, or the lands surrounding the Mediterranean Sea.

In the Greek-speaking world, spectacular human achievements of architecture were selected as the seven wonders. The monuments were chosen for their beauty, engineering skills, or just sheer size. These are the Seven Wonders of the Ancient World:

The Hanging Gardens of Babylon: A palace that may have been built between 604–562 B.C. by Babylonian King Nebuchadnezzar II on the bank of the Euphrates (in what is now Iraq)

The Great Pyramid at Giza: The 481-foot-high (175.75-meter) tomb built by and for Pharaoh Khufu of Egypt around 2560 B.C.

The Statue of Zeus at Olympia: A huge representation of the Greek god at the site of the Olympics, sculpted about 430 B.C. and adorned with ivory, gold, and other precious metals

The Temple of Artemis at Ephesus: A great marble temple and sanctuary built around 550 B.C. (in what is now Turkey) honoring the Greek goddess Artemis

The Mausoleum at Halicarnassus: A tomb on the Aegean Sea (in southwest Turkey) completed around 350 B.C. for Persian King Maussollos

The Colossus of Rhodes: A Statue-of-Liberty-size representation of Helios, the Greek sun-god, built between 294 and 282 B.C. in the harbor off the island of Rhodes

The Pharos of Alexandria: A lighthouse off the coast of Alexandria, Egypt, begun around 290 B.C. by Ptolemy Soter, commander under Alexander the Great, and completed by his son

There are those who argue that other ancient structures are just as worthy, such as the the Great Wall of China, Machu Picchu in Peru, and the Aztec Temple in Tenochtitlan in Mexico. However, though part of our known world today, you now realize that these places were unknown to the ancient Greeks and therefore were not part of *their* world.

Of these seven wonders, only one still stands—The Great Pyramid. The rest have been lost to natural disasters or human destruction. Which "wonder" would you like to learn more about?

The Seven Wonders of the Ancient World: Sign-up Sheet

Directions: Sign up below to research and report on one of the Seven Wonders of the Ancient World. If all the blanks are filled for a topic, make another choice. Use the writing process to prepare your presentation: prewrite, draft, revise, edit, and publish. Then practice reading your final draft out loud. Your teacher will select students to present their findings as a radio reading—reading clearly and fluently, as if reporting on a radio broadcast.

HOT TIP! *Many reporters use the 5W's + H method to plan and draft their work. To plan, write questions you want to find answers to: Who? What? Where? When? Why? How? Take notes as you research. Then, use the answers as the structure of your report. Rearrange and add description as needed.*

The Hanging Gardens of Babylon _____

_____   _____

_____   _____

The Great Pyramid at Giza _____

_____   _____

_____   _____

The Statue of Zeus at Olympia _____

_____   _____

_____   _____

The Temple of Artemis at Ephesus _____

_____   _____

_____   _____

The Mausoleum at Halicarnassus _____

_____   _____

_____   _____

The Colossus of Rhodes _____

_____   _____

_____   _____

The Pharos of Alexandria _____

_____   _____

_____   _____

The Shipwrecked Sailor (2200 B.C.)

Objective

√ Students will enhance comprehension and fluency by participating in reading and listening to an oral reading presentation in reader's theater format.

Preparation

√ Ask students to have their copies of the world map (pages 188–189) from previous lessons.

√ Copy *The Shipwrecked Sailor: A Tale for Reader's Theater* (pages 40–42) for each student.

√ For optional use, copy *Vocabulary Time Travel* (page 43) for each student.

Fluency Suggestions and Activities

To help students analyze the text and read with comprehension and fluency, present the historical background and preteach the vocabulary on the following page before starting the fluency activity.

1. Ask students to find Egypt on their maps. Point out that Egypt was, and still is, located in northern Africa. Discuss the topography. Have students speculate about the climate and the challenges it presented to the people living there thousands of years ago.

2. Distribute copies of *The Shipwrecked Sailor: A Tale for Reader's Theater* (pages 40–42). Ask students to follow along as you read the tale aloud. Be sure to read it with appropriate expression and fluency. Follow by asking students to identify the story's main elements: setting, characters, problem, and solution. Ask students how they think this tale could best be presented orally. If no one suggests it, tell students that the story has been rewritten as a script, and therefore it will be presented as reader's theater.

3. Read the story again, this time with volunteers reading the parts of Master, Sailor, and Serpent. Have all students read the part of Narrator. If students stumble, do not comment or correct them. At the end of the reading, ask the group to self-evaluate and offer positive feedback on expressiveness, reading rate, loudness, and clarity.

4. Direct students to practice reading the entire script orally. You may suggest that they read with someone at home, taking different parts for each reading. Tell students that, after practicing several times, they should each choose a part that they would be ready to perform and that you will be choosing individuals for a performance (at a certain time). When the time comes, have all students stand who have prepared for the part of Sailor. (These are likely to be your best readers.) Choose one. Do the same for the other parts. The part of Narrator is small, and Master even smaller. Give these parts to students who enjoy the drama but are not necessarily the best readers.

5. Invite students' family and friends to come to class to hear the presentation. For the actual presentation, have four volunteers prepare an introduction that explains (1) what the audience will be hearing, (2) where it came from, (3) the purpose for practicing and presenting the tale orally, and (4) who the characters are and who is portraying them.

The Shipwrecked Sailor (cont.)

History Connection

In a country such as the United States, which is just over 200 years old, it is hard to imagine a history of a people and government that dates back more than 5,000 years. By 3500 B.C., a bustling town already existed along the Nile River. Egyptians began writing in hieroglyphics at least 200 years prior to 3000 B.C. From there, the history of Egypt is divided into dynasties, or eras under certain ruling families. In all, 31 dynasties ruled Egypt from approximately 3000 B.C. to 300 B.C.—a period of 2,700 years! Remarkably, the age of Pharaohs, gods, goddesses, pyramids, and mummies that so fascinates us to this day was over even before we started counting the years forward with the birth of Christ.

The tale of *The Shipwrecked Sailor* dates back to 2200 B.C., the era known as the Golden Age of Egypt (Dynasties III–VI). It was during this period, from 2686 to 2181 B.C., that a number of the large pyramids were constructed, including the Great Pyramid at Giza, which is still standing.

Vocabulary Connection

Discuss unfamiliar vocabulary encountered in the text. Begin with these and then add any others you feel need to be reviewed or introduced. Discuss the words' meanings and how they are used specifically in the context of the material.

- **cubit**—a unit of measure for length; approximately 17–22 inches (43–56 centimeters)
- **lazuli**—deep blue (from *lapis lazuli*—a deep-blue gemstone composed of lazurite)
- **obeisance**—gesture of respect, such as a bow of the head; respectful behavior
- **scribe**—a person who writes out someone's words or copies a document by hand

Extension Ideas

- Interject some cross-curricular application by asking students to calculate the approximate lengths of the ship, the waves, the serpent, and the serpent's beard. To do this, students will need to find the references to these measurements in the script, use the definition of *cubit* (above), and then convert the cubits to inches and/or centimeters. Offer "extra credit" for then expressing the answers as feet and inches or decimeters and centimeters.

- Although the language has been somewhat modernized, the basic story in this 4,000-year-old tale could have just as well been written as a current-day pitch for a new book, movie, or game. Challenge students to write a short essay that compares and contrasts the elements of this story as era-specific. Or, let them be creative and write their own adaptations of the ancient tale as updated, modern stories.

- Use *Vocabulary Time Travel* (page 43) to deepen students' understanding of vocabulary words related to ancient Egypt. Answer Key (page 43): 1. canopic jars 2. dynasty 3. Egyptologist 4. hieroglyphics 5. amulet 6. ba 7. ka 8. pharaoh 9. Book of the Dead 10. obelisk 11. sphinx 12. papyrus 13. inundation 14. Uraeus 15. sarcophagus

Name _____

The Shipwrecked Sailor: A Tale for Reader's Theater

An ancient Egyptian tale (2200 B.C.) condensed and edited for reader's theater

All: **A sailor had just returned to his master after a harrowing experience. Nearly breathless the servant said,**

Sailor: Let thy heart be satisfied, O my lord, for that we have come back to the country; after we have been long on board, and rowed much, the prow has at last touched land. All the people rejoice and embrace us one after another. Moreover, we have come back in good health, and not a man is lacking; we have returned in peace to our land. Hear me, my lord; then go and tell the tale to the majesty.

All: **With a puzzled look upon his face, the servant's lord replied,**

Master: Thy heart continues still its wandering words! But although the mouth of a man may save him, his words may also cover his face with confusion. Will you do then as your heart moves you? That is, tell the story!

All: **The sailor responded gladly, anxious to relay his experience.**

Sailor: Now I shall tell that which has happened to me, to my very self. I was going to the mines of Pharaoh, and I went down on the sea in a ship of 150 cubits long and 40 cubits wide, with 150 sailors of the best of Egypt who had seen heaven and earth, and whose hearts were stronger than lions. They had said that the wind would not be contrary, or that there would be none. But as we approached the land, the wind arose, and threw up waves eight cubits high. As for me, I seized a piece of wood; but those who were in the vessel perished, without one remaining. A wave threw me on an island, and after that I had been three days alone, without a companion beside my own heart. I laid in a thicket, and the shadow covered me. Then I stretched my limbs to try to find something for my mouth. I found there figs and grain, melons of all kinds, fishes, and birds. Nothing was lacking. And I satisfied myself; and left on the ground that which was over, of what my arms had been filled withal. I dug a pit, I lighted a fire, and I made a burnt offering unto the gods.

Suddenly I heard a noise as of thunder, which I thought to be that of a wave of the sea. The trees shook, and the earth was moved. I uncovered my face, and I saw that a serpent drew near. He was 30 cubits long, and his beard greater than two cubits; his body was overlaid with gold, and his color as that of true lazuli. He coiled himself before me. Then he opened his mouth, while that I lay on my face before him, and he said to me,

The Shipwrecked Sailor: A Tale for Reader's Theater *(cont.)*

Serpent: What has brought you, what has brought you, little one, what has brought you? If you say not speedily what has brought you to this isle, I will make you know yourself; as a flame you shall vanish, if you do not tell me something I have not heard, or which I already of before you.

Sailor: Then he took me in his mouth and carried me to his resting place, and laid me down without any hurt. I was whole and sound, and nothing was gone from me. Then he opened his mouth against me, while that I lay on my face before him, and he said,

Serpent: What has brought you, what has brought you, little one, what has brought you to this isle which is in the sea, and of which the shores are in the midst of the waves?

All: **And then the sailor told the serpent the story of how he came to be there. The wind, the water, the shipwreck—and clinging to a piece of wood until washed ashore by a wave, only he survived. Upon hearing this, the serpent felt compassion for the man and said,**

Serpent: Fear not, fear not, little one, and make not your face sad. If you have come to me, it is God who has let you live. For it is He who has brought you to this isle of the blest, where nothing is lacking, and which is filled with all good things. See now, you shall pass one month after another, until you shall be four months in this isle. Then a ship shall come from your land with sailors, and you shall leave with them and go to your country, and you shall live until you die in your town.

All: **Then the serpent decided to continue the conversation by telling the man his own sad story.**

Serpent: Converse is pleasing, and he who tastes of it passes over his misery. I will therefore tell you of that which is in this isle. I am here with my brethren and my children around me; we are 75 serpents, children, and kindred; without naming a young girl who was brought unto me by chance, and on whom the fire of heaven fell, and burned her to ashes. As for you, if you are strong, and if your heart waits patiently, you shall press your infants to your bosom and embrace your wife. You shall return to your house which is full of all good things, you shall see your land, where you will live among your kind.

Sailor: Then I bowed in my obeisance, touched the ground before him, and said to the serpent, 'I shall tell of your presence unto Pharaoh, I shall make him know of your greatness, and I shall bring for you ships full of all kinds of the treasures of Egypt, as is comely to do unto a god, a friend of men in a far country, of which men know not.' Then he smiled at my speech, because of that which was in his heart, for he said to me:

The Shipwrecked Sailor:
A Tale for Reader's Theater *(cont.)*

Serpent: That is well but, when you shall depart from this place, you shall never more see this isle; it shall be changed into waves.

Sailor: And behold, when the ship drew near, according to all that he had told me before, I got up into a high tree, to strive to see those who were within it. Then I came and told him this matter, but it was already known unto him before. Then he said to me,

Serpent: Farewell, farewell, go to your house, little one, see again your children, and let your name be good in your town; these are my wishes for you.

Sailor: Then I bowed myself before him, and held my arms low before him, and he, he gave me gifts of all kinds of precious things. I embarked all in the ship which was come, and bowing myself, I prayed God for him. Then he said to me,

Serpent: Behold you shall come to your country in two months.

All: **After this, the sailor went down to the shore unto the ship, and called to the sailors who were there. Then on the shore, he rendered adoration to the master of this isle and to those who dwelt therein.**

Sailor: When we shall come, in our return, to the house of Pharaoh, in the second month, according to all that the serpent has said, we shall approach unto the palace. And I shall go in before Pharaoh, I shall bring the gifts which I have brought from this isle into the country. Then he shall thank me before the fullness of the land. Grant then unto me a follower, and lead me to the courtiers of the king. Cast your eye upon me after that I have both seen and proved this. Hear my prayer, for it is good to listen to people. It was said unto me, 'Become a wise man, and you shall come to honor,' and behold I have become such.

All: **Thus, the story is finished from its beginning unto its end as it was found, written by the scribe of cunning fingers.**

Name_____

Vocabulary Time Travel

These terms are related to the study of Ancient Egypt. Match each word to its meaning.

hieroglyphics	ba	dynasty	Book of the Dead	Uraeus
canopic jars	sphinx	amulet	sarcophagus	papyrus
inundation	ka	obelisk	Egyptologist	pharaoh

_____ 1. Jars used to hold the internal organs that were removed from the body before the mummification process.

_____ 2. A succession of kings, usually from the same family or related by blood.

_____ 3. A scientist who specializes in the study of ancient Egypt; usually an archaeologist—one who studies artifacts.

_____ 4. The form of writing used by ancient Egyptians, consisting mainly of pictorial symbols for animals, gods, and tools.

_____ 5. A charm-like object used on mummies to protect them from bad spirits and bring them luck in the afterlife.

_____ 6. The spirit or soul of a living person, usually symbolized by a bird with a human head.

_____ 7. The spirit or soul of the person that leaves the body upon its death and survives in the afterlife.

_____ 8. The title of an Egyptian king.

_____ 9. A collection of hymns, prayers, and magical spells to assist the dead in reaching the netherworld safely.

_____ 10. A four-sided pillar tapering into a pyramid or rounded shape at the top, used for inscriptions of honor.

_____ 11. The depiction of a creature with a lion's body and the head of a person, bird, or ram.

_____ 12. A tall, grassy plant that grows in wet or marshy lands; the material made from this plant on which writing was recorded.

_____ 13. The seasonal flooding of the Nile River.

_____ 14. The sacred serpent (cobra) on the headdress of Egyptian rulers and gods, which was a symbol of sovereignty and protected the wearer from enemies.

_____ 15. The stone container, which was often elaborately decorated, that housed a mummy and its coffin.

Hymn to the Nile (2100 B.C.)

Objective
√ Students will participate in a cumulative reading exercise to practice and increase fluency.

Preparation
√ Ask students to have their copies of the world map (pages 188–189) from previous lessons.

√ Copy *Excerpts from "Hymn to the Nile"* (page 48) and *Elements of Fluency* (page 49) for each student.

√ For the optional Side Trip, copy *History of Plumbing in Egypt* (pages 50–51) for each student.

Fluency Suggestions and Activities

To help students analyze the text and read with comprehension and fluency, present the historical background and preteach the vocabulary on the following page before starting the fluency activity.

1. Ask students to again locate Egypt on their maps (pages 188–189). Point out that the Nile River runs through Egypt, which is a hot, dry desert. The river, therefore, is the lifeblood of the people—their source of water for their crops, their animals, and themselves. The Nile rises and falls seasonally, so that at times the surrounding land is parched and at others flooded. Since the ancient Egyptians' lives depended on the Nile, they revered it as a living being and implored it to sustain them. "Hymn to the Nile" is an example of this.

2. Distribute copies of *Excerpts from "Hymn to the Nile"* (page 48). (The full text version is provided for your reference on pages 46–47.) Tell students that this is a portion of a longer work, edited for clarity and consistency, but that it retains much of the original language and all of the spirit. Explain that, after practicing, the class will perform a choral reading of the hymn in a special form called cumulative reading. This means that one student starts the reading, more and more join in as the reading progresses, and by the last part everyone is reading together.

3. Begin by asking students to follow along as you demonstrate reading the hymn fluently. When you are finished, ask students to share their definitions of fluency. Accept several answers. Then distribute copies of *Elements of Fluency* (page 49), and let students rate their own levels of fluency in each category. Have them make a personal plan for improvement, and then save this self-evaluation in their notebooks for a later time.

4. In small cooperative groups, have students practice reading the *Excerpts from "Hymn to the Nile."* You may suggest several methods: reading through the paragraphs, reading in pairs, and reading in unison. Encourage students to also practice reading it aloud at home.

5. Finally, at an appointed time, ask your principal or any staff member to meet your class in an area suitable for choral reading, such as in an all-purpose room or outside on the school grounds. Just prior to the actual presentation, choose the starting reader (R1) and assign the remaining students a reader number (R2–R7) to show them the place in the hymn at which they should join in the reading. The final "plea" to the Nile should be read in unison by the whole group.

Hymn to the Nile (cont.)

History Connection

The Nile River was an essential element to the appearance of the early Egyptian society, and crucial to its continuation. The inundation, or annual flooding, of the Nile made the land surrounding it extremely fertile for growing wheat and other crops to feed the population. The water attracted game and fowl and enabled the people to keep livestock. In addition, the Nile gave the Egyptians an efficient and convenient way to transport people and goods.

The early Egyptians were both confounded by and grateful for the annual flooding, which mysteriously, though predictably, happened in the heat of summer. The waters overflowed and fertilized the crops. Though sometimes producing too much flooding or not quite enough, the annual event inspired Egyptians' awe. They worshiped the river, offered it sacrifices, and treated it like a living being who cared for them and would respond to their needs. Whatever the Egyptians believed about the Nile, no one can deny that it served them well.

Vocabulary Connection

Discuss unfamiliar vocabulary encountered in the text. Begin with these and then add any others you feel need to be reviewed or introduced. Discuss the words' meanings and how they are used specifically in the context of the material.

- **inundation**—a flood of water; an overwhelming accumulation of something
- **alights**—lands upon after a flight
- **perpetuity**—the state of being unchanged over time
- **herbage**—vegetation, especially leafy or edible plants (note that the *h* is silent)
- **granaries**—region where grain is abundant; a place for storing grain
- **mart**—marketplace
- **mettle**—strength of character; courage; spirit

Extension Ideas

- Try giving this project to your students who need a challenge. Have them invent a board game called "In Pursuit of the Nile." Direct them to research geographical, historical, and other trivia facts about the Nile, and then use them to create game cards. Instruct them to design a board for the game and develop rules and directions for playing.
- For those students who prefer puzzles, invite them refer back to *Vocabulary Time Travel* (page 43) to design a crossword or word search using the words in that activity.
- **Side Trip:** Use this optional activity to motivate and engage students who are less than enthusiastic about reading or history. Assign this group of students to prepare and deliver to the rest of the class a presentation of the article *History of Plumbing in Egypt* (pages 50–51).

Name_____

Hymn to the Nile (2100 b.c.)

Hail to thee, O Nile! Who manifests thyself over this land, and comes to give life to Egypt! Mysterious is thy issuing forth from the darkness, on this day whereon it is celebrated! Watering the orchards created by Re, to cause all the cattle to live, you give the earth to drink, inexhaustible one! Path that descends from the sky, loving the bread of Seb and the first-fruits of Nepera, You cause the workshops of Ptah to prosper!

Lord of the fish, during the inundation, no bird alights on the crops. You create the grain, you bring forth the barley, assuring perpetuity to the temples. If you cease your toil and your work, then all that exists is in anguish. If the gods suffer in heaven, then the faces of men waste away.

Then He torments the flocks of Egypt, and great and small are in agony. But all is changed for mankind when He comes; He is endowed with the qualities of Nun. If He shines, the earth is joyous, every stomach is full of rejoicing, every spine is happy, every jaw-bone crushes (its food).

He brings the offerings, as chief of provisioning; He is the creator of all good things, as master of energy, full of sweetness in his choice. If offerings are made it is thanks to Him. He brings forth the herbage for the flocks, and sees that each god receives his sacrifices. All that depends on Him is a precious incense. He spreads himself over Egypt, filling the granaries, renewing the marts, watching over the goods of the unhappy.

He is prosperous to the height of all desires, without fatiguing Himself therefore. He brings again his lordly bark; He is not sculptured in stone, in the statutes crowned with the uraeus serpent, He cannot be contemplated. No servitors has He, no bearers of offerings! He is not enticed by incantations! None knows the place where He dwells, none discovers his retreat by the power of a written spell.

No dwelling (is there) which may contain you! None penetrates within your heart! Your young men, your children applaud you and render unto you royal homage. Stable are your decrees for Egypt before your servants of the North! He stanches the water from all eyes and watches over the increase of his good things.

Where misery existed, joy manifests itself; all beasts rejoice. The children of Sobek, the sons of Neith, the cycle of the gods which dwells in him, are prosperous. No more reservoirs for watering the fields! He makes mankind valiant, enriching some, bestowing his love on others. None commands at the same time as himself. He creates the offerings without the aid of Neith, making mankind for himself with multiform care.

He shines when He issues forth from the darkness, to cause his flocks to prosper. It is his force that gives existence to all things; nothing remains hidden for him. Let men clothe themselves to fill his gardens. He watches over his works, producing the inundation during the night. The associate of Ptah . . . He causes all his servants to exist, all writings and divine words, and that which He needs in the North.

Hymn to the Nile *(cont.)*

It is with the words that He penetrates into his dwelling; He issues forth at his pleasure through the magic spells. Your unkindness brings destruction to the fish; it is then that prayer is made for the (annual) water of the season; Southern Egypt is seen in the same state as the North. Each one is with his instruments of labor. None remains behind his companions. None clothes himself with garments, The children of the noble put aside their ornaments.

The night remains silent, but all is changed by the inundation; it is a healing-balm for all mankind. Establisher of justice! Mankind desires you, supplicating you to answer their prayers; You answer them by the inundation! Men offer the first-fruits of corn; all the gods adore you! The birds descend not on the soil. It is believed that with your hand of gold you make bricks of silver! But we are not nourished on lapis-lazuli; wheat alone gives vigor.

A festal song is raised for you on the harp, with the accompaniment of the hand. Your young men and your children acclaim you and prepare their (long) exercises. You are the august ornament of the earth, letting your bark advance before men, lifting up the heart of women in labor, and loving the multitude of the flocks.

When you shine in the royal city, the rich man is sated with good things, the poor man even disdains the lotus; all that is produced is of the choicest; all the plants exist for your children. If you have refused (to grant) nourishment, the dwelling is silent, devoid of all that is good, the country falls exhausted.

O inundation of the Nile, offerings are made unto you, men are immolated to you, great festivals are instituted for you. Birds are sacrificed to you, gazelles are taken for you in the mountain, pure flames are prepared for you. Sacrifice is mettle to every god as it is made to the Nile. The Nile has made its retreats in Southern Egypt, its name is not known beyond the Tuau. The god manifests not his forms, He baffles all conception.

Men exalt him like the cycle of the gods, they dread him who creates the heat, even him who has made his son the universal master in order to give prosperity to Egypt. Come (and) prosper! Come (and) prosper! O Nile, come (and) prosper! O you who make men to live through his flocks and his flocks through his orchards! Come (and) prosper, come, O Nile, come (and) prosper!

He brings the offerings, as chief of provisioning; He is the creator of all good things, as master of energy, full of sweetness in his choice. If offerings are made it is thanks to Him. He brings forth the herbage for the flocks, and sees that each god receives his sacrifices. All that depends on Him is a precious incense. He spreads himself over Egypt, filling the granaries, renewing the marts, watching over the goods of the unhappy.

Name _____

Excerpts from "Hymn to the Nile"

Edited for clarity and consistency for cumulative choral reading

R1: Hail to thee, O Nile! Who manifests thyself over this land and comes to give life to Egypt! Mysterious is thy issuing forth from the darkness; on this day it is celebrated! You water the orchards created by Re, cause all the cattle to live, and give the earth to drink, inexhaustible one!

R1, R2: Lord of the fish, during the inundation, no bird alights on the crops. You create the grain, you bring forth the barley, assuring perpetuity to the temples. If you cease your toil and your work, then all that exists is in anguish. If the gods suffer in heaven, then the faces of men waste away.

R1, R2, R3: When you torment the flocks of Egypt, great and small are in agony. But all is changed for mankind when you come. The earth is joyous, every stomach is full of rejoicing, every spine is happy, every jaw chews.

R1, R2, R3, R4: Offerings are made to you. You bring forth the herbage for the flocks, and see that each god receives his sacrifices. You spread yourself over Egypt, filling the granaries, renewing the marts, watching over the goods of the unhappy.

R1, R2, R3, R4, R5: Where misery existed, joy manifests itself; all beasts rejoice. No more reservoirs for watering the fields! You make mankind valiant, enriching some, bestowing your love on others. None commands the way you do.

R1, R2, R3, R4, R5, R6: O inundation of the Nile, offerings are made unto you, men are immolated to you, great festivals are instituted for you. Birds are sacrificed to you, gazelles are taken for you in the mountain, pure flames are prepared for you. Sacrifice is mettle to every god as it is made to you. You, the Nile, have made your retreats in Southern Egypt, where beyond the Tuau, your name is not known. You do not manifest all your forms; you baffle all conception.

All: **Men exalt you like the cycle of the gods; they dread he who creates the heat, even he who has made his son the universal master in order to give prosperity to Egypt. Now, come. Come and prosper! Come and prosper! O Nile, come and prosper! O you who enable us to live through the flocks and through the orchards! Come and prosper, come, O Nile, come and prosper!**

Name_____

Elements of Fluency

Fluency is the ability to express something effortlessly and clearly. Well, that clearly takes some effort! The way to achieve fluency is through practice. What elements comprise fluency? In other words, what differentiates fluency from reading aloud?

1. **Rate of Reading**

   Is the speed too fast or too slow (for the intended audience)?

   Is the speed at a rate that makes the material easy to understand?

   Is the speed consistent so that the listener is neither waiting, nor trying to keep up?

   If 1 is *terrible*, and 10 is *outstanding*, what score do you give yourself? _____

2. **Loudness**

   Is the reading too soft?

   Is the reading too loud?

   Does the reading loudness match the size of the audience?

   If 1 is *whispering* and 10 is *shouting*, what number do you give yourself? _____

3. **Accuracy**

   Does the reader pronounce the words correctly?

   Does the reader skip words or change them?

   If 1 is way *off*, and 10 is *right on*, what score do you give yourself? _____

4. **Smoothness**

   Does the reading flow smoothly?

   Does the reader use phrasing (chunking) and punctuation clues?

   If 1 is *choppy*, and 10 is *smooth*, what number do you give yourself? _____

5. **Expression**

   Does the reading reflect the mood and tone of the writing?

   Does the reader use emphasis and inflection to communicate feeling or thought?

   If 1 is *like a robot*, and 10 is *expressive*, what score do you give yourself? _____

When reading aloud, which element do you think is your strongest?_____

Which one do you think needs the most improvement? _____

Make a plan for improving your overall fluency. List three things you will do:

1. _____

2. _____

3. _____

Name_____

History of Plumbing in Egypt

If you have ever wondered how the people of ancient times "took care of business," this article, originally printed in *Plumbing & Mechanical* magazine, gives us some insight.

Work with your group to prepare a presentation of the history of plumbing for the class:

1. Read the article. Mark any words you do not know or understand. Use whatever sources you can (dictionary, online search, Egyptian references, etc.) to find the words' meanings and pronunciations.
2. Read the article several more times, both silently and aloud until you can read it fluently.
3. Decide together how to divide the reading among the group for the presentation.
4. Practice reading your part alone and with the group.
5. When everyone is ready, present your reading to the class.

History of Plumbing—Egypt

Egypt and the Nile: From ancient joddlldld dk dtimes, the rise and fall of the River Nile portended periods of famine or good fortune for the peoples of Egypt. Other than wells, the River Nile is the only source of water in the country. During an idyllic year, the flooding of the Nile would begin in July, and by September its receding waters woggguld deposit a rich, black silt in its wake for farming. Before taming the river, however, the ancient Egyptians had to overcome the river's peculiar problem.

movement of the ground. When the Nile is the lowest, the ground completely dries up. When it floods, the water seeps into the dry soil and causes the ground to rise as much as a foot or two like some bloated sponge. As the inundation subsides, the ground settles again to its original dry level, but never settles evenly.

The name Egypt means "Two Lands," reflecting the two separate kingdoms of Upper and Lower prehistoric Egypt—a delta region in the north and a long length of sandstone and limestone in the south. In 3000 B.C., a single ruler, Menes, unified the entire land and set the stage for an impressive civilization that lasted 3,000 years. He began with the construction of basins to contain the flood water, digging canals and irrigation ditches to reclaim the marshy land.

From these earliest of times, so important was the cutting of a dam that the event was heralded by a royal ceremony. King Menes is credited with diverting the course of the Nile to build the city of Memphis on the site where the great river had run. By 2500 B.C., an extensive system of dikes, canals, and sluices had developed. It remained in use until the Roman occupation, circa 30 B.C.–A.D. 641.

History of Plumbing in Egypt (cont.)

For pure water, the Egyptians depended upon wells. Their prowess in divining hidden sources is evident in the "Well of Joseph," constructed about 3000 B.C. near the Pyramids of Giza. Workers had to dig through 300 feet of solid rock to tap into the water.

Plumbing for the Dead: Egypt's pyramid-temples, which have withstood thousands of years of time, also attest to the skill of the ancient construction workers. The earliest pyramids were built from 2660 to 2500 B.C., a period running parallel with the Sumer-Mesopotamians when they achieved their greatest advances in civilization. Yet any cultural ties that Egypt had with Mesopotamia had vanished by this period.

By 2500 B.C. the Egyptians were pretty adept with drainage construction, accentuated by the significance that water played in their priestly rituals of purification and those affecting the burial of the kings. According to their religion, to die was simply to pass from one state of life to another. If the living required food, clothing and other accoutrements of daily life, so did the dead. Thus, it's not surprising that archaeologists have discovered bathrooms in some tombs.

Excavators of the mortuary temple of King Suhura at Abusir discovered niches in the walls and remnants of stone basins. These were furnished with metal fittings for use as lavatories. The outlet of the basin closed with a lead stopper attached to a chain and a bronze ring. The basin emptied through a copper pipe to a trough below. The pipe was made of one-sixteenth-inch beaten copper to a diameter of a little under two inches. A lap joint seam hammered it tight.

Also found within a pyramid temple built by King Tutankhamen's father-in-law at Abusir was a brass drain pipe running from the upper temple along the connecting masonry causeway to the outer temple on the river.

Excavators have discovered a tomb that supposedly contains the body of Osiris before he became a god. It contains the dividing line between Life and Death, i.e., a deep moat containing water that surrounds all sides of the figure of the god on his throne. After 5,000 years, water still fills the canal through underground pipes from the River Nile.

From *Plumbing & Mechanical*, July 1989. Used with permission of the publisher.

Herodotus's Description of Mummification

From Herodotus's *The Histories* (~450 B.C.)

Objective

√ Students will demonstrate fluency in reading aloud a personally rewritten version of an expository primary source.

Preparation

√ Enlist 3–5 adults or older students to serve as the judges' panel for the presentation activity.

√ Copy *Description of Mummification* (page 54) and *WANTED: Editor for Really Old Manuscript* (page 55) for each student.

Fluency Suggestions and Activities

To help students analyze the text and read with comprehension and fluency, present the historical background and preteach the vocabulary on the following page before starting the fluency activity.

1. Distribute copies of Herodotus's *Description of Mummification* (page 54). Give students a moment to preview it, and then ask if they have any comments. Hopefully, some will notice the obvious inconsistencies and errors. If not, continue without pointing them out.

2. Ask students to follow along as you read the description. Students will likely be engrossed in the content, so use the first reading as an opportunity to discuss it, check students' comprehension, and just have a conversation about mummification.

3. For the second reading, ask students to focus on how the content is written. Does it flow smoothly? Is it easy to understand? Is the placement of the punctuation helpful to the reader? Is the language and spelling correct and appropriate?

4. Distribute copies of *WANTED: Editor for Really Old Manuscript* (page 55). Read the information and directions at the top of the page. Explain to students that they will be asked to read aloud their final draft for a panel of judges. (You may want to identify the judges here to allay any apprehension.) The judges will compare students' rewritten version to the original (*Description of Mummification* on page 54), and determine which is easier to read with fluency. Prior to presentation time, ask for a student volunteer to be the "reader" of the original version for the panel. Allow that student to practice reading the original in lieu of doing a revision.

5. Assemble the judges at presentation time. (If you have a large number of students, you may want to do the presentations in groups at different times.) Give them a few sample comments or questions they might ask the reader when he or she is finished reading aloud. For example, "Your first paragraph reads much more smoothly than the original. What did you change to make it that way?" When you are ready to begin, have the volunteer read the original manuscript aloud. Then let the judges call on students to read their versions. If you like, have the students who are listening take notes about the versions they hear and vote for the best revision in that group.

Herodotus's Description of Mummification (cont.)

History Connection

When a body dies, it begins to rot. The ancient Egyptians believed that a living thing had a soul or spirit, called a *Ka*, that did not die, but survived the body. This Ka needed a resting place, and the physical body it inhabited in life was ideal. The mummification process was a way to prevent the body from decaying and preserve it for the Ka. Not only the rich or royal were mummified, but common people practiced mummification, too. Perhaps even more interesting is the fact that not only people were mummified, but animals as well.

Though the earliest Egyptian mummies date back to about 3500 B.C., the earliest description of mummification procedures were written by the historian Herodotus of Halicarnassus. Herodotus visited Egypt around 450 B.C. and wrote down the mummification process as was told to him by Egyptian priests. His description of mummification appears in his work *The Histories*.

Vocabulary Connection

Discuss unfamiliar vocabulary encountered in the text. Begin with these and then add any others you feel need to be reviewed or introduced. Discuss the words' meanings and how they are used specifically in the context of the material. (*spelling corrected)

- **flank**—area of the body between the last rib and the hip
- **aromatics**—a class of chemical compounds
- **bruised**—crushed or pounded
- **myrrh, cassia, frankincense**—resins derived from plants
- **natrum**—sodium bicarbonate (baking soda), also spelled *natron*
- **sepulchral**—relating to burial vaults (from *sepulcher*)
- **disembowelling**—cutting open the stomach and removing internal organs, especially the intestines
- **clyster**—process of removing contents of intestines; enema

Extension Ideas

- The practice of mummification was not exclusively Egyptian. Send your students on a "Mummy Search." Challenge them to find out which other ancient cultures practiced mummification, when, and why. If you like, offer a small prize or special privilege to the individual or team who finds the most interesting and enlightening information.

- Ask students to name an influential woman from ancient Egypt, and they will likely answer Cleopatra. It may surprise them to know that a woman named Hatshepsut was Pharaoh in the 18th Dynasty. Challenge them to find out about her life and accomplishments.

Name_____

Description of Mummification

From Herodotus's *The Histories* (~450 B.C.)

The mode of embalming, according to the most perfect process, is the following:- They take first a crooked piece of iron, and with it draw out the brain through the nostrils, thus getting rid of a portion, while the skull is cleared of the rest by rinsing with drugs; next they make a cut along the flank with a sharp Ethiopian stone, and take out the whole contents of the abdomen, which they then cleanse, washing it thoroughly with palm wine, and again frequently with an infusion of pounded aromatics. After this they fill the cavity with the purest bruised myrrh, with cassia, and every other sort of spicery except frankincense, and sew up the opening. Then the body is placed in natrum for seventy days, and covered entirely over. After the expiration of that space of time, which must not be exceeded, the body is washed, and wrapped round, from head to foot, with bandages of fine linen cloth, smeared over with gum, which is used generally by the Egyptians in the place of glue, and in this state it is given back to the relations, who enclose it in a wooden case which they have had made for the purpose, shaped into the figure of a man. Then fastening the case, they place it in a sepulchral chamber, upright against the wall. Such is the most costly way of embalming the dead.

If persons wish to avoid expense, and choose the second process, the following is the method pursued:- Syringes are filled with oil made from the cedar-tree, which is then, without any incision or disembowelling, injected into the abdomen. The passage by which it might be likely to return is stopped, and the body laid in natrum the prescribed number of days. At the end of the time the cedar-oil is allowed to make its escape; and such is its power that it brings with it the whole stomach and intestines in a liquid state. The natrum meanwhile has dissolved the flesh, and so nothing is left of the dead body but the skin and the bones. It is returned in this condition to the relatives, without any further trouble being bestowed upon it.

Scott Rothstein/Shutterstock, Inc.

The third method of embalming, which is practised in the case of the poorer classes, is to clear out the intestines with a clyster, and let the body lie in natrum the seventy days, after which it is at once given to those who come to fetch it away.

Name_____

WANTED: Editor for Really Old Manuscript

Herodotus wrote in Greek. The text you have is the unedited original translation into English. While reading Herodotus's description, you probably noticed that it could use editing and proofreading to bring it up to standard English conventions. Imagine now that Herodotus has asked you to revise the work for republication in English. You will need to revise for sentence structure and organization, as well as proofread for spelling, capitalization, punctuation, and word usage. As you work on this, keep in mind the fact that there are many volumes in *The Histories*. All you have to do is revise one tiny description!

Use the rest of this page for your notes and ideas. You may want to jot down words you need to check, try out rewritten sentences, or make notes about the meanings of some terms used. When you are ready, write your draft on another sheet of paper. Then, of course, give it a final edit before writing your final draft.

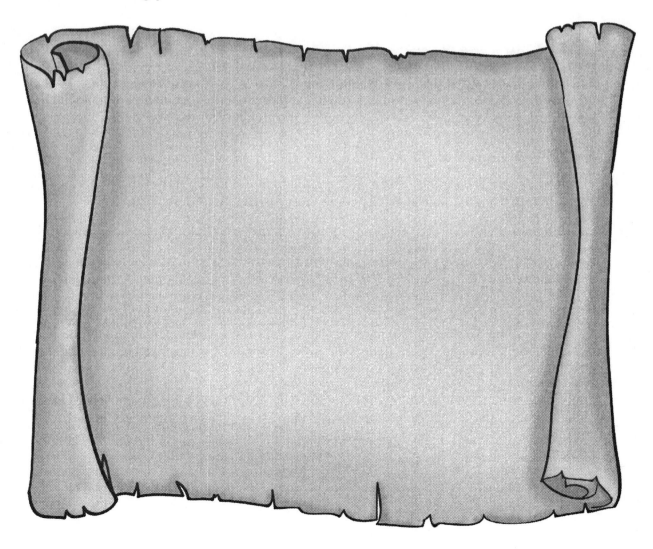

Exodus from Egypt

Excerpt from the Hebrew Scriptures, Book of Exodus

Objective

√ Students will deliver a choral reading presentation in call and response form, focusing on pacing and tracking to increase fluency.

Preparation

√ Make copies of *A Presentation: The Story of the Exodus from Egypt* (pages 58–60) and *Making Connections* (page 61) for each student.

√ Invite religious and other leaders in your community to be the audience for the performance. This presentation could be especially effective if given around Passover, or as a culminating activity in or for a class studying Egypt.

√ For the optional Extension Activity, copy *Go Down, Moses* (pages 62–63) for each student.

Fluency Suggestions and Activities

To help students analyze the text and read with comprehension and fluency, present the historical background and preteach the vocabulary on the following page before starting the fluency activity.

1. Distribute copies of *A Presentation: The Story of the Exodus from Egypt* (pages 58–60). Explain to students that the main text of Part 1: Let My People Go is taken directly from the Hebrew Scriptures, which is also in the Old Testament of the Christian Bible. The refrain, "Let my people go!" has been added for dramatic effect. Begin with a practice reading in which you read aloud the text parts and students respond with the refrain. Remind students that they will need to track and keep pace in order to know when to come in with the refrain.

2. Introduce Part 2: The Passover. Tell students that this is another part of the story, this time taken directly from the Scriptures. Conduct the first reading as described above.

3. Have students complete *Making Connections* (page 61) to check their comprehension.

4. Explain to students that they will present both parts of the story for an audience, but the eight main reading parts will be performed by individuals. Direct students to prepare to audition for at least one individual reading part by practicing reading that part until they can do so fluently. Remind them that they will not be memorizing anything, just reading it smoothly, accurately, and with expression. Then have each student sign up to audition for one of the eight individual parts. This will ensure that students practice and prepare at least one section, even if they do not perform it.

5. After giving students sufficient time to practice, hold auditions for the parts. This gives you an opportunity to hear each student read and assess his or her fluency. Choose one student to perform each part at the presentation. Then practice as a group several times before the actual performance.

Exodus from Egypt (cont.)

History Connection

The Exodus is a narrative that is in both the Torah (Hebrew Scriptures) and the Christian Bible (Old Testament). It tells the story of the Hebrews' release and pilgrimage from Egypt in search of the "promised land." Moses, a Hebrew prophet, leads the enslaved Israelites out of Egypt, across the Red Sea, and into the Sinai Desert. It is there that he receives the Ten Commandments. Moses himself is widely believed to be the author, but the story we read may have been a compilation of works.

Scholars—religious and secular—are unable to agree on specifically when the Exodus itself occurred. The time between 1491 and 1440 B.C. is most favored, but it is still in question. For some, another subject of great debate is the content itself. Should this story, or any ancient story, be taken literally (as fact) or more as literature from which larger lessons can be drawn?

Vocabulary Connection

Discuss unfamiliar vocabulary or phrases encountered in the text. Begin with these and then add any others you feel need to be reviewed or introduced. Discuss the words' meanings and how they are used specifically in the context of the material.

- **"lay this to heart"**—consider, think over
- **lintel**—the horizontal beam over a door that supports the weight of the wall
- **leaven**—a substance used to make bread rise, such as yeast
- **"loins girded"**—the area between the waist and legs covered or wrapped in cloth
- **ordinance**—law; formal religious ceremony
- **hyssop**—an aromatic herb similar to mint

Extension Idea

- The song "Go Down, Moses" (pages 62–63) makes an excellent bridge to connect different times and places in history. Although created by slaves in the American South, it retells the story of the Exodus. People who have been enslaved, no matter when or where, experience similar feelings about their plight. From being told the story of the Exodus in the Bible, American slaves adopted the story and applied it to their own conditions. The American slaves were able to express their own anguish indirectly, by setting to song the story of Moses and his efforts to free his own kind from oppression. As an optional extension, invite your students to prepare for and perform "Go Down, Moses" as poetry or as a song. Students could add this performance to the regular presentation or perform it separately.

Name_____

A Presentation: The Story of the Exodus from Egypt

Excerpt from the Hebrew Scriptures, Book of Exodus

Part 1: Let My People Go

R1: And the LORD said to Moses, "See, I make you as God to Pharaoh; and Aaron your brother shall be your prophet. You shall speak all that I command you; and Aaron your brother shall tell Pharaoh to let the people of Israel go out of his land. But I will harden Pharaoh's heart, and though I multiply my signs and wonders in the land of Egypt, Pharaoh will not listen to you; then I will lay my hand upon Egypt and bring forth my hosts, my people the sons of Israel, out of the land of Egypt by great acts of judgment. And the Egyptians shall know that I am the LORD, when I stretch forth my hand upon Egypt and bring out the people of Israel from among them." And Moses and Aaron did so; they did as the LORD commanded them . . .

All: **Let my people go!**

R2: And the LORD said to Moses and Aaron, "When Pharaoh says to you, 'Prove yourselves by working a miracle,' then you shall say to Aaron, 'Take your rod and cast it down before Pharaoh, that it may become a serpent.'" So Moses and Aaron went to Pharaoh and did as the LORD commanded; Aaron cast down his rod before Pharaoh and his servants, and it became a serpent. Then Pharaoh summoned the wise men and the sorcerers; and they also, the magicians of Egypt, did the same by their secret arts. For every man cast down his rod, and they became serpents. But Aaron's rod swallowed up their rods. Still Pharaoh's heart was hardened, and he would not listen to them; as the LORD had said.

All: **Let my people go!**

R3: Then the LORD said to Moses, "Pharaoh's heart is hardened, he refuses to let the people go. Go to Pharaoh in the morning, as he is going out to the water; wait for him by the river's brink, and take in your hand the rod which was turned into a serpent. And you shall say to him, 'The LORD, the God of the Hebrews, sent me to you, saying, "Let my people go, that they may serve me in the wilderness; and behold, you have not yet obeyed." Thus says the LORD, "By this you shall know that I am the LORD: behold, I will strike the water that is in the Nile with the rod that is in my hand, and it shall be turned to blood, and the fish in the Nile shall die, and the Nile shall become foul, and the Egyptians will loathe to drink water from the Nile'". And the LORD said to Moses, "Say to Aaron, 'Take your rod and stretch out your hand over the waters of Egypt, over their rivers, their canals, and their ponds, and all their pools of water, that they may become blood; and there shall be blood throughout all the land of Egypt, both in vessels of wood and in vessels of stone.'"

A Presentation: The Story of the Exodus from Egypt *(cont.)*

All: **Let my people go!**

R4: Moses and Aaron did as the LORD commanded; in the sight of Pharaoh and in the sight of his servants, he lifted up the rod and struck the water that was in the Nile, and all the water that was in the Nile turned to blood. And the fish in the Nile died; and the Nile became foul, so that the Egyptians could not drink water from the Nile; and there was blood throughout all the land of Egypt. But the magicians of Egypt did the same by their secret arts; so Pharaoh's heart remained hardened, and he would not listen to them; as the LORD had said. Pharaoh turned and went into his house, and he did not lay even this to heart. And all the Egyptians dug round about the Nile for water to drink, for they could not drink the water of the Nile.

All: **Let my people go!**

Part 2: The Passover

All: **The LORD said to Moses and Aaron in the land of Egypt,**

R5: "This month shall be for you the beginning of months; it shall be the first month of the year for you. Tell all the congregation of Israel that on the tenth day of this month they shall take every man a lamb according to their fathers' houses, a lamb for a household; and if the household is too small for a lamb, then a man and his neighbor next to his house shall take according to the number of persons; according to what each can eat you shall make your count for the lamb. Your lamb shall be without blemish, a male a year old; you shall take it from the sheep or from the goats; and you shall keep it until the fourteenth day of this month, when the whole assembly of the congregation of Israel shall kill their lambs in the evening. Then they shall take some of the blood, and put it on the two doorposts and the lintel of the houses in which they eat them. They shall eat the flesh that night, roasted; with unleavened bread and bitter herbs they shall eat it. Do not eat any of it raw or boiled with water, but roasted, its head with its legs and its inner parts. And you shall let none of it remain until the morning, anything that remains until the morning you shall burn. In this manner you shall eat it: your loins girded, your sandals on your feet, and your staff in your hand; and you shall eat it in haste.

All: **It is the LORD's passover.**

R6: "For I will pass through the land of Egypt that night, and I will smite all the first-born in the land of Egypt, both man and beast; and on all the gods of Egypt I will execute judgments: I am the LORD. The blood shall be a sign for you, upon the houses where you are; and when I see the blood, I will pass over you, and no plague shall fall upon you to destroy you, when I smite the land of Egypt.

A Presentation: The Story of the Exodus from Egypt *(cont.)*

All: **"This day shall be for you a memorial day, and you shall keep it as a feast to the LORD; throughout your generations you shall observe it as an ordinance for ever.**

R7:   "Seven days you shall eat unleavened bread; on the first day you shall put away leaven out of your houses, for if any one eats what is leavened, from the first day until the seventh day, that person shall be cut off from Israel. On the first day you shall hold a holy assembly, and on the seventh day a holy assembly; no work shall be done on those days; but what every one must eat, that only may be prepared by you. And you shall observe the feast of unleavened bread, for on this very day I brought your hosts out of the land of Egypt . . ."

All: **Then Moses called all the elders of Israel, and said to them,**

R8:   "Select lambs for yourselves according to your families, and kill the passover lamb. Take a bunch of hyssop and dip it in the blood which is in the basin, and touch the lintel and the two doorposts with the blood which is in the basin; and none of you shall go out of the door of his house until the morning. For the LORD will pass through to slay the Egyptians; and when he sees the blood on the lintel and on the two doorposts, the LORD will pass over the door, and will not allow the destroyer to enter your houses to slay you. You shall observe this rite as an ordinance for you and for your sons for ever. And when you come to the land which the LORD will give you, as he has promised, you shall keep this service. And when your children say to you, 'What do you mean by this service?' you shall say, 'It is the sacrifice of the LORD's passover, for he passed over the houses of the people of Israel in Egypt, when he slew the Egyptians but spared our houses.'"

All: **And the people bowed their heads and worshiped.**

Name _____

Making Connections

1. How did the spiritual beliefs of the Egyptians differ from those of the Hebrews in Egypt at the time of Moses?

   _____

   _____

   _____

2. The word *exodus* means "departure." Explain why Moses wanted to lead his people out of Egypt.

   _____

   _____

   _____

3. Why would making the Nile's water unusable be an effective means of persuasion?

   _____

   _____

   _____

4. Although it is known that the Exodus took place under Moses's guidance, the question of whether or not the events described are accurate in terms of historical fact or more narrative embellishment, is a hotly debated topic. What is your opinion and why? (Remember, an opinion is neither right nor wrong.)

   _____

   _____

   _____

5. What modern group of people still observe events described in the Book of Exodus as religious holidays? _____ One of the holidays still observed is Passover. Explain the derivative of the name.

   _____

   _____

   _____

6. During the period of slavery in the United States, a popular song among slaves was "Go Down, Moses," which retells the story of the Exodus from Egypt. The slaves in America were not of Hebrew descent. Why do you think this song had such widespread appeal?

   _____

   _____

   _____

Name _____

Go Down, Moses

R1: When Israel was in Egypt's land,
Let my people go!
Oppressed so hard they could not
    stand,
Let my people go!

**All: Go down, Moses,
Way down in Egypt's land.
Tell old Pharaoh
To let my people go!**

R2: "Thus spoke the Lord," bold Moses
    said
"Let my people go!
If not, I'll smite your firstborn dead
Let my people go!"

**All: Go down, Moses,
Way down in Egypt's land.
Tell old Pharaoh
To let my people go!**

R3: No more shall they in bondage toil
Let my people go!
Let them come out with Egypt's spoil
Let my people go!

**All: Go down, Moses,
Way down in Egypt's land.
Tell old Pharaoh
To let my people go!**

R4: The Lord told Moses what to do
Let my people go!
To lead the Hebrew children through
Let my people go!

**All: Go down, Moses,
Way down in Egypt's land.
Tell old Pharaoh
To let my people go!**

R5: O come along Moses, you'll not
    get lost
Let my people go!
Stretch out your rod and come
    across.
Let my people go!

**All: Go down, Moses,
Way down in Egypt's land.
Tell old Pharaoh
To let my people go!**

R6: As Israel stood by the water side
Let my people go!
At God's command it did divide
Let my people go!

**All: Go down, Moses,
Way down in Egypt's land.
Tell old Pharaoh
To let my people go!**

R7: When they reached the other
    shore
Let my people go!
They sang a song of triumph o'er
Let my people go!

**All: Go down, Moses,
Way down in Egypt's land.
Tell old Pharaoh
To let my people go!**

R8: Pharaoh said he'd go across
Let my people go!
But Pharaoh and his host were
    lost
Let my people go!

Go Down, Moses (cont.)

All: **Go down, Moses,**
        Way down in Egypt's land.
        Tell old Pharaoh
        To let my people go!

R9:   O let us all from bondage flee
        Let my people go!
        And let us all in Christ be free
        Let my people go!

All: **Go down, Moses,**
        Way down in Egypt's land.
        Tell old Pharaoh
        To let my people go!

R10:   You need not always weep and mourn
        Let my people go!
        And wear these slav'ry chains forlorn
        Let my people go!

All: **Go down, Moses,**
        Way down in Egypt's land.
        Tell old Pharaoh
        To let my people go!

R11:   Your foes shall not before you stand
        Let my people go!
        And you'll possess fair Canaan's land
        Let my people go!

All: **Go down, Moses,**
        Way down in Egypt's land.
        Tell old Pharaoh
        To let my people go!

The Library of Congress

Ancient Greek Olympics

Objective

√ Students will participate in a cooperative learning activity to enhance comprehension and improve expression by engaging in reader's theater.

Preparation

√ Ask students to have their copies of the world map (pages 188–189) from previous lessons.

√ Copy *Reader's Theater: The Most Illustrious of Athletes* (pages 66–67) and *In My Opinion* (page 68) for each student.

Fluency Suggestions and Activities

To help students analyze the text and read with comprehension and fluency, present the historical background and preteach the vocabulary on the following page before starting the fluency activity.

1. Have students take out the maps they have been using to locate the places they are studying. Assist them, as needed, to find Greece.

2. Distribute copies of *Reader's Theater: The Most Illustrious of Athletes* (pages 66–67). After sharing the information in the History Connection section on how the script was prepared, explain to students that the presentation is divided into 16 reading parts. Although it is to be read by different students, the presentation should flow so smoothly that it retains the coherence of one fluent work.

3. Demonstrate fluency by asking students to follow along as you read the script. Remind them to pay attention to the words and how the words are said. Then assign parts to pairs of students. Reread the script, this time with the students reading their respective parts. After this first read, do a whole-group critique. Ask students to comment on what went well and how it could be improved.

4. Provide opportunities for students to practice their specific parts and also to read the script together. After each full reading, offer feedback on the fluency of the reading and the smoothness of the transitions.

5. Tie the past to the present by timing the presentation of *Reader's Theater: The Most Illustrious of Athletes* to coincide with an athletic event currently in the news. The Olympics would be ideal, of course, but topics in the script can easily be applied to competition and heroism today in such things as major league sports, competitive weightlifting, and wrestling. The audience for your presentation could be a physical education teacher or class, a school athletic team or club, or even an invited guest from the community who is a personal trainer or athletic coach.

6. During or after the presentation, invite students to engage in critical thinking about related topics. The *In My Opinion* activity (page 68) offers opinion statements for students' reflection and reaction. Students' answers will vary. You may wish to follow up the activity with a class discussion.

Ancient Greek Olympics (cont.)

History Connection

The words of three noted Greek writers of the period are incorporated into the reader's theater presentation, "The Most Illustrious of Athletes." The first is Strabo's *Geography*. Completed in the first century, this is an extensive work in Greek—spanning 17 volumes—and is an encyclopedia of the geographical knowledge of Strabo's time. In his discussion of the Olympics, Strabo gives a description of Milo of Kroton [Croton], a popular hero and multiple-time victor of the ancient Olympics in the sixth century B.C.

Pausanias was a geographer of Ancient Greece who traveled and wrote in the second century. His lengthy *Description of Greece* includes detailed information about Grecian topography, monuments, and traditional legends. Pausanias observed Greece firsthand, and while describing various statues and memorials, he reveals bits of the historical background behind them. His legendary account of Milo adds a more colorful picture of the man and his legacy.

Finally, a single philosophical comment on physical strength is included to offer another perspective. It is from Diodorus Siculus's *History*, an historical library of information collected and written in the first century B.C. It is notable that this text predates the others and takes the view of Milo's feats as a waste of strength rather than something to hold in awe.

The quotes included in the reader's theater presentation form a bridge from ancient history to modern times. They illustrate the connection between attitudes toward the present-day Olympics and athletic heroes and those of Ancient Greece.

Vocabulary Connection

Discuss unfamiliar vocabulary encountered in the text. Begin with these and then add any others you feel need to be reviewed or introduced. Discuss the words' meanings and how they are used specifically in the context of the material.

- **illustrious**—famous; outstanding
- **quoit**—a ring used in a game of quoits, in which the ring is tossed onto a post
- **demise**—death

Extension Idea

- Write on a chart each of the contemporary terms listed below. Challenge students to explain their modern meanings, and then find out the specific connection each has to ancient Greece.

Olympic proportions   Achilles' heel   Hippocratic Oath   Spartan effort   Trojan horse

Name _____

Reader's Theater:
The Most Illustrious of Athletes

Narrated explanatory text in plain type and original source material in italics

R1: In the years leading up to the late eighth century B.C., many of the kingdoms that were part of Greece's glory had fallen, and Greece was in disarray. The institution of the Olympics, a combination of athletic competition and religious festival honoring the god Zeus, served to reignite pride and nationalism at a time when Greece was in need of a spark.

R2: Olympia was the logical site for the games. First, it was one of the oldest religious centers where Greeks honored their gods. In addition, its geographic location made it easy to reach from near and far. People came from all over the ancient world to watch and participate in the games.

R3: The Olympics restored honor and recognition to Greece. In fact, for one month prior to the start of the games, an international truce was observed in order to allow people to travel and arrive safely. To this day, the Olympics are expected to be a time and place in which international differences are set aside.

R4: Today we consider the athletes who train and compete in the Olympics international heroes. As spectators we marvel at their abilities and cheer them on to victory. Individuals we had never before heard of become household names. But, what was it like in ancient times? Strabo, an early Greek writer, gives us a glimpse in his description of Croton, a city in ancient Greece:

R5: *. . . [At] one Olympian festival the seven men who took the lead over all others in the stadium-race were all Crotoniates and therefore the saying "The last of the Crotoniates was the first among all other Greeks" seems reasonable. And this, it is said, is what gave rise to the other proverb, "more healthful than Croton," the belief being that the place contains something that tends to health and bodily vigor, to judge by the multitude of its athletes. Accordingly, [Croton] had a very large number of Olympic victors,. . .And its fame was increased by. . .Milo, who was the most illustrious of athletes.*

R6: So the early Olympians were heroes as well. Perhaps this Milo of Croton was something like our modern-day superathletes—his accomplishments so impressive that they became legendary. Apparently, Milo's fame lasted into the second century, during which another early Greek writer, Pausanias, came upon a statue of him and tells us the legend behind it:

R7: *The statue of Milo the son of Diotimus was made by Dameas, also a native of [Croton]. Milo won six victories for wrestling at Olympia, one of them among the boys; at Pytho he won six among the men and one among the boys. He came to Olympia to wrestle for the seventh time, but did not succeed in mastering Timasitheus, a fellow-citizen who was also a young man, and who refused, moreover, to come to close quarters with him.*

Reader's Theater:
The Most Illustrious of Athletes *(cont.)*

R8: *It is further stated that Milo carried his own statue into the Altis. His feats with the pomegranate and the quoit are also remembered by tradition. He would grasp a pomegranate so firmly that nobody could wrest it from him by force, and yet he did not damage it by pressure. He would stand upon a greased quoit, and make fools of those who charged him and tried to push him from the quoit.*

R9: Pausanias gives us these accounts of Milo's strength and agility. But grasping a fruit and balancing on a ring does not make Milo a legend. So, Pausanias tells us a few more stories about the feats of Milo:

R10: *He would tie a cord round his forehead as though it were a ribbon or a crown. Holding his breath and filling with blood the veins on his head, he would break the cord by the strength of these veins.*

R11: *It is said that [Milo] would let down by his side his right arm from the shoulder to the elbow, and stretch out straight the arm below the elbow, turning the thumb upwards, while the other fingers lay in a row. In this position, then, the little finger was lowest, but nobody could bend it back by pressure.*

R12: If these feats still are not enough to exalt Milo to superhuman hero status, Pausanias adds the amazing circumstances of his demise.

R13: *They say that he was killed by wild beasts. The story has it that he came across in the land of Crotona a tree-trunk that was drying up; wedges were inserted to keep the trunk apart. Milo in his pride thrust his hands into the trunk, the wedges slipped, and Milo was held fast by the trunk until the wolves—a beast that roves in vast packs in the land of Crotona—made him [his] prey. Such was the fate that overtook Milo.*

R14: What parts of these accounts are true, exaggerated, or just plain made-up doesn't really matter. What we can tell from these words, written nearly 2,000 years ago, is that human nature hasn't changed. The Olympics—then and now—are a spectacle that both excites and mollifies the competitive nature of people. The ancient people, just like the people of today, gave outstanding athletes star status.

R15: There's one more thing that hasn't changed—the tendency of men to acquire and use strength for no purpose other than to show off or impress others. A comment by another Greek historian, Diodorus Siculus, dismisses Milo's enormous strength as wasted. Although written in the first century B.C., it could have just as easily been written yesterday:

R16: *It is no great thing to possess strength, whatever kind it is, but to use it as one should.*

Name _____

In My Opinion

Directions: Read each statement of opinion. Remember that, unlike a fact, an opinion is neither right nor wrong. Decide if you agree or disagree. Write your opinion and two sentences to support it.

1. Demonstrations of strength used only for show are a waste of that strength.

_____

_____

_____

_____

2. Athletic competition is a good way to bring together people of different cultures and beliefs.

_____

_____

_____

_____

3. Physical excellence is not as valuable as academic excellence.

_____

_____

_____

_____

4. Athletes make good role models and heroes for young people.

_____

_____

_____

_____

5. Women have no business competing in athletics at the same level as men.

_____

_____

_____

_____

Aesop's Fables

Objective

√ Students will read passages fluently after practicing and monitoring fluency with repeated readings.

Preparation

√ Make copies of *Fables from Aesop* (pages 71–72) and *Fluent in Fables* (page 73) for each student.

√ Provide tape recorders for recording readings, if possible.

√ For optional use, provide additional resources containing retellings of Aesop's fables.

Fluency Suggestions and Activities

To help students analyze the text and read with comprehension and fluency, present the historical background and preteach the vocabulary on the following page before starting the fluency activity.

Note: The six fables on pages 71–72 are selected from over 600 attributed to Aesop. These are arranged in ascending order of length and difficulty so that students of various fluency levels can use them.

1. After reading the information about fables and Aesop in the History Connection section on the following page, distribute copies of *Fables from Aesop* (pages 71–72). Although the texts are short and not particularly difficult to read, they do contain some dialogue and unconventional syntax. Model fluent reading of each fable, pointing out these features.

2. Tell students that, like anything else, fluency improves with practice. Distribute copies of *Fluent in Fables* (page 73). Have students look at the directions with you. Explain that the activity is like a contract. At this point you have three options: (1) assign specific fables from those offered, so that you control the amount of reading each student is required to do; (2) allow students to choose for themselves which two fables they would like to focus on; or (3) assign one fable from those provided and direct students to find and choose a second fable from another source.

3. After making sure that students understand the directions and have filled in the titles of the two fables they will be using, give them several days to complete their repeated readings and commentary. One option listed is for students to record their reading. If you have access to tape recorders, provide them. If not, allow students to do this at home or in the library. If tape recording is not practical, have students use a listener as directed.

4. Fables are popular with and enjoyable for all ages. Hold a Fable Fest for your presentation. If you can arrange to visit a class of younger students, make it a traveling Fable Fest. Choose students to present the six selected fables, plus any others they would like to read aloud. Note: A lesson later in this book presents "Five Old Tales from India" (pages 103–106), a selection of short stories similar to fables. If you plan to use the tales from India, you may want to have students delay presenting Aesop's fables until you have added the Indian tales to the repertoire. You could then expand your presentation into a multicultural read-aloud festival.

Aesop's Fables *(cont.)*

History Connection

Fables are a form of narrative used throughout history not only for entertainment, but also as tools for teaching values. They are especially effective since the message, or moral, is demonstrated in the story, rather than delivered directly as a lecture or advice from someone claiming to have higher moral ground or authority. In their pure form, fables achieve this by having the actions of the characters—whether people, animals, or even animated objects—mimic human behavior. Through the story and the symbolism, the reader or listener picks up the intended message through subtle means, sometimes even unconsciously.

Aesop, arguably the most renown fabulist, is considered among the greats of ancient Greece. But unlike Socrates, Plato, and other philosophers of considerable education and status, Aesop was born a slave. He used his wit and wisdom to raise himself from the obscurity and indignity of servitude to a position of fame and respect. Today, we still recognize the follies of human behavior that Aesop so cleverly pointed out, and we continue to enjoy retellings of Aesop's fables.

Vocabulary Connection

Discuss unfamiliar vocabulary encountered in the text. Begin with these and then add any others you feel need to be reviewed or introduced. Discuss the words' meanings and how they are used specifically in the context of the material.

- **imprudence**—lack of wisdom or judgment
- **filberts**—fruit of the hazelnut tree; hazelnuts
- **lamented**—expressed regret or disappointment
- **gaunt**—extremely thin and bony in appearance
- **spoil, spoils**—valuables or property seized in a conflict; reward or benefit of winning
- **felling**—cutting or chopping down
- **Mercury**—(also Hermes) a god who acted as messenger between humans and other gods
- **contrived**—deceptively planned; accomplished by clever or deceitful scheme

Extension Ideas

- Ask students to look up the term *personification*. Have them find out what it means, and then explain how this literary device was used in Aesop's fables. Direct them to give specific examples from both Aesop's fables and at least one other piece of literature.
- Aesop's fables were designed to point out human frailties and teach more desirable approaches. Challenge pairs or small groups of students to brainstorm a list of words that name or describe character traits. Direct them to classify those words as more desirable or less desirable.

Name _____

Fables from Aesop

Selected fables of Aesop (born ~650 B.C.)

Aesop's Fable: The Boy Bathing

A boy bathing in a river was in danger of being drowned. He called out to a passing traveler for help, but instead of holding out a helping hand, the man stood by unconcernedly, and scolded the boy for his imprudence. "Oh, sir!" cried the youth. "Pray help me now and scold me afterwards."

Moral: *Counsel without help is useless.*

Aesop's Fable: The Dog and the Shadow

A dog, crossing a bridge over a stream with a piece of flesh in his mouth, saw his own shadow in the water and took it for that of another Dog, with a piece of meat double his own in size. He immediately let go of his own, and fiercely attacked the other Dog to get his larger piece from him. He thus lost both: that which he grasped at in the water, because it was a shadow; and his own, because the stream swept it away.

Moral: *Better to have something than greed for more.*

Aesop's Fable: The Boy and the Filberts

A boy put his hand into a pitcher full of filberts. He grasped as many as he could possibly hold, but when he tried to pull out his hand, he was prevented from doing so by the neck of the pitcher. Unwilling to lose his filberts, and yet unable to withdraw his hand, he burst into tears and bitterly lamented his disappointment. A bystander said to him, "Be satisfied with half the quantity, and you will readily draw out your hand."

Moral: *Do not attempt too much at once.*

Aesop's Fable: The Dog and the Wolf

A gaunt Wolf was almost dead with hunger when he happened to meet a House-dog who was passing by. "Ah, Cousin," said the Dog. "I knew how it would be; your irregular life will soon be the ruin of you. Why do you not work steadily as I do, and get your food regularly given to you?"

"I would have no objection," said the Wolf, "if I could only get a place."

"I will easily arrange that for you," said the Dog; "come with me to my master and you shall share my work."

So the Wolf and the Dog went towards the town together. On the way there the Wolf noticed that the hair on a certain part of the Dog's neck was very much worn away, so he asked him how that had come about.

Fables from Aesop (cont.)

Aesop's Fable: The Dog and the Wolf (cont.)

"Oh, it is nothing," said the Dog. "That is only the place where the collar is put on at night to keep me chained up; it chafes a bit, but one soon gets used to it."

"Is that all?" said the Wolf. "Then good-bye to you, Master Dog."

Moral: *Better to be hungry and free than fed but captive.*

Aesop's Fable: The Lion's Share

The Lion went once a-hunting along with the Fox, the Jackal, and the Wolf. They hunted and they hunted till at last they surprised a Stag, and soon took its life. Then came the question of how the spoil should be divided. "Quarter me this Stag," roared the Lion; so the other animals skinned it and cut it into four parts. Then the Lion took his stand in front of the carcass and pronounced judgment: The first quarter is for me in my capacity as King of Beasts; the second is mine as arbiter; another share comes to me for my part in the chase; and as for the fourth quarter, well, as for that, I should like to see which of you will dare to lay a paw upon it."

"Humph," grumbled the Fox as he walked away with his tail between his legs; but he spoke in a low growl. "You may share the labors of the great, but you will not share the spoil."

Moral: *The size of the reward should match the size of the effort.*

Aesop's Fable: Mercury and the Woodman

A Woodman was felling a tree on the bank of a river, when his axe, glancing off the trunk, flew out of his hands and fell into the water. As he stood by the water's edge lamenting his loss, Mercury appeared and asked him the reason for his grief. On learning what had happened, out of pity for his distress, Mercury dived into the river and, bringing up a golden axe, asked him if that was the one he had lost. The Woodman replied that it was not, and Mercury then dived a second time, and, bringing up a silver axe, asked if that was his. "No, that is not mine either," said the Woodman. Once more Mercury dived into the river, and brought up the missing axe. The Woodman was overjoyed at recovering his property, and thanked his benefactor warmly; and the latter was so pleased with his honesty that he made him a present of the other two axes.

When the Woodman told the story to his companions, one of these was filled with envy of his good fortune and determined to try his luck for himself. So he went and began to fell a tree at the edge of the river, and presently contrived to let his axe drop into the water. Mercury appeared as before, and, on learning that his axe had fallen in, he dived and brought up a golden axe, as he had done on the previous occasion. Without waiting to be asked whether it was his or not, the fellow cried, "That's mine, that's mine," and stretched out his hand eagerly for the prize: but Mercury was so disgusted at his dishonesty that he not only declined to give him the golden axe, but also refused to recover for him the one he had let fall into the stream."

Moral: *Honesty is the best policy.*

Name_____

Fluent in Fables

Directions: To improve your reading fluency, choose two fables of Aesop on which to concentrate. First explain and summarize each fable in your own words. Then practice reading each fable with the correct expression, phrasing, tone, volume, and speed. Read it aloud three different times by either recording yourself or reading it to another person. Finally, either evaluate your own reading from the recordings, or ask for feedback from the person who listened to you read. Write these comments in the sections below.

Title of fable one: _____

Explanation and summary: _____

_____

_____

_____

Comments on first reading: _____

_____

Comments on second reading: _____

_____

Comments on third reading: _____

_____

Title of fable two: _____

Explanation and summary: _____

_____

_____

_____

Comments on first reading: _____

_____

Comments on second reading: _____

_____

Comments on third reading: _____

_____

Plato and Socrates

Objective
√ Students will read passages fluently and accurately in a choral reading activity, focusing on tone, expression, and voice.

Preparation
√ Make a transparency of *A Conversation with Socrates* (page 76).
√ Copy *A Conversation with Socrates* (page 76) and *In Other Words* (page 77) for each student.

Fluency Suggestions and Activities

To help students analyze the text and read with comprehension and fluency, present the historical background and preteach the vocabulary on the following page before starting the fluency activity.

Note: You may want to tie this presentation to a week near summer or late spring when the trees and flowers are in bloom. Or you may want to present in the dead of winter when everyone is longing for summer. Depending on what you choose, students can present to each other (outside under a tree, for example) or to a social studies class studying Greece.

1. Prepare students for reading the selection with this introduction: More than 2,000 years after his time, Socrates remains an internationally recognized name and respected philosopher and teacher. Yet there are no writings by Socrates. What we know of him is from the writing of his student Plato, who went on to become the teacher of another great philosopher, Aristotle. The passage you are about to read is written by Plato about a conversation between Socrates and his friend Phaedrus.

2. Display the transparency of *A Conversation with Socrates* (page 76). Before reading, be sure to point out and discuss the vocabulary words. Then read the text aloud word by word, with no variation in your tone, expression, or voice. When you are finished, ask students in what form this selection is written (dialogue). Ask them to suggest ways you could have read it differently to make it sound more interesting.

3. The selection lends itself well to what Dr. Timothy Rasinski calls Say It Like the Character (*The Fluent Reader*, page 89). This means reading with expression as a means to get the most out of the text. Read the passage again. This time invite a capable student to take the part of Phaedrus as you read the part of Socrates. Unlike before, read with fluency—varying your expression and voice to match the content. Pause for emphasis and to create a natural-sounding conversational tone.

4. Choose one of the following ways to have students practice and present the selection:
   - Let pairs of students use the Say It Like the Character strategy.
   - Choose one student to read the part of Socrates, and have the rest of the class read in unison the part of Phaedrus.
   - Divide the class into two groups, so each group reads one part as choral call and response.
   - Organize a reverse cumulative choral reading. Begin with everyone reading, and have students drop out at each successive part, until a single student is left reading the final part spoken by Socrates.

Plato and Socrates (cont.)

History Connection

Along with Plato and Aristotle, Socrates (~469–399 B.C.) is considered one of ancient Greece's three greatest philosophers. The ideas of all three are studied to this day. Of these "great thinkers," Socrates came first. Socrates did not lecture, but rather taught through informal conversations. He used questioning of traditional beliefs and ideas to make his students think. Among the young men who were his pupils was Plato (~427–347 B.C.). When Socrates was put on trial for such things as "corrupting the youth," he was sentenced to death. Plato attended the trial. One of Plato's most famous works, *Apology*, recounts the events. Socrates did not put his teaching and ideas in writing, so there are no written records by Socrates. However, Plato was deeply affected by the life and death of his mentor, so he took it upon himself to write about the teachings and beliefs of Socrates. Although written after Socrates's death, Plato often wrote in the conversational style that Socrates used. One of these works is called *Phaedrus*—which is a conversation between Socrates and one of his pupils. In addition to dialogue, Plato took care to describe the setting so vividly that readers almost cannot help feeling that they are there. This text is a description of the place where Socrates and Phaedrus go to sit and talk about life.

Vocabulary Connection

Discuss unfamiliar vocabulary encountered in the text. Begin with these and then add any others you feel need to be reviewed or introduced. Discuss the words' meanings and how they are used specifically in the context of the material.

- **plane tree**—a tall, leafy deciduous tree
- **Boreas**—in Greek mythology, the north wind that carried off **Orithyia** (also **Oreithyia**), daughter of a legendary king of Athens
- **fancy**—imagine
- **maidens**—young, unmarried women
- **agnus castus**—a leafy shrub with dense branches and clusters of purple flowers
- **Achelous**—patron deity of the river of the same name and ruler of all rivers
- **Nymphs**—in mythology, minor goddesses or spirits of nature inhabiting areas of natural beauty such as woods, mountains, and rivers
- **cicadae**—large-winged insects that live in trees and tall grass (the male makes a shrill sound)

Extension Ideas

Have students choose one of these activities:

- List all the sensory words you can find in the passage.
- Make a detailed drawing of the scene.
- Write a paragraph about a pleasant memory this description triggers or about how you would spend an hour if you found yourself in the place described.

Name _____

A Conversation with Socrates

Excerpt from *Phaedrus* (360 B.C.)

Socrates: Let us turn aside and go by the Ilissus; we will sit down at some quiet spot.

Phaedrus: I am fortunate in not having my sandals, and as you never have any, I think that we may go along the brook and cool our feet in the water; this will be the easiest way, and at midday and in the summer it is far from being unpleasant.

Socrates: Lead on, and look out for a place in which we can sit down.

Phaedrus: Do you see the tallest plane-tree in the distance?

Socrates: Yes.

Phaedrus: There are shade and gentle breezes, and grass on which we may either sit or lie down.

Socrates: Move forward.

Phaedrus: I should like to know, Socrates, whether the place is not somewhere here at which Boreas is said to have carried off Orithyia from the banks of the Ilissus?

Socrates: Such is the tradition.

Phaedrus: And is this the exact spot? The little stream is delightfully clear and bright; I can fancy that there might be maidens playing near.

Socrates: But let me ask you, friend: have we not reached the plane-tree to which you were conducting us?

Phaedrus: Yes, this is the tree.

Socrates: By Here, a fair resting-place, full of summer sounds and scents. Here is this lofty and spreading plane-tree, and the agnus castus high and clustering, in the fullest blossom and the greatest fragrance; and the stream which flows beneath the plane-tree is deliciously cold to the feet. Judging from the ornaments and images, this must be a spot sacred to Achelous and the Nymphs. How delightful is the breeze—so very sweet; and there is a sound in the air shrill and summerlike which makes answer to the chorus of the cicadae. But the greatest charm of all is the grass, like a pillow gently sloping to the head. My dear Phaedrus, you have been an admirable guide.

Name_____

In Other Words

When you read Plato's description of the area where Socrates and his friend go to talk, you can almost imagine being there. An effective description includes precise, vivid words that rouse the senses.

Focus on the final paragraph of the excerpt, in which Plato describes the setting. First write how Plato described each element. Then write your own descriptions. You may want to use a thesaurus to help you choose precise, vivid words that target the senses.

Item	Plato's Description	Your Description
tree		
flowering shrub (Agnus castus)		
stream		
breeze		
sound in the air		
grass		

Alexander the Great

Objective

√ Students will participate in a cooperative learning group to read and rewrite text as a script and then perform it as reader's theater.

Preparation

√ Choose a panel of judges from administration, staff, and/or parents.

√ Make copies of *Alexander the Great as a Boy* (page 80) for each student plus the panel of judges.

√ Copy *Life of Alexander: "Alexander and the Wild Horse" for Reader's Theater* (page 81) for each student.

√ For optional use, copy *Fluency Evaluation* (page 82) for the judging panel.

√ For the optional Side Trip, copy *Homer and the Odyssey* (page 83) for selected students.

Fluency Suggestions and Activities

To help students analyze the text and read with comprehension and fluency, present the historical background and preteach the vocabulary on the following page before doing the fluency activity.

1. Distribute copies of *Alexander the Great as a Boy* (page 80). Point out that the preface tells some background information about Alexander. Read aloud the preface as students follow along, and then take a few moments to discuss Alexander in more detail. Tell students that Plutarch wrote *Parallel Lives*, which includes *Life of Alexander* and *Life of Caesar*. Plutarch lived several hundred years after Alexander, so his writing was history, not contemporary first-hand knowledge.

2. Next read the excerpt from Plutarch's *Life of Alexander*, having students follow as you model fluent reading of the story. Afterward, discuss the language used in the English translation (*dost, thou, art, thine, knowest, shouldst, thy, thee*). Ask students to update these terms as we would say them today. Finally, address any other vocabulary as needed.

3. Ask students to identify the form in which the story is written (running text). Ask them to suggest how it might be reformatted not only to show quotations correctly, but also for ease of reading. If no one suggests reader's theater or script, offer it yourself.

4. Distribute copies of the reader's theater worksheet *Life of Alexander: "Alexander and the Horse" for Reader's Theater* (page 81). Assign each student to a group, and have students write their names and group numbers where indicated on the page. Continue explaining the directions as shown. Explain that groups will work cooperatively to create a reader's theater script from the text. Allow students to update the language so that it is more understandable for an audience today. Finally, tell students that they will be presenting their final work as reader's theater before a panel of judges. Explain who the judges will be and how their performances will be evaluated—either informally by judges' comments or formally with the *Fluency Evaluation* (page 82).

Alexander the Great (cont.)

History Connection

Note: The basic background for reading the excerpt from Plutarch's *Life of Alexander* appears on the student page. The following is additional information.

Alexander's parents, Philip and Olympias, were devoted to Alexander. However, they were not particularly devoted to each other. Philip was frequently off on conquests, and although proud of his son's exceptionalities, the two spent little time together. Alexander was closer to his mother, who fed his ego, and he grew to become fanatical about wanting to outdo his father's accomplishments. Phillip encouraged him and must have placed a great deal of trust in his son's abilities at a young age. This is evidenced by the fact that, during an absence, Philip left Alexander in charge of the whole kingdom—with the power to rule in his name—when Alexander was just 16. When Philip was assassinated (perhaps at the will of Olympias), 20-year-old Alexander was permanently in power and well prepared to use it. When encountered by resistance by anyone—outside and even within his own kingdom—Alexander was ruthless. For those who thought this handsome young man should not have been taken seriously, it did not take long to change their minds. Alexander was fearless in pursuing what he believed to be his destiny. After many successes, he even came to believe that he was a god and invincible.

Plutarch's story tells how young Alexander acquired a horse, Bucephalas. It is interesting to note that Alexander is said to have ridden Bucephalas in every battle he fought in Greece and Asia. In 326 B.C., when Alexander was fighting a battle in India, Bucephalas was wounded and died. Alexander, in a rare expression of sentiment, was grief stricken.

Vocabulary Connection

Discuss unfamiliar vocabulary encountered in the text. Begin with these and then add any others you feel need to be reviewed or introduced. Discuss the words' meanings and how they are used specifically in the context of the material.

- **talents**—ancient units of weight and money
- **intractable**—unruly; strong-willed and resistant to control or discipline
- **rashness**—acting without thought to consequences
- **mantle**—cloak

Extension Ideas

- Have students find out the meaning of the phrase "self-fulfilling prophecy." Then ask them to write a paragraph stating if they believe this applies to Alexander, and why or why not.
- **Side Trip:** This optional extension activity is for capable students who are also interested in ancient history or classic literature. Have pair of students use *Homer and the Odyssey* (page 83) to prepare a presentation on Homer and an excerpt from the *Odyssey* for the rest of the class.

Name _____

Alexander the Great as a Boy

Excerpts from *Parallel Lives* by Plutarch (~A.D. 100)

Preface: *Alexander III of Macedon was born in 356 B.C., to Philip II and his wife Olympias in the northern Greek kingdom of Macedonia. His father, Philip, believed that Alexander was destined for greatness and therefore, even as child, began to groom him for his destiny. Alexander was educated formally by Aristotle and proved to be unusually bright, intense, and perceptive. Whether true, exaggerated, or plain fiction, tales about Alexander abound with details of his many attributes—from his distinctive physical looks to his exceptional abilities. When Alexander was only 20 years old, his father Philip was assassinated. Alexander not only took the reins of the kingdom of Greece, but fearlessly proceeded to conquer an area that spanned three continents and incorporated two million square miles. Alexander was many things, but most notably a military genius. Through his relentless efforts, he managed to change the ancient world in just a few short years. Alexander only lived to be 32, but experienced and accomplished more than mere men had done in several lifetimes. For these and many other reasons, he is known as Alexander the Great.*

Incident from the "Life of Alexander" by Plutarch

Once upon a time Philoneicus the Thessalian brought Bucephalas, offering to sell him to Philip for thirteen talents, and they went down into the plain to try the horse, who appeared to be savage and altogether intractable, neither allowing any one to mount him, nor heeding the voice of any of Philip's attendants, but rearing up against all of them. Then Philip was vexed and ordered the horse to be led away, believing him to be altogether wild and unbroken; but Alexander, who was near by, said: "What a horse they are losing, because, for lack of skill and courage, they cannot manage him!" At first, then, Philip held his peace; but as Alexander many times let fall such words and showed great distress, he said: "Dost thou find fault with thine elders in the belief that thou knowest more than they do or art better able to manage a horse?" "This horse, at any rate," said Alexander, "I could manage better than others have." "And if thou shouldst not, what penalty wilt thou undergo for thy rashness?" "Indeed," said Alexander, "I will forfeit the price of the horse."

There was laughter at this, and then an agreement between father and son as to the forfeiture, and at once Alexander ran to the horse, took hold of his bridle-rein, and turned him towards the sun; for he had noticed, as it would seem, that the horse was greatly disturbed by the sight of his own shadow falling in front of him and dancing about. And after he had calmed the horse a little in this way, and had stroked him with his hand, when he saw that he was full of spirit and courage, he quietly cast aside his mantle and with a light spring safely bestrode him. Then, with a little pressure of the reins on the bit, and without striking him or tearing his mouth, he held him in hand; but when he saw that the horse was rid of the fear that had beset him, and was impatient for the course, he gave him his head, and at last urged him on with sterner tone and thrust of foot. Philip and his company were speechless with anxiety at first; but when Alexander made the turn in proper fashion and came back to them proud and exultant, all the rest broke into loud cries, but his father, as we are told, actually shed tears of joy, and when Alexander had dismounted, kissed him, saying: "My son, seek thee out a kingdom equal to thyself; Macedonia has not room for thee."

Name_____

Life of Alexander: "Alexander and the Wild Horse" for Reader's Theater

Group #_____ Names _____

Directions: Working as a cooperative group, rewrite Plutarch's account of the story of Alexander and the wild horse as a reader's theater script. Break up the text, edit it for clarity, and rewrite it so that everyone in your group has a reading part. Use the space below for drafting. Be prepared to perform a fluent reading of your script by the following date: _____. Each of you will need a clean copy of your finalized script at that time.

_____

_____

_____

_____

_____

_____

_____

_____

_____

_____

_____

_____

_____

_____

_____

_____

_____

_____

_____

_____

_____

_____

Name_____

Fluency Evaluation

Directions: Below are two forms for evaluating your group's reading fluency. After you have practiced, use the first one to see how you are doing and to make any adjustments. Use the second one with your final performance. Then compare the results. Did your fluency improve?

Group Names: _____

Evaluation 1

Our reading was   very smooth   somewhat smooth   choppy

Our reading rate was   too slow   too fast   just right

We misread these words: _____

_____

Did we read with appropriate expression?   yes   no

Our improvement plan: _____

_____

_____

Evaluation 2

Our reading was   very smooth   somewhat smooth   choppy

Our reading rate was   too slow   too fast   just right

We misread these words: _____

_____

Did we read with appropriate expression?   yes   no

Our improvement plan: _____

_____

_____

Name_____

Homer and the Odyssey

Directions: In this challenge, you will look at an excerpt from the ancient work and not only read it, but try to get its meaning. Work with your partner to prepare a presentation about Homer and the *Odyssey* for your class.

1. Do some background research. Find out the answers to these questions: Who was Homer? When and where did he live? What does *odyssey* mean? What is an epic? When was the *Odyssey* written? What is it about? How long is the entire work?

2. Read the excerpt below. What it is describing? Mark the words you do not understand. Use whatever sources you can to decipher their meanings.

3. Write an introduction that explains to your audience the background information you found and what they are about to hear.

4. Rewrite the excerpt as a poem for two voices (using alternating lines).

5. Practice reading it aloud with your partner until you can read it fluently and expressively.

6. When you are both ready, present your introduction and poem to the class.

Excerpt from the *Odyssey* by Homer *translation by Alexander Pope (1688–1744)*

And now, rejoicing in the prosperous gales
With beating heart Ulysses spreads his sails;
Placed at the helm he sate, and mark'd the skies,
Nor closed in sleep his ever-watchful eyes.
There view'd the Pleiads, and the Northern Team,
And great Orion's more refulgent beam.
To which, around the axle of the sky,
The Bear, revolving, points his golden eye:
Who shines exalted on the ethereal plain,
Nor bathes his blazing forehead in the main.
Far on the left those radiant fires to keep
The nymph directed, as he sail'd the deep.
Full seventeen nights he cut the foaming way:
The distant land appear'd the following day:
Then swell'd to sight Phaeacia's dusky coast,
And woody mountains, half in vapours lost;
That lay before him indistinct and vast,
Like a broad shield amid the watery waste.

Courtesy of the United States Naval Observatory Library

Arrian's Description of India
From the third century B.C.

Objective
√ Students will listen to an oral preview reading of the text, practice reading using a taped version for oral support, and then read a selection orally aloud with the tape.

Preparation
√ Ask students to have their copies of the world map (pages 188–189) from previous lessons.

√ Prepare tape recordings of the different sections of text, modeling fluent reading. Be sure to read with clarity and expression and at a natural rate.

√ Make copies of *India: The Caste System* (pages 86–87) for each student.

√ Enlist the help of parent volunteers or support staff to listen to students' readings and do a quick, half-page evaluation. Make copies of *Oral Support Reading Evaluation* (page 88) and cut apart into half pages.

√ For the optional Side Trip, copy *Reflection on Society* (page 89) for each student.

Fluency Suggestions and Activities

To help students analyze the text and read with comprehension and fluency, present the historical background and preteach the vocabulary on the following page before doing the fluency activity.

Note: The selection from Arrian's writing is a description of the caste system in ancient India. The text appears as written except that it has been divided into sections that describe each caste. Require each student to prepare one section to read aloud. The length of the sections varies widely—from quite long to very short. This gives you the opportunity to assign sections by students' individual abilities to handle text. For example, you may want your ELLs to read one of the shorter sections, while your advanced students tackle the longer ones.

1. Have students locate India on their world maps. Assist them as needed.

2. For the oral preview, play the taped reading of the entire selection while students follow along on their copies.

3. Assign each student a section. Have students mark their assigned sections on their copies. Make the tape recordings available to students. Direct them to listen to the recording of their section several times while reading out loud along with it. Dr. Timothy Rasinski calls this strategy Oral Support Reading (*The Fluent Reader*, p. 123).

4. Enlist the help of parent volunteers or support staff to listen to each student read along with the tape. Provide evaluation sheets for listeners to record their assessments, and then share them with students. Have students fill in the bottom line. If you don't have volunteers who can help, try listening to a few students read each day. Another option is to set aside a separate time period for listening while the rest of the students complete the optional Side Trip activity on the following page.

Arrian's Description of India *(cont.)*

History Connection

Arrian is the English name given to Lucius Flavius Arrianus 'Xenophon', who was a Greek historian and philosopher of the Roman period. His description of India is extensively based on the writings of Megasthanese, a Greek ambassador who spent several years in India and recorded his observations in a work called *Indica*. Though large portions of Megasthanese's original writings are lost, Arrian relied upon these as firsthand source material for his historical writing. It is widely believed that Arrian's work is more factually accurate than some of the other early historians who incorporated more hearsay and embellishment into their accounts.

Megasthanese wrote his book *Indica* in the third century B.C. Arrian constructed his history 300 years or so later using extracts and quotes directly from Megasthanese. In this selection, Arrian describes the caste system Megasthanese observed in India. The caste system is a social structure of rank that is rigid and is maintained from one generation to the next. Although the caste system is entwined with Hindu beliefs, it applies to everyone. The caste of a person is generally tied to their occupation, but its deeper significance is the rank of perceived "purity" vs. "pollution." The system to some extent remains intact today, much the same as Arrian described it. However, in more recent times another rank was added—that of no caste, which came to be known as "untouchables." In this lowest class were people who performed "polluting tasks," such as butchers. Although outlawed now, it was considered defiling to even touch an "untouchable."

In traditional Hindu law texts, all castes are loosely grouped into four classes. In order of hierarchy, these are the Brahmans (priests and scholars), the Kshatriyas (warriors and rulers), the Vaisyas (merchants, farmers, and traders), and the Sudras (laborers, including artisans, servants). The classes no longer strictly correspond to traditional professions. In modern times, the importance of caste has declined somewhat in India. Travel and food service have brought people of every caste in contact with one another, so it is impossible to be certain of the caste of a person. There are no particular castes linked to the modern professions of bank clerk, postal worker, teacher, and lawyer. However, castes have shown no sign of disappearing, mainly because of the system of marriage. Almost all Hindu marriages in India are arranged, and almost all arranged marriages occur between people of the same caste.

Vocabulary Connection

Discuss unfamiliar vocabulary encountered in the text that you feel need to be reviewed or introduced. Discuss the words' meanings and how they are used specifically in the context of the material.

Extension Ideas

- The country of India brings to mind images of tigers and elephants. Have students find the significance of these animals to past and present Indians.
- **Side Trip:** Use *Reflection on Society* (page 89) as an extension activity to stimulate critical thinking. Here students read a quote by a respected Indian religious leader, analyze its meaning, and then write a personal response to the quote. Prompt questions are included.

Name_____

India: The Caste System

Excerpts from *Arrian's Description of India* (Megasthanese's *Indica*)

Section 1

The Indians generally are divided into seven castes. Those called the wise men are less in number than the rest, but chief in honor and regard. For they are under no necessity to do any bodily labor; nor to contribute from the results of their work to the common store; in fact, no sort of constraint whatever rests upon these wise men, save to offer the sacrifices to the gods on behalf of the people of India. Then whenever anyone sacrifices privately, one of these wise men acts as instructor of the sacrifice, since otherwise the sacrifice would not have proved acceptable to the gods. These Indians also are alone expert in prophecy, and none, save one of the wise men, is allowed to prophesy. And they prophesy about the seasons of the year, or of any impending public calamity: but they do not trouble to prophesy on private matters to individuals, either because their prophecy does not condescend to smaller things, or because it is undignified for them to trouble about such things. And when one has thrice made an error in his prophecy, he does not suffer any harm, except that he must forever hold his peace.

Section 2

Then next to these come the farmers, these being the most numerous class of Indians; they have no use for warlike arms or warlike deeds, but they till the land; and they pay the taxes to the kings and to the cities, such as are self-governing; and if there is internal war among the Indians, they may not touch these workers, and not even devastate the land itself; but some are making war and slaying all comers, and others close by are peacefully ploughing or gathering the fruits or shaking down apples or harvesting.

Section 3

The third class of Indians are the herdsmen, pasturers of sheep and cattle, and these dwell neither by cities nor in the villages. They are nomads and get their living on the hillsides, and they pay taxes from their animals; they hunt also birds and wild game in the country.

Section 4

The fourth class is of artisans and shopkeepers; these are workers, and pay tribute from their works, save such as make weapons of war; these are paid by the community. In this class are the shipwrights and sailors, who navigate the rivers.

India: The Caste System *(cont.)*

Section 5

The fifth class of Indians is the soldiers' class, next after the farmers in number; these have the greatest freedom and the most spirit. They practice military pursuits only. Their weapons others forge for them, and again others provide horses; others too serve in the camps, those who groom their horses and polish their weapons, guide the elephants, and keep in order and drive the chariots. They themselves, when there is need of war, go to war, but in time of peace they make merry; and they receive so much pay from the community that they can easily from their pay support others.

Section 6

The sixth class of Indians are those called overlookers. They oversee everything that goes on in the country or in the cities; and this they report to the King, where the Indians are governed by kings, or to the authorities, where they are independent. To these it is illegal to make any false report; nor was any Indian ever accused of such falsification.

Section 7

The seventh class is those who deliberate about the community together with the King, or, in such cities as are self-governing, with the authorities. In number this class is small, but in wisdom and uprightness it bears the palm from all others; from this class are selected their governors, district governors, and deputies, custodians of the treasures, officers of army and navy, financial officers, and overseers of agricultural works. To marry out of any class is unlawful—as, for instance, into the farmer class from the artisans, or the other way; nor must the same man practice two pursuits; nor change from one class into another, as to turn farmer from shepherd, or shepherd from artisan. It is only permitted to join the wise men out of any class; for their business is not an easy one, but of all most laborious.

Oral Support Reading Evaluation

Directions: You have practiced reading aloud your assigned section along with the taped reading. Now read it to your audience (listener). Your listener will fill out Part 1 as you read. Then afterward you will complete Part 2 about your own presentation.

Name _____ I am reading aloud Section #_____

Part 1: Listener completes

   ◆   Was my reading in sync with the taped reading?   *yes*   *mostly*   *somewhat*

   ◆   Did I stumble or trip on words?   *not at all*   *a few*   *a lot*

   ◆   Did I use pauses and phrasing correctly?   *yes*   *mostly*   *somewhat*

   ◆   Was the volume of my voice appropriate?   *just right*   *too loud*   *too soft*

   ◆   Did I read with appropriate expression?   *yes*   *mostly*   *somewhat*

   ◆   Could you understand what my section was about?   *yes*   *somewhat*   *not really*

Part 2: Reader completes

   ◆   Overall, I think I read this passage   *very well*   *fairly well*   *not so well*

   ◆   I think my listener evaluated my reading   *accurately*   *not accurately*

- -

Oral Support Reading Evaluation

Directions: You have practiced reading aloud your assigned section along with the taped reading. Now read it to your audience (listener). Your listener will fill out Part 1 as you read. Then afterward you will complete Part 2 about your own presentation.

Name _____ I am reading aloud Section #_____

Part 1: Listener completes

   ◆   Was my reading in sync with the taped reading?   *yes*   *mostly*   *somewhat*

   ◆   Did I stumble or trip on words?   *not at all*   *a few*   *a lot*

   ◆   Did I use pauses and phrasing correctly?   *yes*   *mostly*   *somewhat*

   ◆   Was the volume of my voice appropriate?   *just right*   *too loud*   *too soft*

   ◆   Did I read with appropriate expression?   *yes*   *mostly*   *somewhat*

   ◆   Could you understand what my section was about?   *yes*   *somewhat*   *not really*

Part 2: Reader completes

   ◆   Overall, I think I read this passage   *very well*   *fairly well*   *not so well*

   ◆   I think my listener evaluated my reading   *accurately*   *not accurately*

Name_____

Reflection on Society

❝*Sectarianism, bigotry, and its horrible descendant, fanaticism, have long possessed this beautiful earth. They have filled the earth with violence, drenched it often and often with human blood, destroyed civilization, and sent whole nations to despair. Had it not been for these horrible demons, human society would be far more advanced than it is now.*❞

—Swami Vivkananda, India, 1893

First use what you know about word roots and a dictionary to define these words:

sectarianism: _____

bigotry: _____

fanaticism: _____

Read the quote again, and write in your own words what it means.

_____

_____

_____

_____

_____

_____

Now read the quote aloud and reflect on the meaning. Think about when it was said. Does it still apply today? Has it applied to other times throughout history? The speaker was from India. Does the quote apply only to India? To other countries? To all societies? What does this quote say to you about the nature of human beings past, present, and future? Discuss the quote and these questions with a friend or adult.

Finally, on a clean sheet of paper, write about your reactions to this quote. Be sure to describe your feelings, thoughts, and reflections on its meaning. Read your reflections aloud to someone in your family.

One Law There Is

A poem by King Bhartrihari, written in A.D. 100

Objective

√ Students will participate in a cumulative reading exercise to practice and increase fluency.

Preparation

√ Prepare a chart or transparency of *One Law There Is* (page 92) with no breaks between stanzas.

√ Copy *One Law There Is* (page 92), *One Law, One Puzzle* (page 93), and *The King's Law* (page 94) for each student.

Fluency Suggestions and Activities

To help students analyze the text and read with comprehension and fluency, present the historical background and preteach the vocabulary on the following page before starting the fluency activity.

1. After sharing the information in the History Connection section, distribute copies of *One Law There Is* (page 92). Tell students that this poem, written in India in the year A.D. 100, is a very brief and to-the-point explanation of Hindu belief. If you like, expand your discussion by asking students what was going on in other parts of the world at this time.

2. Read aloud the preface and then the poem. Model your reading so that the poem flows smoothly, despite it being visually broken up. Remind students that, unless it is done intentionally, a poem should not sound "sing-song-y." To avoid this, the reader should not automatically pause at the end of each line, but continue until the thought is complete. Read the poem aloud two more times—the first time pausing after each line, and the second time reading through until each thought is complete.

3. Explain to students that, after practicing, the class will perform a choral reading of the poem in a form called reverse cumulative reading. This means that the reading is started with all students, and a few drop out as the reading progresses. By the end, a single student is reading alone.

4. Display the chart or transparency of the poem. Work as a class to determine where the natural breaks are and mark the divisions. On the transparency or chart, label each section with a letter. Then assign each student a letter. Explain that when the class reads the poem together, students should stop reading at the end of the section marked with their letter.

5. Rehearse several times as a group until the reading flows. When the group is ready, invite a colleague to hear your students' reverse cumulative choral reading of *One Law There Is*.

6. Follow up this activity by having students complete *The King's Law* (page 94), to analyze the poem. Answer Key (page 94): 1. A 2. B 3. A 4. B

One Law There Is (cont.)

History Connection

One of the tenets of Hinduism is that to achieve one's highest state, one must first understand beauty and morality and then renounce desire, pleasure, and material comforts in order to free one's mind from mortal concerns.

Bhartrihari traya Shataka was king of Ujjaini in the first century. Originally a rich, powerful man who enjoyed the luxuries of life, he later chose to renounce all worldly pleasures for the spiritual path of Hinduism. Bhartrihari went on to express his beliefs in hundreds of verses, many of which focus on renunciation. He became one of India's most inspirational yogis (spiritual teachers), and his work is still widely read today.

King Bhartrihari wrote in Sanskrit, which is a language that is clear and concise. Even in translation, the messages are simple and direct. For example, Bhartrihari's verse below can be read and easily understood as well today as when it was written nearly 2,000 years ago.

> With enjoyment, comes fear of disease
> With social position, fear of disfavor
> With riches, fear of hostile people (kings)
> With honor, fear of humiliation
> With power, fear of enemies
> With beauty, fear of old age
> With scholarship, fear of challengers
> With virtue, fear of traducers
> With the identification with body, fear of death
> Everything in this world is done with fear
> Renunciation alone makes one fearless.

Vocabulary Connection

Discuss unfamiliar vocabulary encountered in the text. Have students complete the crossword puzzle on *One Law, One Puzzle* (page 93). Below is a list of the terms in the puzzle and their matching clues (meanings). *See notation below the verse on page 92.

alter—change; **abide**—stand; remain as is; **discard**—throw away; toss out; **don**—put on; **doth**—does; **doff**—remove; cast off; **marred**—stained; flawed; **kindle**—ignite; provoke; *****infold**—enclose; surround; enfold; **unfold**—make clear gradually; develop over time

Extension Idea

• Read the above verse to students. Ask them to repeat the last two lines after you. Begin an informal conversation about whether or not Bhartrihari was on to something by saying that fear is what motivates all behavior. Ask students to think of things we choose to do or choose to avoid doing. Are they motivated by fear in some way?

Name _____

One Law There Is

A poem by King Bhartrihari, written in A.D. 100

Preface: *King Bhartrihari abandoned the luxuries of his throne and made his home in the forest, where he could meditate at his will and be free from the honors and temptations of life in a palace. This poem is one of many he wrote related to his philosophy of life. His writings are respected for their simple but powerful messages about Hindu beliefs.*

> ONE law there is: no deed perform
> To others that to thee were harm;
> And this is all, all laws beside
> With circumstances alter or abide.
>
> Like as our outworn garments we discard,
> And other new ones don;
> So doth the Soul these bodies doff when marred
> And others new put on.
>
> Fire doth not kindle It, nor sword divides,
> Nor winds nor waters harm;
> Eternal and unchanged the One abides,
> And smiles at all alarm.
>
> Like as a goldsmith beateth out his gold
> To other fashions fairer than the old,
> So may the Spirit, learning ever more,
> In ever nobler forms his life infold.*

*The word *infold* may be a lesser-used form of the word *enfold*; or it may be meant to be *unfold*. To infold, or enfold, means to wrap completely around; unfold can mean to develop over time. Either term can be interpreted as making sense within the context of the verse.

Name_____

One Law, One Puzzle

Directions: Bhartrihari's poem "One Law There Is" may be short, but it contains a few words that you need to understand precisely in order to get the meaning of the verse. Use the list of terms from the poem and the clues below to solve this crossword puzzle.

alter	abide	discard	don	doth	doff	marred	kindle	infold	unfold

ACROSS

1. change
2. enclose; surround, enfold
5. ignite; provoke
6. make clear gradually; develop over time
7. stained; flawed
9. put on

DOWN

1. stand; remain as is
3. remove; cast off
4. throw away; toss out
8. does

What do you think?

After reading the verse again with better understanding, what do you think the last line of the poem means and why?

_____

_____

_____

_____

Name_____

The King's Law

The poem "One Law There Is" was written almost 2,000 years ago. Although it was translated into English much later, sometimes old writings are still hard to understand because you are not used to the words used. Below each stanza are two summaries, but only one is accurate. Circle the letter of the one that best says what you think the king meant.

> ONE law there is: no deed perform
> To others that to thee were harm;
> And this is all, all laws beside
> With circumstances alter or abide.

A. Treat others as you would want to be treated; no exceptions.

B. Only harm others if they harm you first; but that depends on the circumstances.

> Like as our outworn garments we discard,
> And other new ones don;
> So doth the Soul these bodies doff when marred
> And others new put on.

A. If you do something bad, your soul is marred, but you can cover it up on the outside.

B. It's okay to make mistakes if you learn from them, and replace your old ways with new ones.

> Fire doth not kindle It, nor sword divides,
> Nor winds nor waters harm;
> Eternal and unchanged the One abides,
> And smiles at all alarm.

A. If you are at peace with yourself and don't concern yourself with outside influences (greed, envy, pleasure, material things), they will have no power over you.

B. Don't be afraid of fire or swords or wind or water; they cannot harm you.

> Like as a goldsmith beateth out his gold
> To other fashions fairer than the old,
> So may the Spirit, learning ever more,
> In ever nobler forms his life infold.

A. You should keep up with the times and go along with what is in fashion.

B. To learn is to continuously transform into something better.

Buddha and His Teachings

Objective

√ Students will participate in one of two choral read-and-refrain fluency activities, with special emphasis on reading rate and flow.

Preparation

√ Make as many copies as needed of one or both of these scripts: *Buddha's Wheel of Sacred Law— The Eightfold Path* (pages 98–99) and *Words of Truth* (page 100).

√ For the optional Extension Activity, provide plain white paper plates.

Fluency Suggestions and Activities

To help students analyze the text and read with comprehension and fluency, present the historical background and preteach the vocabulary on the following page before starting the fluency activity.

Note: This lesson contains two separate choral reading scripts. The suggested way to use them is to divide your class into two groups (perhaps by reading level) and have each group read and prepare its choral presentation separately (if possible, without the other group hearing it ahead of time). The oral presentation will then consist of each group performing for the other.

1. Be sure to share with students the background story about the Buddha in the History Connection section on the following page. Next divide your class in two groups. If you group your students by ability or reading level, you can have as few as 11 in either group and the remaining number of students in the other group.

2. Physically separate the groups—at least on opposite sides of the room, if not completely separate—and distribute the scripts. If you do not have access to another adult in the room to work with one of the groups, you can alternate previewing the text and vocabulary with each group. For example, while you read with one group, you could have the other students find and highlight the vocabulary words in their scripts.

3. Model fluent reading of the scripts at least once for each group. Then either allow them to work cooperatively on their own to pick reading parts and practice, or assign parts if you prefer. As students practice, have them read in what Dr. Timothy Rasinski calls *mumble reading*, which in this case has to be less of a mumble and more of a hushed tone, but with clear pronunciation. If necessary, guide students through the pattern of alternating between a single reader and the group refrain.

4. For the actual presentation, you may want to increase motivation by offering some reward or special privilege to the group who is better prepared. If you do this, to avoid being perceived as biased, you should probably ask a colleague or administrator to decide which group's performance deserves the award for effort.

Buddha and His Teachings (cont.)

History Connection

Siddhartha Gautama may have lived from 566 to 486 B.C. (According to more recent research, revised dates are 490–410 B.C.). He was born a prince, and stories tell of premonitions of him becoming either a powerful king or a buddha who relieves the suffering of men. His father, wanting him to be king, indulged him with anything he wanted, but kept him in the palace sheltered from outside influences. The prince married, had a child, and lived royally, but he was not happy. It was not until he was a young man that he laid eyes upon the world outside the palace. In doing so, he was stunned and profoundly affected by the suffering and sadness he saw.

The prince decided to renounce all his worldly goods, and even left his wife and child to go out into the world and find a way to conquer suffering. First, he took the path of self-denial and hardship hoping that, by clearing away all distractions, he might find the answers he sought.

But still he could not make sense of things. Then, while meditating under a tree, Siddhartha suddenly understood. It was like awakening from a deep, dark sleep and seeing the light for the first time. Everything seemed clear. He knew what to do. Siddhartha spent the rest of his life sharing his enlightenment through teachings. He became known as the Buddha, which means "one who is awakened." Buddhism has remained a philosophy that millions still follow today.

Vocabulary Connection

Discuss unfamiliar vocabulary encountered in the text. Begin with these and then add any others you feel need to be reviewed or introduced. Discuss the words' meanings and how they are used specifically in the context of the material.

Script 1: *Buddha's Wheel of Sacred Law—The Eightfold Path*

- **self-indulgence**—excessive gratification of one's own desires or whims
- **noble**—relating to excellence of character or having high moral principles
- **malicious**—with harmful intent
- **harmony**—pleasant arrangement; happy agreement

Script 2: *Words of Truth*

- **meditating**—deeply concentrating with controlled thought
- **cultivate**—to grow or develop something; to nurture
- **miser**—person who hoards money, unwilling to spend or share; a selfish person
- **liberality**—with generosity or unselfish giving
- **negligence**—acting without thought or regard; uncaring so as to cause harm
- **wrought**—done in a skillful way; brought about
- **appeased**—brought to a state of peace and quiet

Buddha and His Teachings (cont.)

Extension Idea

- Extend this lesson into art and math. After the performances, ask students to recall the names of the eight components of the Middle Path, or Wheel of Sacred Law. Write these on the board (out of order, as shown).

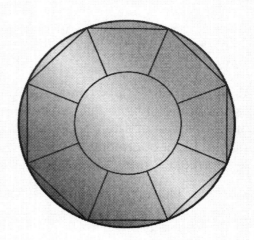

  Right Speech

  Right Thought

  Right Mindfulness

  Right Concentration

  Right Effort

  Right Livelihood

  Right Understanding

  Right Action

Then give each student a plain white paper plate. Challenge them to suggest how they could divide it into eight equal sections. For example, they could fold it in half three times, or use a protractor to determine angle degrees needed for each section to be exactly one-eighth ($360° \div 8 = 45°$). After ideas are presented, let students divide their plates. Have them number the sections on the front, and label the back with their names and the title Buddha's Wheel of Sacred Law—The Eightfold Path.

Next choose a random component and read aloud the description only. Ask students which of the eight components you just described. Tell students to write their answers in the correct numbered section on their wheels. Example: Say, "Buddha's fourth tenet says to conduct oneself in a way that is moral, honorable, and peaceful. One should show kindness, be considerate of others, and behave in a manner that promotes harmony. Write this rule's name in the section you marked number 4." (Right Action)

Continue presenting the remaining seven of Buddha's sacred laws, until students have filled in the all the sections. Conclude the lesson by reminding students that Buddha's proposals take self-discipline and are not just for Buddhists. The messages are more philosophical than religious; they are more about people in general than about any particular beliefs about god.

Name _____

Buddha's Wheel of Sacred Law— The Eightfold Path

The teachings of the Buddha

R1: The Buddha believed that neither self-indulgence nor total self-denial was the appropriate path to take in life. Instead, he taught a more middle-of-the-road approach, because it avoids extremes in the search for happiness—either through material and sense-pleasures, or through self-imposed hardship and rejection of all that is material in hopes of becoming purely spiritual.

R2: It was through personal experience that the Buddha discovered the Middle Path, "which gives vision and knowledge, which leads to Calm, Insight, Enlightenment, Nirvana." Because of its eight interdependent components, it is sometimes represented by a wheel with eight connecting spokes. It is also called the Wheel of Sacred Law or the Noble Eightfold Path.

R3: They are not steps in the sense of learning one before the next, but rather traits to be developed at the same time to the greatest extent possible by the individual person. Each is linked with the others, so that together the person develops respect for him or herself as well as all others. These eight concepts form the Buddha's Eightfold Path.

All: **Number 1—Right Understanding**

R4: Right Understanding means looking at and accepting things as they really are, seeing each thing's true nature without labels or judgments. Understanding is different from knowledge, which is using intelligence to learn and remember information.

All: **Number 2—Right Thought**

R5: Right Thought means not thinking of oneself as detached from all other beings. Understanding others leads to thinking about them with regard and tolerance. This applies to individuals, groups, and societies. Right Thought is that which connects one to all and commands respect for all.

All: **Number 3—Right Speech**

R6: Right Speech means avoiding telling lies, talking poorly of someone else, using harsh, rude, impolite, malicious, and abusive language, and refraining from idle, useless, foolish gossip or babble. Right Speech is thoughtful, gentle, meaningful, and useful.

All: **Number 4—Right Action**

R7: Right Action means conducting oneself in a way that is moral, honorable, and peaceful. One should show kindness, be considerate of others, and behave in a manner that promotes harmony.

Buddha's Wheel of Sacred Law— The Eightfold Path *(cont.)*

All: **Number 5—Right Livelihood**

R8: Right Livelihood means one should abstain from making one's living through a profession that brings harm to others.

All: **Number 6—Right Effort**

R9: Right Effort means making a willful effort to prevent evil and unwholesome states of mind, to correct it when it already exists, and to do what one can to promote and cause good, wholesome, and harmonious states of mind in oneself and others.

All: **Number 7—Right Mindfulness**

R10: Right Mindfulness means being diligently aware of activities of the body, one's sensations and feelings, the activities of the mind, and one's ideas, thoughts, and conceptions.

All: **Number 8—Right Concentration**

R11: Right Concentration means recognizing and discarding unwholesome and negative feelings, such as ill-will, desire, worry, and doubt, and concentrating first on filling oneself with joy and happiness. Once that is achieved, one then concentrates on acquiring tranquility and harmony within oneself and among his or her surroundings.

Buddha's Wheel of Sacred Law—The Middle Path

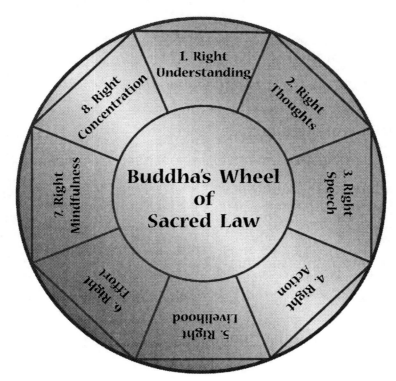

Name _____

Words of Truth

Selected teachings from the *Dhammapada*

R1:   In the year 601 B.C., while meditating under a tree, Siddhartha Gautama had a spiritual awakening. He shared his enlightenment by teaching others.

R2:   Soon he became known as the "Buddha" (one who is awakened). The Buddha offered advice to others about how to live peacefully, free of suffering.

All: **Now we will share with you some of his ideas:**

R3:   *The best of all paths is the Eightfold Path. Entering upon the path you will make an end of pain.*

All: **This is the teaching of the Buddha.**

R4:   *Not to do any evil, to cultivate good, to purify one's mind. . .*

All: **This is the teaching of the Buddha.**

R5:   *Whosoever offend an innocent person, pure and guiltless, his evil comes back on that fool like a fine dust thrown against the wind.*

All: **This is the teaching of the Buddha.**

R6:   *The man of little learning grows like a bull; his flesh grows, but not his wisdom.*

All: **This is the teaching of the Buddha.**

R7:   *Happy indeed we live without hate amongst the hateful. We live free from hatred amidst hateful men.*

All: **This is the teaching of the Buddha.**

R8:   *Conquer anger by love, evil by good; conquer the miser with liberality, and the liar with truth.*

All: **This is the teaching of the Buddha.**

R9:   *Do not follow mean things. Do not dwell in negligence. Do not embrace false views.*

All: **This is the teaching of the Buddha.**

R10:   *Neither mother, nor father, not any other relative, can do a man such good as is wrought by a rightly directed mind.*

All: **This is the teaching of the Buddha.**

R11:   *Hatred is never appeased by hatred in this world; it is appeased by love. This is an eternal law.*

All: **These are the teachings of the Buddha.**

Tales from Ancient India

Objective

√ Students will read passages fluently after practicing and monitoring fluency with repeated readings.

Preparation

√ Copy *Five Old Tales from India* (pages 103–106) and *Improving My Fluency* (page 107) for each student.

Fluency Suggestions and Activities

To help students analyze the text and read with comprehension and fluency, present the historical background and preteach the vocabulary on the following page before starting the fluency activity.

Note: The five tales differ in length and difficulty so that students of various fluency levels can use them. On the following page, an overview is included with the vocabulary for each story.

1. Distribute copies of *Five Old Tales from India* (pages 103–106). Begin by modeling fluent reading of each tale. Be sure to use "storytelling" form—dramatic voice inflection, emphasis, expression, and so on.

2. Tell students that, like anything else, fluency improves with practice. Distribute copies of *Improving My Fluency* (page 107). Have them look at the directions with you. Explain that the activity is like a contract. At this point you have the option of assigning specific tales from those offered, so that you control the difficulty and amount of reading each student is required to do, or allowing students to choose one of the tales for themselves.

3. After making sure that students understand the directions and have filled in the title of the tale they have chosen, assign or let them choose partners. Distribute copies of the tales as needed, and give students time to practice.

4. In the Aesop's Fables (pages 69–73) lesson earlier in this book, the suggested presentation was to have a Fable Fest and perform for younger students. That lesson also suggested combining the performance of fables with these tales from India for a multicultural read-aloud festival. If possible, either go to an elementary class or invite one to yours to listen to your students read the stories in a dramatic performance of fluency. If this is not possible, when students have practiced and read their tale three times with their partners, have them switch partners for a final dramatic reading.

Tales from Ancient India *(cont.)*

History Connection

Although different cultures evolve independently in various times and places, using storytelling as an entertaining way of teaching values is a common thread. As you read the old tales from India, you will notice similarities to familiar stories from other cultures, such as Aesop's fables.

The word *storytelling* implies spoken, rather than written, delivery. At first the tales were passed along orally from generation to generation. Only later were some written down. Although they are enjoyable to read on our own, there remains something especially appealing about hearing a story aloud. Is it the dramatic expression of the storyteller? Is it the personal connection between the storyteller and the listener? It is perhaps both, and much more.

Vocabulary Connection

Discuss unfamiliar vocabulary. Begin with these and then add any others as you see fit. Discuss the words' meanings and how they are used specifically in the context of the material.

Tale 1: Although this is one of the longer tales, there are no difficult vocabulary words.

Tale 2: This tale is medium length, with one or two possibly unfamiliar terms.
- **blacksmith**—person who melts and forms metals into objects, such as horseshoes
- **humoring**—doing what someone wants in order to keep that person content

Tale 3: This tale is short, but contains several possibly unfamiliar terms:
- **pannier**—a large basket placed on the back to carry things (usually in pairs on animals)
- **provoked**—caused a reaction (Note: It does not always mean to cause *anger*.)
- **bearing**—pushing down upon with weight; testing support or strength

Tale 4: This tale is medium length and of medium difficulty.
- **plumage**—the feathers of a bird
- **moved**—feeling of emotional tenderness or pity
- **avaricious**—greedy for money, wealth, or riches

Tale 5: This tale is long and has the most difficult vocabulary.
- **credulous**—gullible; easy to fool
- **fret**—worry; be agitated about
- **supplications**—humble requests of someone who has the power to grant them
- **metamorphosis**—to change from one form into another
- **jeering**—laughing, shouting, and making fun of
- **dupe**—someone who has been tricked or deceived
- **presumption**—disrespectful; overconfident

Extension Idea

- Many of these vocabulary words have multiple meanings. Have students look up selected words, find another meaning for each, and then use the word in two sentences showing the different meanings.

Name _____

Five Old Tales from India

Tale 1: Watering the Garden

It was just before New Year's in Benares, in northern India. Everyone in the city was getting ready for the three-day celebration, including the gardener of the king's pleasure garden.

There was a large troop of monkeys living in this pleasure garden. So they wouldn't have to think too much, they always followed the advice of their leader, the monkey king.

The royal gardener wanted to celebrate the New Year's holiday, just like everybody else. So he decided to hand over his duties to the monkeys.

He went to the monkey king and said, "Oh, king of monkeys, my honorable friend, would you do a little favor for me? New Year's is coming. I, too, wish to celebrate. So I must be away for three full days. Here in this lovely garden, there are plenty of fruits and berries and nuts to eat. You and your subjects may be my guests, and eat as much as you wish. In return, please water the young trees and plants while I'm gone."

The monkey king replied, "Don't worry about a thing, my friend! We will do a terrific job! Have a good time!"

The gardener showed the monkeys where the watering buckets were kept. Feeling confident, he left to celebrate the holiday. The monkeys called after him, "Happy New Year!"

The next day, the monkeys filled up the buckets, and began watering the young trees and plants. Then the king of the monkeys addressed them: "My subjects, it is not good to waste water. Therefore, pull up each young tree or plant before watering. Inspect it to see how long the roots are. Then give more water to the ones with long roots, and less water to the ones with short roots. That way we will not waste water, and the gardener will be pleased!"

Without giving it any further thought, the obedient subjects followed their king's orders.

Meanwhile, a wise man was walking by outside the entrance to the garden. He saw the monkeys uprooting all the lovely young trees and plants, measuring their roots, and carefully pouring water into the holes in the ground. He asked, "Oh foolish monkeys, what do you think you're doing to the king's beautiful garden?"

They answered, "We are watering the trees and plants, without wasting water! We were commanded to do so by our lord king."

The man said, "If this is the wisdom of the wisest among you—the king—what are the rest of you like? Intending to do a worthwhile deed, your foolishness turns it into disaster!"

Five Old Tales from India (cont.)

Tale 2: The Man in the Moon

There was a blacksmith once who complained: "I am not well, and my work is too warm. I want to be a stone on the mountain. There it must be cool, for the wind blows and the trees give a shade."

A wise man who had power over all things replied: "Go you, be a stone." And he was a stone, high up on the mountain-side. It happened that a stone-cutter came that way for a stone, and when he saw the one that had been the blacksmith, he knew that it was what he sought, and he began to cut it. The stone cried out: "This hurts! I no longer want to be a stone. A stone-cutter I want to be. That would be pleasant."

The wise man, humoring him, said, "Be a cutter." Thus he became a stone-cutter, and as he went seeking suitable stone, he grew tired, and his feet were sore. He whimpered, "I no longer want to cut stone. I would be the sun; that would be pleasant."

The wise man commanded, "Be the sun." And he was the sun. But the sun was warmer than the blacksmith, than a stone, than a stone-cutter, and he complained, "I do not like this. I would be the moon. It looks cool."

The wise man spoke yet again, "Be the moon." And he was the moon. "This is warmer than being the sun," murmured he, "for the light from the sun shines on me ever. I do not want to be the moon. I would be a smith again. That, verily, is the best life."

But the wise man replied, "I am weary of your changing. You wanted to be the moon; the moon you are, and it you will remain."

And in yon high heaven lives he to this day.

Tale 3: Let's See on Which Side the Camel Sits

Once a greengrocer and a potter jointly hired a camel and each filled one side of the pannier with his goods. The camel as he went along the road took a mouthful every now and then, as he had a chance, from the greengrocer's bag of vegetables. This provoked a laugh from the potter, who thought he had the best of the bargain.

But the time came for the camel to sit, and he naturally sat on the heavier side, bearing down on the pots, and also to have his mouth free to operate on the bag of greens. This caused the pots to break in the bag, and then the greengrocer had all the laugh to himself.

Vera Bogaerts/Shutterstock, Inc.

Five Old Tales from India *(cont.)*

Tale 4: The Peacock and the Tortoise

Once upon a time a peacock and a tortoise became great friends. The peacock lived on a tree on the banks of the stream in which the tortoise had his home; and daily the peacock after he had a drink of water danced near the stream and displayed his brightly colored plumage for the amusement of his friend.

Michael Kempf/Shutterstock, Inc.

One unfortunate day, a bird-catcher who was on the prowl caught the peacock and was about to take him away to the market. The unhappy bird begged of his captor to allow him to bid his friend the tortoise good-bye, as it would be the last time he would see him. The bird-catcher allowed him his prayer and took him to the tortoise, who was greatly moved to see his friend a captive. The tortoise asked the bird-catcher to let the peacock go; but he laughed at the request, saying that was his means of livelihood. The tortoise then said, "If I make you a handsome present, will you let my friend go?"

Jeremy R. Smith/Shutterstock, Inc.

"Certainly," answered the bird-catcher, "that is all I want." Whereupon the tortoise dived into the water and in a few seconds came up with a handsome pearl, which, to the great astonishment of the bird-catcher, he handed to him. This was beyond his expectations, and he let the peacock go immediately.

A short time after, the avaricious man came back and told the tortoise that he thought he had not paid enough for the release of his friend, and threatened that, unless a match to that pearl was obtained for him, he would again catch the peacock. The tortoise, who had already advised his friend to betake himself to a distant jungle on being set free, was greatly enraged at the greed of this man.

"Well," said the tortoise, "if you insist on having another pearl like it, give it to me and I will fish you out an exact match for it." The cupidity of the bird-catcher prevented his reasoning that "one in the hand was equal to two in the bed of the stream," and he speedily gave the pearl to the wily tortoise, who swam out with it saying, "I am no fool to take one and give two!" and forthwith disappeared, leaving the bird-catcher to be sorry ever after for his covetousness.

Five Old Tales from India (cont.)

Tale 5: The Washerman and the Donkey

A story is told of an over-credulous washerman who was childless. This preyed upon his mind very much and was a permanent cause of unhappiness.

One day, in the course of his work, he went to the house of the town kazi (or magistrate). He heard the kazi reproaching one of his pupils in this wise: "Not long ago you were a jackass; I made a man of you," etc. The washer-man did not wait to hear the rest. He hastened home with all speed and told his wife that he had made a discovery which they were to lose no time in utilizing.

"The kazi, my dear," said the washerman, "can make a man of a donkey. Why should we fret any longer for a child? Let us take our donkey to him and beg of him to transform him." The washerman and his wife, with their donkey, were shortly after this conversation on their way to the kazi.

Their mission being explained with many supplications, the kazi, quick-sighted, and with an eye to business, accepted the charge, and promised to effect the metamorphosis in a year. The washerman on his part promised to give his services free for that period. A year passed in waiting and in happy hopes. On the appointed day the washerman and his companion presented themselves before the kazi. The kazi took them aside and pointed out a strong young man among his pupils. "There," he whispered to the washerman, "is your donkey. You see the change: now persuade him and take him home."

The washerman and his wife flew to their newly created son, and with many endearing terms prepared to embrace him and made other affectionate advances. Amazed at this unaccountable conduct of these low people, the lad resisted at first, but as they persisted, he grew furious. After receiving many a cuff from the lad, a happy idea struck the washerman's wife: turning to her husband she said, "Go you and fetch his peg, rope, and grain-bag; perhaps they may remind him of what he was once." The washerman in hot haste went home and fetched them. But it seemed to make matters worse.

The washerman held up each of these articles to the young man's view, and said, in the most persuasive tone he could command, "Come home, my son. Do you forget the day you were my donkey? This was the peg to which I would tether you, this your tether rope, and this your food-bag; come to your home!"

By this time a jeering crowd had gathered round the young man, and this so infuriated him that he turned to and gave the washerman the soundest thrashing he had ever received in his life. The poor dupe of a washerman—the story says—went home thoroughly convinced that what fate had ordained it was useless to fight against, looking upon his punishment as a just return for his presumption.

Name_____

Improving My Fluency

The Old Tale from India that I am going to read is _____

My partner, _____, will listen to me read it aloud three different times, and fill out this evaluation after the second and third readings.

Fluency	Second Reading	Third Reading
Improved accuracy		
Improved speed		
Smoother reading		
Improved expression		

In between the second and the third reading. . .

1. Have your partner write one compliment about your second reading and one suggestion for practice before the third reading.

   Compliment: _____

   _____

   _____

   Suggestion: _____

   _____

   _____

2. Write at least two things you are going to do to improve your fluency between the second and the third time you read the tale.

   Improvement plan:_____

   _____

   _____

   _____

   _____

   _____

San Zi Jing (Three Character Classic)

Excerpts from the collection of sayings

Objective

√ Students will participate in creating and reading aloud fluently a big book of verses.

Preparation

√ Ask students to have their copies of the world map (pages 188–189) from previous lessons.

√ Copy *San Zi Jing (Three Character Classic)* (pages 110–111) for each student.

√ Have available rulers and art materials. For creating the big book described on page 111, provide 12 sheets of large drawing paper (11 x 17 inches), and for advertising and the book cover provide 3–5 sheets of poster paper.

√ For the optional Side Trip, copy *Lun Yu—The Analects of Confucius* (page 112) for each student.

Fluency Suggestions and Activities

To help students analyze the text and read with comprehension and fluency, present the historical background and preteach the vocabulary on the following page before starting the fluency activity.

1. Have students locate China on their world maps. Distribute copies of *San Zi Jing (Three Character Classic)* (pages 110–111). Ask students to look at the title, which is written in simplified Chinese characters. Have them look at the pronunciation given below the characters and attempt to say the words *San Zi Jing*. (If you have any students in your class who know Chinese, call upon them to help!) Next explain that the translation of the title, *Three Character Classic*, refers to verses written in lines that contain three Chinese characters. *Characters* here means Chinese writing symbols, not story characters. Of course, the three characters in each line are lost when the verses are translated into English.

2. Ask students to follow along as you read the first verse aloud. Take a moment to allow students to comment or clarify, then have them join you in rereading the verse aloud. Continue in this manner through the rest of the verses.

3. Direct students' attention to the activity described at the end of the verses. Explain that big books engage young children in reading because the words and pictures are big enough for all to see as the books are read. Select times and a place, such as the library or all-purpose room, for presentation. Tell students that some of them will be assigned to advertising— making and hanging posters inviting the school community to the presentations.

4. Assign pairs of students to individual verses. Give the remaining students the jobs of materials supervisor, advertising, cover artist, and book assembly coordinator. Then give students time to create their big book pages as described and practice reading their verses. Hold two oral performances, with alternating partners. At the end, assemble the big book, and either give it to a younger class for their library, or hold a drawing among your own students to determine who gets to keep the book.

San Zi Jing (Three Character Classic) *(cont.)*

History Connection

Confucius (551–479 B.C.) was a famous Chinese thinker and social philosopher, whose teachings deeply influenced East Asian life and thought. Confucianism is a philosophy emphasizing personal and governmental morality, correctness of social relationships, justice, and sincerity. The *San Zi Jing (Three Character Classic)* was written in the thirteenth century and attributed to Wang Yinglin (1223–1296). It is a simplified version of the essentials of Confucian thought suitable for teaching young children. In an address at the Chinese University of Hong Kong, George Yeo, who was Singapore's Minister for Trade and Industry at the time, described his view of the *San Zi Jing*: "For centuries, Chinese children, before they could read or write, were taught to recite the *San Zi Jing* through which the Confucianist idea of society being one big happy family is programmed into young minds. The three-character phrases are like strands of cultural DNA, which are passed on from generation to generation."

Vocabulary Connection

Discuss unfamiliar vocabulary encountered in the text. Begin with these and then add any others you feel need to be reviewed or introduced. Discuss the words' meanings and how they are used specifically in the context of the material.

- **filial**—of children and parents
- **fraternal**—brotherly; with mutual support
- **luminaries**—objects that give off light
- **sovereign**—having power or authority, as in government
- **millet**—cereal-type plant; **glutinous millet**—millet that is sticky like rice

Extension Idea

Side Trip: Confucianism is sometimes difficult for western cultures to understand. Lun Yu—*Analects of Confucius* (page 112) gives students a peek into the mind of Confucius and asks them to use their critical thinking skills to determine the meanings of some of the things "the master" said. If you decide to do this activity, you may want to also preteach this vocabulary:

- **analects**—selected passages combined into a single collection of works, sayings, etc.
- **sanctions**—penalties imposed for breaking a rule or law
- **murmured**—complained; grumbled
- **aspire**—seek, as in to reach a goal
- **principles**—moral values; essentials

Answer Key (page 112): 1. A good person does the right thing not for gain, but just because it is right. 2. A person who is always out for himself will be talked poorly of by others. 3. Don't aspire to be famous, but rather to be worthy of fame. 4. You learn from others—good qualities and bad. Learn one but not the other. 5. Be honest and don't lower your principles just to be accepted. 6. A person who has strong will and determination is hard to stop.

Name _____

San Zi Jing (Three Character Classic)

Original 1910 Giles translation with minor edits

三 字 經

(San)　(Zi)　(Jing)

1. Men at their birth are naturally good.
   Their natures are much the same; their habits become widely different.
   If foolishly there is no teaching, the nature will deteriorate.
   The right way in teaching, is to attach the utmost importance in thoroughness.

2. To feed without teaching is the father's fault.
   To teach without severity is the teacher's laziness.
   If the child does not learn this is not as it should be.
   If he does not learn while young, what will he be when old?

3. In its natural state, jade is of no use.
   If a man does not learn, he cannot know his duty towards his neighbor.
   While young, he should attach himself to his teachers and friends;
   And learn the proper way to behave in all respects.

4. The first thing to learn is filial duty and fraternal love, and then see and hear.
   Learn to count; learn to read.
   Units and tens, then tens and hundreds,
   Hundreds and thousands, thousands and then tens of thousands.

5. The three forces are heaven, earth, and man.
   The three luminaries are the sun, the moon, and the stars.
   The three bonds are the obligation between sovereign and subject,
   The love between father and child, the harmony between husband and wife.

6. We speak of spring and summer, we speak of autumn and winter,
   These four seasons revolve without ceasing.
   We speak of North and South, we speak of East and West,
   These four points, respond to the requirements of the center.

7. We speak of water, fire, wood, metal, and earth.
   These five elements have their origin in number.
   We speak of charity, duty, of propriety, of wisdom, of truth.
   These five virtues must not be compromised.

San Zi Jing (Three Character Classic) *(cont.)*

8. Rice, spike, pulse, wheat, glutinous millet, and common millet,
   These six grains are those which men eat.
   The horse, the ox, the sheep, the fowl, the dog, the pig.
   These six animals are those which men keep.

9. We speak of joy, of anger, we speak of pity, of fear,
   Of love, of hate, and of desire. These are the seven emotions.
   The ground, earthenware, skin, wood, stone, metal,
   Silk, and bamboo yield the eight musical sounds.

10. Great-great grandfather, great-grandfather, grandfather,
    Father and self, self and son, son and grandson,
    From son and grandson on to great grandson and great-great-grandson,
    These are the nine generations of your family.

11. Affection between father and child, harmony between man and wife, . . .
    Friendliness on the part of elder child to younger,
    Respectfulness on the part of younger child to elder,
    Precedence between elders and youngers, as between friend and friend.

12. Respect on the part of the sovereign,
    Loyalty on the part of the subject
    These are the obligations
    That bind all people together.

We speak of spring and summer, we speak of autumn and winter,

These four seasons revolve without ceasing.

We speak of North and South, we speak of East and West,

These four points, respond to the requirements of the center.

You and your partner will create one page for the class big book, *San Zi Jing*, including a nicely printed copy of your verse and a large, colorful illustration.

Your teacher will give you one sheet of large paper. Plan ahead! First draw a very light pencil line down the left side where the pages will be bound together. Next make tiny marks on the left and right edges 11 inches down from the top. This is your illustration space. Below it is your writing space. Then use a ruler to draw four light, evenly spaced lines for the verse. Decide who should do the printing and who should do the art. Put your verse number in the lower right-hand corner, and write your names on the back. After your oral presentation, all the pages will be bound together to make a complete book, which will be given away to a lucky student.

Name _____

Lun Yu–The Analects of Confucius

Analects are selected passages combined into a collection. Below are some analects of Confucius. Read each as it was translated from Chinese into English in 1861 by James Legge (*The Chinese Classics, Vol. 1*). Then read the modern interpretations in the box below. Match each updated explanation to the original by writing it on the correct line.

The Master (Confucius) said,

"The superior man thinks of virtue; the small man thinks of comfort. The superior man thinks of the sanctions of law; the small man thinks of favors which he may receive."

1. _____

"He who acts with a constant view to his own advantage will be much murmured against."

2. _____

"A man should say, 'I am not concerned that I have no place, I am concerned how I may fit myself for one. I am not concerned that I am not known, I seek to be worthy to be known.'"

3. _____

"When I walk along with two others, they may serve me as my teachers. I will select their good qualities and follow them, their bad qualities and avoid them."

4. _____

"Hold faithfulness and sincerity as first principles. Have no friends not equal to yourself. When you have faults, do not fear to abandon them."

5. _____

"The commander of the forces of a large state may be carried off, but the will of even a common man cannot be taken from him."

6. _____

> You learn from others—good qualities and bad. Learn one but not the other.
> A good person does the right thing not for gain, but just because it is right.
> A person who has strong will and determination is hard to stop.
> Don't aspire to be famous, but rather to be worthy of fame.
> A person who is always out for himself will be talked poorly of by others.
> Be honest and don't lower your principles just to be accepted.

Marco Polo's City of Heaven (A.D. 1300)

Excerpts from *The Book of Ser Marco Polo the Venetian concerning the Kingdoms and Marvels of the East*

Objective

√ Students will participate in a divided reading activity focusing on fluency and dramatic expression.

Preparation

√ Copy *The City of Heaven* (pages 115–118) and the blank *Journal of Marco Polo* (page 119) for each student. Note: Some students may need extra blank pages.

√ Copy *Marco Polo Comprehension and Fluency Check* (page 120) for each student.

Fluency Suggestions and Activities

To help students analyze the text and read with comprehension and fluency, present the historical background and preteach the vocabulary on the following page before starting the fluency activity.

1. Distribute copies of *The City of Heaven* (pages 115–118), an excerpt from Marco Polo's description of Kinsay (now Hangchow) during his travels to China. (Note: Because of the length, you may want to save paper by reproducing half as many copies for partners to share.) For the first reading, have students follow along as you read it aloud. Stop along the way to point out instances in which the text requires a change in tone, volume, or word emphasis for dramatic effect.

2. For the second reading, ask for volunteers to read a section and then point out something within the text that gives a clue as to how it should be read. For example, in Part 1 the phrase "first and foremost" signals emphasis on the point to follow.

3. Remind students that Marco Polo journeyed from his home in Italy to China, which at the time was practically unknown to Europeans. Tell them that although the writings of his experiences are in running text, it is easy to imagine that Marco kept a travel journal. Then distribute copies of *Journal of Marco Polo* (page 119). Assign or let students choose one of the labeled parts of the text on which to focus. Go over the directions at the top of the journal page, and make sure all students understand the assignment, including the part about practicing in preparation for an oral performance.

4. You can use *Marco Polo Comprehension and Fluency Check* (page 120) at any point during the lesson—right after the initial reading, in conjunction with the journal-writing activity, or following the presentation.

5. Check students' fluency while they audition for the parts in the performance. Choose one student to read each part in the final presentation. Invite students' parents to come to the dramatic reading. For the performance, have students read directly from their self-created *Journal of Marco Polo*.

Marco Polo's City of Heaven (cont.)

History Connection

This introduction is part of the text translated by Henry Yule and revised by Henri Codier in 1903:

"Marco Polo returned to Venice, his hometown, in 1295 after an absence of twenty-five years in the East. He claimed to have spent seventeen years in the service of Kublai Khan, ruler of the Mongols and of the largest empire in the world. He had many stories to tell. These stories were eventually written down by Rustichiello of Pisa, who heard them while sharing a Genoese prison with Polo, sometime after 1298. Here is the account in the book of Hangchow, called 'Kinsay.' Although Kublai Khan's capital was in the north, at the city later called Beijing, Hangchow had served as the capital of the Southern Song dynasty until 1279 and was a major cultural and political center.

"There is some dispute as to the reliability of the Travels of Marco Polo. Several authorities, including Frances Wood of the British Museum, point out that Polo uses Persian words to describe Chinese sights, omits descriptions of phenomena which would have been hard to miss [for instance footbinding or even the Great Wall], and gives an account of his own career under Kublai Khan, which goes beyond belief. Wood suggests that many of the stories may have been picked up from Persian merchants in caravan stops."

Vocabulary Connection

Discuss unfamiliar vocabulary encountered in the text. Begin with these and then add any others you feel need to be reviewed or introduced. Discuss the words' meanings and how they are used specifically in the context of the source.

- **guilds**—associations of people with common interests, especially in business or trade
- **ordinance**—a law or rule made by an authority; a formal religious ceremony
- **idolaters**—people who worship an object as a god
- **edifice**—a large and complex structure
- **haven**—a place sought for rest, shelter, or protection
- **nativity**—birth or circumstances of birth
- **caparisoned**—decorated; adorned
- **effigies**—carvings, dolls, or other representations of a people or things
- **demesne**—estate; private grounds with a mansion
- **divers**—more than one and of various types

Extension Idea

- Give your students a practical proofreading challenge by asking them to find and correct any errors or nonstandard punctuation or spelling in the original text of their section.

Name _____

The City of Heaven

Excerpts from *The Book of Ser Marco Polo the Venetian concerning the Kingdoms and Marvels of the East*

Description of the Great City of Kinsay, which is the Capital of the Whole Country of Manzi

Preface: Kinsay is the modern Hangchow. Manzi comprised the greater part of China, being all the territory south of the Hwang-Ho (the Yellow River} in the East and the province of Shensi in the West. The notes in [brackets] are clarifications by the translator, and should not be included when read aloud.

Part 1

When you have left the city of Changan and have traveled for three days through a splendid country, passing a number of towns and villages, you arrive at the most noble city of Kinsay, a name which is as much as to say in our tongue "The City of Heaven."

First and foremost, then, the document stated the city of Kinsay to be so great that it hath an hundred miles of compass. [note: probably a hundred Chinese *li,* about .4 miles] And there are in it twelve thousand bridges of stone, for the most part so lofty that a great fleet could pass beneath them. And let no man marvel that there are so many bridges, for you see the whole city stands as it were in the water and surrounded by water, so that a great many bridges are required to give free passage about it. And though the bridges be so high the approaches are so well contrived that carts and horses do cross them.

Part 2

The document aforesaid also went on to state that there were in this city twelve guilds of the different crafts, and that each guild had 12,000 houses in the occupation of its workmen. Each of these houses contains at least 12 men, whilst some contain 20 and some 40—not that these are all masters, but inclusive of the journeymen who work under the masters. And yet all these craftsmen had full occupation, for many other cities of the kingdom are supplied from this city with what they require.

Part 3

The document aforesaid also stated that the number and wealth of the merchants, and the amount of goods that passed through their hands, were so enormous that no man could form a just estimate thereof. And I should have told you with regard to those masters of the different crafts who are at the head of such houses as I have mentioned, that neither they nor their wives ever touch a piece of work with their own hands, but live as nicely and delicately as if they were kings and queens. The wives indeed are most dainty and angelical creatures! Moreover it was an ordinance laid down by the King that every man should follow his father's business and no other, no matter if he possessed 100,000 bezants [*note: a Byzantine coin, often used as a standard coinage*].

The City of Heaven *(cont.)*

Part 4

Inside the city there is a Lake which has a compass of some 30 miles [note: probably 30 *li*] and all round it are erected beautiful palaces and mansions, of the richest and most exquisite structure that you can imagine, belonging to the nobles of the city. There are also on its shores many abbeys and churches of the Idolaters. In the middle of the Lake are two Islands, on each of which stands a rich, beautiful and spacious edifice, furnished in such style as to seem fit for the palace of an Emperor. And when any one of the citizens desired to hold a marriage feast, or to give any other entertainment, it used to be done at one of these palaces. And everything would be found there ready to order, such as silver plate, trenchers, and dishes, napkins and table-cloths, and whatever else was needful. The King made this provision for the gratification of his people, and the place was open to every one who desired to give an entertainment. Sometimes there would be at these palaces a hundred different parties; some holding a banquet, others celebrating a wedding; and yet all would find good accommodation in the different apartments and pavilions, and that in so well ordered a manner that one party was never in the way of another.

Part 5

The houses of the city are provided with lofty towers of stone in which articles of value are stored for fear of fire; for most of the houses themselves are of timber, and fires are very frequent in the city. The people are Idolaters; and since they were conquered by the Great Khan they use paper-money. Both men and women are fair and comely, and for the most part clothe themselves in silk, so vast is the supply of that material, both from the whole district of Kinsay, and from the imports by traders from other provinces. And you must know they eat every kind of flesh, even that of dogs and other unclean beasts, which nothing would induce a Christian to eat.

Part 6

Since the Great Khan occupied the city he has ordained that each of the 12,000 bridges should be provided with a guard of ten men, in case of any disturbance, or of any being so rash as to plot treason or insurrection against him. Each guard is provided with a hollow instrument of wood and with a metal basin, and with a time-keeper to enable them to know the hour of the day or night. And so when one hour of the night is past the sentry strikes one on the wooden instrument and on the basin, so that the whole quarter of the city is made aware that one hour of the night is gone. At the second hour he gives two strokes, and so on, keeping always wide awake and on the look out. In the morning again, from the sunrise, they begin to count anew, and strike one hour as they did in the night, and so on . . .

The City of Heaven *(cont.)*

Part 7

Moreover, within the city there is an eminence on which stands a Tower, and at the top of the tower is hung a slab of wood. Whenever fire or any other alarm breaks out in the city a man who stands there with a mallet in his hand beats upon the slab, making a noise that is heard to a great distance. So when the blows upon this slab are heard, everybody is aware that fire has broken out, or that there is some other cause of alarm. The Khan watches this city with special diligence because it forms the head of all Manzi-, and because he has an immense revenue from the duties levied on the transactions of trade therein, the amount of which is such that no one would credit it on mere hearsay.

Part 8

All the streets of the city are paved with stone or brick, as indeed are all the highways throughout Manzi, so that you ride and travel in every direction without inconvenience. Were it not for this pavement you could not do so, for the country is very low and flat, and after rain 'tis deep in mire and water. But as the Great Khan's couriers could not gallop their horses over the pavement, the side of the road is left unpaved for their convenience. The pavement of the main street of the city also is laid out in two parallel ways of ten paces in width on either side, leaving a space in the middle laid with fine gravel, under which are vaulted drains which convey the rain water into the canals; and thus the road is kept ever dry.

You must know also that the city of Kinsay has some 3,000 baths, the water of which is supplied by springs. They are hot baths, and the people take great delight in them, frequenting them several times a month, for they are very cleanly in their persons. They are the finest and largest baths in the world; large enough for 100 persons to bathe together.

Part 9

And the Ocean Sea comes within 25 miles of the city at a place called Ganfu, where there is a town [*note: it is since covered by the sea, which is much closer*] and an excellent haven, with a vast amount of shipping which is engaged in the traffic to and from India and other foreign parts, exporting and importing many kinds of wares, by which the city benefits. And a great river [*the Ts'ien T'ang*] flows from the city of Kinsay to that sea-haven, by which vessels can come up to the city itself. This river extends also to other places further inland.

The City of Heaven (cont.)

---| **Part 10** |---

I repeat that everything appertaining to this city is on so vast a scale, and the Great Khan's yearly revenues from there are so immense, that it is not easy even to put it in writing, and it seems past belief to one who merely hears it told. But I will write it down for you.

First, however, I must mention another thing. The people of this country have a custom, that as soon as a child is born they write down the day and hour and the planet and sign under which its birth has taken place; so that every one among them knows the day of his birth. And when any one intends a journey he goes to the astrologers, and gives the particulars of his nativity in order to learn whether he shall have good luck or no. Sometimes they will say no, and in that case the journey is put off till such day as the astrologer may recommend. These astrologers are very skillful at their business, and often their words come to pass, so the people have great faith in them.

---| **Part 11** |---

They burn the bodies of the dead. And when any one dies the friends and relations make a great mourning for the deceased, and clothe themselves in hempen garments, and follow the corpse playing on a variety of instruments and singing hymns to their idols. And when they come to the burning place, they take representations of things cut out of parchment, such as caparisoned horses, male and female slaves, camels, armor, suits of cloth of gold (and money), in great quantities, and these things they put on the fire along with the corpse, so that they are all burnt with it. And they tell you that the dead man shall have all these slaves and animals of which the effigies are burnt, alive in flesh and blood, and the money in gold, at his disposal in the next world; and that the instruments which they have caused to be played at his funeral, and the idol hymns that have been chanted, shall also be produced again to welcome him in the next world; and that the idols themselves will come to do him honor.

---| **Part 12** |---

Furthermore there exists in this city the palace of the king who fled, him who was Emperor of Manzi [*the Emperor Tu-Tsong*], and that is the greatest palace in the world, as I shall tell you more particularly. For you must know its demesne hath a compass of ten miles, all enclosed with lofty battlemented walls; and inside the walls are the finest and most delectable gardens upon earth, and filled too with the finest fruits. There are numerous fountains in it also, and lakes full of fish. In the middle is the palace itself, a great and splendid building. It contains 20 great and handsome halls, one of which is more spacious than the rest, and affords room for a vast multitude to dine. It is all painted in gold, with many histories and representations of beasts and birds, of knights and dames, and many marvelous things. It forms a really magnificent spectacle, for over all the walls and all the ceiling you see nothing but paintings in gold. And besides these halls the palace contains 1,000 large and handsome chambers, all painted in gold and divers colors.

Name_____

Journal of Marco Polo

Directions: After reading and becoming familiar with your part, pretend that it is a page in Marco Polo's journal. Use this form to carefully handwrite your part as the journal entry for this day. Then practice reading it aloud again, each time with improved fluency. Be ready to present your part reading with natural flow, good voice quality, and emotional expression.

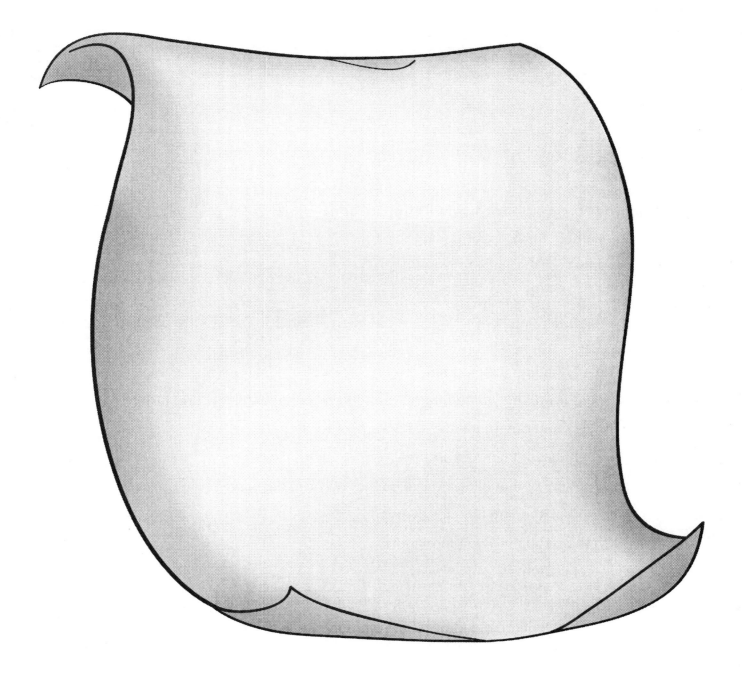

Name _____

Marco Polo Comprehension and Fluency Check

Directions: Go back to *The City of Heaven*, Marco Polo's account of Kinsay, China, and reread as needed to answer these questions:

1. List three "facts" in the account that you think are exaggerations of the truth.

   _____

   _____

   _____

   _____

   _____

   _____

2. Would you consider the style of this writing formal or informal? _____

   Give an example that supports your opinion. _____

   _____

   _____

3. Rank these statements 1–4 to indicate the intended importance of the points made about the city.

   _____ The city had bustling commerce and trade.

   _____ People lived and worked there, but there was peaceful law and order.

   _____ The city had enormous wealth and resources.

   _____ Fire was a common occurrence.

4. Mark an X on any of the following issues that was not described in the excerpt.

   _____ method of keeping time for everyone

   _____ how the people viewed foreigners

   _____ funeral customs

   _____ how the census was kept (an accounting of the population)

5. According to this writing, did Marco Polo want to give his readers more of a favorable or an unfavorable impression of Kinsay? _____ What makes you think so?

   _____

   _____

An Old Chinese Poem

Anonymous, translated by Arthur Whaley, 1919

Objective

√ Students will participate in preparing and presenting a poem for two voices, focusing on conveying mood in oral reading.

Preparation

√ Make a transparency of *An Old Chinese Poem* (page 123).

√ Make copies—one for every two students—of *An Old Chinese Poem* (page 123).

√ For the optional Side Trip, Part 1, copy *When I Went to School in China* (pages 124–126) for each student. Also copy *Assessing Fluency* (page 127) for your reference and *Fluency Evaluation* (page 128) for each student.

√ For the optional Side Trip, Part 2, copy *Try Your Hand at Chinese* (page 129).

Fluency Suggestions and Activities

To help students analyze the text and read with comprehension and fluency, present the historical background and preteach the vocabulary on the following page before starting the fluency activity.

1. Project the transparency of *An Old Chinese poem* (page 123), covering the directions on the bottom so that only the poem is displayed. Point out the blank line at the top and ask students what is missing there (a title). Explain that you will come back to that later.

2. Before reading the poem, review the vocabulary if necessary. Then read the poem aloud fluently, except without a hint of feeling or mood. Ask students how it could be read differently to express the feelings the author wanted the readers to understand—sadness, loss, grief, and suffering. Call on different students to reread 2–4 lines each, with expression. Then reread the whole poem aloud, this time including appropriate voice tone, volume and rate change for emphasis, and pauses for effect.

3. Assign or let students choose partners. Distribute one copy of *An Old Chinese Poem* (page 123) to each pair. Go over the activity directions at the bottom. Tell them that, together, they must rewrite this poem as a script for two voices. Point out that the poem has 16 lines. Students could alternate lines, read groups of lines, or use any other method in which each person reads at least part of the poem. Encourage them to be creative, but to design it so that the way they read it enhances, not detracts from, the listener's understanding of the content and mood. Finally, point out the blank line above the poem. As part of their rewrite, they must add their best idea for a title for the poem.

4. Explain to students that, after practicing, each pair will be asked to read their selected poem in two voices. As each pair reads, the rest of the group will listen and then write down the title that the readers chose. At the end of all the readings, have the class vote for the best title. Give an award to the winning students.

An Old Chinese Poem (cont.)

History Connection

The poem in this lesson is not from any revered collection or famous poet, yet it is considered a classic. It is not about philosophy, religion, or romance. It has no title and does not even mention its subject—war—within the lines. It was written by an unknown author at an unknown time in Chinese history. It is apropos that it is anonymously written and pinpoints no time, place, or particulars about the war because the feeling it expresses could apply to someone coming home from any war, at any time, and in any place. Victory may matter to the opposing sides, but on a personal level, the outcome of war—won or lost—can be the same. This poem shows that for the individual human beings involved, war does not end in glory, but in grief.

Vocabulary Connection

Discuss unfamiliar vocabulary encountered in the text. Begin with these and then add any others you feel need to be reviewed or introduced. Discuss the words' meanings and how they are used specifically in the context of the source.

- **fourscore**—eighty (a score is equal to 20)
- **mallows**—flowering plants with fine hairs on the stems and disk-shaped fruit
- **porridge**—grain ground or crushed into flakes or powder; oatmeal

Extension Ideas

- **Side Trip, Part 1:** Using *When I Went to School in China* (pages 124–126), take your students on a fascinating trip to China in the late 1880s. This high-interest story, which is set up like a magazine article, will capture even your reluctant readers' attention as they compare their own experiences to that of a young man, Yan Phou Lee. If you like, have students choose a paragraph to practice reading for a fluency check-up. *Assessing Fluency* (page 127) and *Fluency Evaluation* (page 128) are provided for your convenience and record-keeping.
- **Side Trip, Part 2:** Perhaps your students would enjoy trying to recreate some simple Chinese characters, such as the ones below—reproduced for students to practice on *Try Your Hand at Chinese* (page 129). If you or your students have a special interest in this subject, a reference called CEDICT (Chinese English Dictionary) is accessible online at **www.mandarintools.com/cedict.html.**

人 rén : man; person; people
學 xué : learn; study
冬 dong : winter
夏 xià : summer

善 shàn : good
友 you : friend
春 chun : spring
秋 qiu : autumn; fall

An Old Chinese Poem

Anonymous, translated by Arthur Whaley, 1919

Title: _____

At fifteen I went with the army,
At fourscore I came home.
On the way I met a man from the village,
I asked him who there was at home.
That over there is your house,
All covered over with trees and bushes.
Rabbits had run in at the dog-hole,
Pheasants flew down from the beams of the roof.
In the courtyard was growing some wild grain;
And by the well, some wild mallows.
I'll boil the grain and make porridge,
I'll pluck the mallows and make soup.
Soup and porridge are both cooked,
But there is no one to eat them with.
I went out and looked towards the east,
While tears fell and wetted my clothes.

Activity Directions:

1. This activity requires working cooperatively with a partner. Write your names here:

   _____   _____

2. Read the poem again. Decide how you want to divide it for presentation as a poem for two voices. Each of you must have parts to read aloud.

3. Put your heads together to come up with a title for the poem. You may want to brainstorm your ideas and then choose the one you both feel is the best.

4. Rewrite the poem as you decided, in the form of a script for two voices. Each of you needs a copy of the full script with the speaker names identified for your performance. Be sure to include your chosen title on the scripts.

5. Both with your partner and on your own, practice reading the poem aloud. Focus on fluency and especially on how to express the mood and emotion of the poem.

6. Be prepared to read your script to the class. Remember that this means *performing* your reading, not just saying the words! At the end, reveal to the group the title you chose. The class will vote for the best title.

Name_____

When I Went to School in China

In the 1870s the Chinese government sent 120 boys to the United States to attend American schools. Among these children—the first Chinese citizens sent to learn in the United States—was Yan Phou Lee, the author of "When I Went to School in China." In 1880, Yan Phou Lee entered Yale University—the same year he wrote this story.

When I Went to School in China, 1880
by Yan Phou Lee

Schools in China are generally kept by private gentlemen. The Government provides for advanced scholars only. But since the one qualification for office is education, and the avenue to literary distinction and public honors lies through competitive examinations, the encouragement that the Government extends to education and learning can be estimated only by that eager pursuit of knowledge which is common to all classes, and by the veneration in which scholars and scholarships are held.

Therefore it is not strange that schools are to be found everywhere, in small hamlets as in large towns, although the Government appropriates no funds for the establishment of common schools; and although no such thing is known as "compulsory education," there is a general desire, even among the poorer classes, to give their children "a little schooling." Schools of the lower grades never boast more than one teacher each. The combination system of a head master and several assistants does not work well in China. The schoolmaster in China must be absolute. He is monarch of all he surveys; in his sphere there is none to dispute his rights. You can always point him out among a thousand by the scholar's long gown, by his stern look, by his bent form, by his shoulders rounded by assiduous study. He is usually near-sighted, so that an immense pair of spectacles also marks him as a trainer of the mind. He generally is a gentleman who depends on his teaching to make both ends meet—his school is his own private enterprise—for no such thing exists in China as a "school-board,"—and if he be an elegant penman, he increases the weight of his purse by writing scrolls; if he be an artist, he paints pictures on fans. If he has not taken a degree, he is a perennial candidate for academic honors, which the Government only has a right to confer.

A tuition fee in China varies according to the ability and reputation of the teacher, from two dollars to twenty dollars a year. It varies also according to the age and advancement of the pupil. The older he be, the more he has to pay. The larger sum I have named is paid to private tutors. A private tutor is also usually invited to take his abode in the house of the wealthy pupil; and he is also permitted to admit a few outsiders. During festivals and on great occasions, the teacher receives presents of money as well as of eatables from his pupils. And always he is treated with great honor by all, and especially by the parents of the pupils. For the future career of their children may, in one sense, be said to be in his hands. One who teaches thirty or forty boys at an average tuition fee of four dollars is doing tolerably well in China; for with the same amount he can buy five or six times as much of provisions or clothing as can be bought in America.

Schools usually open about three weeks after the New Year's Day, and continue till the middle of the twelfth month with but a few holidays sprinkled in. However, if the teacher be a candidate for a literary degree, usually a vacation of about six weeks is enjoyed by the pupils in summer. During the New Year festival, a month is given over to fun and relaxation. Unlike the boys and girls of America, Chinese pupils have no Saturdays as holidays, no Sundays as rest days. School is in session daily from 6 to 10 A.M., at which time all go home to breakfast. At 11 A.M., all assemble again. At 1 P.M. a recess of about an hour is granted to the pupils to get lunch. From 2 P.M. to 4 P.M. is held the afternoon session. This of course is only approximate, as no teacher is bound to a fixed regularity. He is at liberty to regulate his hours as he chooses. At 4 P.M., the school closes for the day.

When I Went to School in China (cont.)

Schools are held either in a private house or in the hall of a temple. The ancestral temples which contain the tablets of deceased ancestors are usually selected for schools, because they are of no other use and because they are more or less secluded and are generally spacious. In a large hall, open on one side towards a court, and having high ceilings supported by lofty pillars beside the brick walls, you may see in the upper right-hand corner a square wooden table, behind which is the wooden chair; this is the throne of his majesty—the schoolmaster. On this table are placed the writing material consisting of brushes, India ink, and ink-wells made of slate. After pouring a little water in one of these wells the cake of ink is rubbed in it until it reaches a certain thickness, when the ink is ready to be used. The brushes are held as a painter's brushes are.

In conspicuous view are the articles for inflicting punishment; a wooden ruler to be applied to the head of the offender and sometimes to the hands, also a rattan stick for the body. Flogging with this stick is the heaviest punishment allowed; for slight offenses the ruler is used upon the palms, and for reciting poorly, upon the head.

The room at large is occupied by the tables and stools of the pupils, chairs being reserved for superiors. The pupils sit either facing the teacher or at right angles to him. Their tables are oblong in form and if much used will show the carving habits and talents of their occupants. Usually the pupils are all of one sex, for girls seldom attend other schools than those kept in the family, and then only up to eleven or twelve years of age. They are taught the same lessons as their brothers. The boys range all the way from six or seven up to sixteen or seventeen years of age, in an ordinary school; for there is no such thing as organizing them into classes and divisions; each one is studying for himself. Still there are schools in which all the pupils are advanced; and there are others which have none but beginners. But they are rare.

I began to go to school at six. I studied first the three primers: the "Three Character Classic," the "Thousand-words Classic," and the "Incentive to Study." They were in rhyme and meter, and you might think they were easy on that account. But no! they were hard. There being no alphabet in the Chinese language, each word had to be learned by itself. At first all that was required of me was to learn the name

of the character and to recognize it again. Writing was learned by copying from a form written by the teacher; the form being laid under the thin paper on which the copying was to be done. The thing I had to do was to make all the strokes exactly as the teacher had made them. It was a very tedious operation. I finished the three primers in about a year, not knowing what I really was studying. The spoken language of China has outgrown the written; that is, we no longer speak as we write. The difference is like that between the English of today and that of Chaucer's time [*late1300s*].

I then took up the "Great Learning," written by a disciple of Confucius, and then the "Doctrine of the Mean" by the grandson of Confucius. These textbooks are rather hard to understand sometimes, even in the hands of older folks; for they are treatises on learning and philosophy. I then passed on to the "Life and Sayings of Confucius," known as the "Confucian Analects" to the American scholars. These books were to be followed by the "Life and Sayings of Mencius" and the "Five Kings"—five classics, consisting of books of history, divination, universal etiquette, odes, and the "Spring and Autumn," a brief and abstract chronicle of the times by Confucius. I had to learn all my lessons by rote; commit them to memory for recitation the day following. We read from the top right-hand corner downwards, and then begin at the top with the next line, and so on. Moreover, we begin to read from what seems to you the end of the book. All studying must be done aloud. The louder you speak or shriek, the more credit you get as a student. It is the only way by which Chinese teachers make sure that their pupils are not thinking of something else or are not playing under the desks.

Now let me take you into the school where I struggled with the Chinese written language for three years. Oh! those hard characters which refused to yield their meaning to me. But I gradually learned to make and to recognize their forms as well as their names. This school was in the ancestral hall of my clan and was like the one I have described. There were about a dozen of us youngsters placed for the time being under the absolute sway of an old gentleman of threescore-and-six [66]. He had all the outward marks of a scholar; and in addition, he was cross-eyed, which fact threw an element of uncertainty into our schemes of fun. For we used to like to "get ahead" of the old gentleman, and there were a few of us always ready for any lark.

When I Went to School in China (cont.)

It is 6 A.M. All the boys are shouting at the top of their voices, at the fullest stretch of their lungs. Occasionally, one stops and talks to some one sitting near him. Two of the most careless ones are guessing pennies; and anon a dispute arises as to which of the two disputants writes a better having given his book to another, repeats it for a trial. All at once the talking, the playing, the shouting ceases. A bent form slowly comes up through the open court. The pupils rise to their feet. A simultaneous salutation issues from a dozen pairs of lips. All cry out, "Lao Tse" (venerable teacher)! As he sits down, all follow his example. There is no roll-call. Then one takes his book up to the teacher's desk, turns his back to him and recites. But see, he soon hesitates; the teacher prompts him, with which he goes on smoothly to the last and returns to his seat with a look of satisfaction. A second one goes up, but, poor fellow, he forgets three times; the teacher is out of patience with the third stumble, and down comes the ruler, whack! whack! upon the head. With one hand feeling the aching spot and the other carrying back his book, the discomfited youngster returns to his desk to re-con [relearn] his lesson.

This continues until all have recited. As each one gets back to his seat, he takes his writing lesson. He must hold his brush in a certain position, vertically, and the tighter he holds it the more strength will appear in his handwriting. The schoolmaster makes a tour of inspection and sees that each writes correctly; writing is as great an art in China as painting and drawing are in other countries, and good specimens of fine writing are valued as good paintings are here. After the writing lesson it is time to dismiss school for breakfast. On re-assembling, the lesson for the day is explained to each one separately. The teacher reads it over, and the pupil repeats it after him several times until he gets the majority of the words learned. He then returns to his desk and shouts anew to get the lesson fixed in his memory. The more advanced scholars are then favored with the expounding of Confucius' "Analects" or some literary essay. After the teacher concludes, each is given a passage of the text to explain. In this way the meaning of words and sentences is learned and made familiar. The afternoon session is passed by the older pupils in writing compositions in prose or in verse, and by the younger in learning the next day's task. This is the regular routine, the order of exercises, in Chinese schools.

Grammar, as a science, is not taught, nor are the mathematics. Language and literature occupy the child's attention, as I have shown, for the first five or six years; afterwards essay-writing and poetry are added. For excellence in these two branches, public prizes are awarded by the resident literary sub-chancellor. But public exhibitions and declamations are unknown, though Chinese fathers sometimes visit the schools. The relations of the sexes are such that a Chinese mother never has the presumption to appear at the door of a schoolroom in order to acquaint herself with the progress of her child's education. Parents furnish the textbooks as a rule. They are bound into volumes and printed usually with immovable type.

The pupils usually behave well. If not, the rattan stick comes promptly into use. Chinese teachers have a peculiar method of meting out punishment. I remember an episode in my school life which illustrates this. One afternoon, when the old schoolmaster happened to be away longer than his wont after the noon recess, some of the boys began to "cut up." The fun reached its height in the explosion of some fire-crackers. As they went off, making the hall ring with the noise, the teacher came in, indignant, you may be sure. His defective eyes darted about and dived around to fix upon the culprit; but as he did not happen to be in the line of their vision, the guilty boy stole back to his seat undetected. The old gentleman then seized the rattan and in a loud voice demanded who it was that had let off the crackers. And when nobody answered, what do you suppose he did? He flogged the whole crowd of us, saying that he was sure to get hold of the right one and that the rest deserved a whipping for not making the real offender known. Truly, the paths of Chinese learning in my day were beset with thorns and briers!

Student Directions: You have just heard the article read aloud. Now reread it on your own. Use a highlighter or colored pen to mark any words you need to look up. Then, choose one paragraph from the article on which to focus. Practice reading it aloud several times—until you can read it fluently. Your teacher may ask you to read it aloud and evaluate your oral reading skills.

Assessing Fluency

Directions: Use the information below as you complete the *Fluency Evaluation* on page 128.

Passage: On this line, record the name of the passage that the student read.

Smooth Reading: Listen as the student reads the passage. Pay attention to the manner in which he or she reads. Briefly respond to these questions:

- Does the student hesitate between words?
- Does the reading sound choppy?
- Does the student have a consistent pace when reading?

Reading Rates: The goal of fluency is not to read as quickly as possible, but rather to read at a comfortable pace. Listen as the student reads the passage.

- Does the student read at a rate that is pleasant to listen to and easy to comprehend?

Accuracy: As the student reads, pay attention to the number of mistakes made. The student should receive a positive comment if he or she is able to read with 80–90% accuracy. Students who receive below this may need some pointers about their common mistakes.

Expression: Part of fluent reading involves the ability to read with expression. This might involve varying the tone of voice when reading. This might also involve varying the sound of the voice when different characters speak. As the student reads, consider the following questions:

- Does the student read in monotone?
- Does the student vary his or her tone of voice?
- Does the student vary his or her voice when reading dialogue?

Student's Comments: This portion of the chart is important to complete because it encourages self-evaluation. After the student reads the passage, ask him or her the questions below and record pertinent responses:

- How do you feel about the way you read the passage?
- Was the passage difficult for you?
- Was your reading choppy or smooth?
- Did you read slowly or at a quick pace?
- Did you make many mistakes?
- How do you feel about your use of expression?

Student Name _____

Fluency Evaluation

Passage: _____

Smooth Reading: _____

_____

_____

_____

Reading Rates: _____

_____

_____

_____

Accuracy: _____

_____

_____

_____

Expression: _____

_____

_____

_____

Student's Comments: _____

_____

_____

_____

_____

Name_____

Try Your Hand at Chinese

English and many other languages are based on an alphabet which, through combinations of letters, forms words. Chinese, however, is based on characters that have individual meanings of their own. From ancient times, writing in Chinese was considered an art. Form and precision of each stroke was like painting a picture. Today, both traditional and simplified Chinese characters can be read and written on a computer. This activity will give you a chance to try your hand at copying the characters. Perhaps you will begin to appreciate the skill and art of writing in Chinese.

人	善
rén : man; person; people	**shàn : good**
學	友
xué : learn; study	**you : friend**
冬	春
dong : winter	**chun : spring**
夏	秋
xià : summer	**qiu : autumn; fall**

Julius Caesar

Excerpts from writings about Caesar

Objective

√ Students will deliver a choral reading presentation in divided reading, call-and-response style, focusing on dramatic refrain to increase comprehension and fluency.

Preparation

√ Ask students to have their copies of the world map (pages 188–189) from previous lessons.

√ Copy *Hail Caesar!* (pages 132–133) and *Analyzing "Hail, Caesar!"* (page 134) for each student.

Fluency Suggestions and Activities

To help students analyze the text and read with comprehension and fluency, present the historical background and preteach the vocabulary on the following page before starting the fluency activity.

1. To check students' levels of prior knowledge, ask them to locate Rome on their world maps. Assist students in finding the Mediterranean Sea and then the country of Italy. Direct them to put a dot or star on the map in the approximate location of Rome (about halfway down the "front" of the boot, slightly inland). Explain that by the time of Caesar's death in 44 B.C., the Roman Empire already controlled most of the lands bordering the Mediterranean, and that it would expand even further under his successors, Augustus and Marcus Aurelius.

2. Distribute copies of *Hail Caesar!* (pages 132–133), which contains excerpts of historical writing about Caesar. Tell students that it has been divided into sections for individuals to read. The short refrains will be read in unison. Explain that first, you will read it orally to demonstrate how it should be read, and that they only need to join in for the refrain. Have the group discuss the text and complete *Analyzing "Hail, Caesar!"* (page 134). (Students' answers will vary.)

3. Be sure to have shared the History Connection and reviewed the vocabulary on the following page. Tell students that they will all participate in the performance, even though the nine main reading parts will be performed by individuals. Direct students to prepare to audition for at least one individual reading part by practicing reading that part until they can do so fluently. Then have each student sign up to audition for one of the eight individual parts. This will ensure that students practice reading at least one section, even if they do not perform it.

4. After giving students sufficient time to practice, hold auditions for the parts. This gives you an opportunity to hear each student read and assess his or her fluency. Choose one student to perform each part, and practice as a group several times before the actual performance. Invite another class who is studying, or has studied, Rome to your performances. If possible, plan your presentation for around the "Ides of March" (March 15th), the day on which Caesar was murdered.

Julius Caesar (cont.)

History Connection

Julius Caesar was a Roman military and political leader who played a key role in the transformation of the Roman Republic into the Roman Empire. His conquest of Gaul extended the Roman world all the way to the Atlantic Ocean, paving the way for the first Roman invasion of Britannia in 55 B.C. He is widely considered to be one of the greatest military geniuses of all time, as well as a brilliant politician and one of the ancient world's strongest leaders. In 42 B.C., two years after his assassination, the Roman Senate officially proclaimed him a Roman deity.

Vocabulary Connection

Discuss unfamiliar vocabulary or phrases encountered in the text. Begin with these and then add any others you feel need to be reviewed or introduced. Discuss the words' meanings and how they are used specifically in the context of the material.

- **munificence**—characterized by great generosity
- **purified**—rid of that which is harmful, inferior, or unwanted
- **extortion**—obtained illegally by threat, or force
- **censor**—an ancient Roman official
- **grants**—legal favors or privileges
- **frugality**—avoidance of waste; involving little expense
- **litters**—couches on poles carried by people used to transport someone
- **foreboding**—a premonition or feeling that something terrible is about to happen
- **basely**—without moral principles or proper social values
- **tumult**—noisy commotion, often upon disturbing news or information
- **oration**—formal public speech
- **funeral pyre**—a pile of wood or other material on which a body is cremated

Note: This is an excellent opportunity to give students a first glimpse of the usefulness of footnotes. Twelve numbered notations that explain content references or help with pronunciation have been inserted with simple accompanying notes. Take a few moments to show students how to use these notes to help them better read and understand the selection.

Extension Idea

- Point out the speaking directions in parentheses for the responses in the last portion of the reading. Example: ALL: (*with hushed foreboding*) Beware the Ides of March. Challenge students to come up with words and phrases that would describe how to say each "Hail, Caesar," so it reflects the mood that the speaker would elicit. Let students practice in the suggested ways, and then choose one as a "stage direction" to write next to each part. Examples: Hail, Caesar! (*triumphantly*); Hail, Caesar! (*with enthusiasm*); Hail, Caesar! (*cheering*)

Name_____

"Hail, Caesar!"
A Presentation about Julius Caesar

Excerpts from historical writings about Caesar with explanatory notes

R1:   On his return from Africa, Caesar celebrated four triumphs, on four successive days; one over the Gauls[1], one over of Egypt, one over Pharnaces[2], and one over Juba[3]. He gratified his armed followers with liberal gifts, and pleased the people by his great munificence. They were feasted at a splendid banquet, at which were 22,000 tables, each table having three couches, and each couch three persons. Then followed shows in the circus and theatre, combats of wild beasts and gladiators, in which the public especially delighted.

All: **Hail, Caesar!**

R2:   Honors were now heaped upon Caesar without stint. A thanksgiving of forty days was decreed. His statue was placed in the Capitol. Another was inscribed to Caesar the Demigod. A golden chair was allotted to him in the Senate-House. The name of the fifth month (Quintilis) of the Roman calendar was changed to Julius (July). He was appointed Dictator for two years, and later for life. He received for three years the office of Censor, which enabled him to appoint Senators, and to be guardian of manners and morals. Julius Caesar had already been made Tribune for life, and Pontifex[4] Maximus. In a word, he was king in everything excepting name.

All: **Hail, Caesar!**

R3:   One of Caesar's most remarkable and durable reforms at this period was the revision of the calendar. The Roman method of reckoning time had been so inaccurate, that now their seasons were more than two months behind. Caesar established a calendar, which, with slight changes, is still in use. It went into operation January 1st, 45 B.C. He employed Sosigenes, an Alexandrian astronomer, to superintend the reform.

All: **Hail, Caesar!**

R4:   While Sosigenes was at work on the calendar, Caesar purified the Senate. Many who were guilty of extortion and corruption were expelled, and the vacancies filled with persons of merit....

All: **Hail, Caesar!**

R5:   Upon his return from Spain, Caesar granted pardon to all who had fought against him, the most prominent of whom were Cassius, Brutus, and Cicero.

All: **Hail, Caesar!**

R6:   He increased the number of the Senate to nine hundred. He cut off the corn grants, which nursed the city mob in idleness. He sent out impoverished men to colonize old cities. He rebuilt Corinth[5], and settled eighty thousand Italians on the site of Carthage[6].

All: **Hail, Caesar!**

R7:   As a censor of morals he was very rigid. His own habits were marked by frugality. The rich young patricians were forbidden to be carried about in litters, as had been the custom. Libraries were formed. Eminent physicians and scientists were encouraged to settle in Rome.

"Hail, Caesar!"
A Presentation about Julius Caesar (cont.)

R7: The harbor of Ostia[7] was improved, and a road constructed from the Adriatic to the Tyrrhenian Sea[8], over the Apennines[9]. A temple to Mars[10] was built, and an immense amphitheatre was erected at the foot of the Tarpeian Rock[11]. But, in the midst of all this useful activity . . .

All: *(in hushed, foreboding tone)* **Beware the Ides of March**

R7: he was basely murdered.

R8: On the morning of the Ides (15th) of March, 44 B.C., as Caesar entered the Senate and took his seat, he was approached by the conspirators, headed by Tullius Cimber, who prayed for the pardon of his exiled brother; and while the rest joined him in the request, he, grasping Caesar's hand, kissed his head. As Caesar attempted to rise, Cimber dragged his cloak from his shoulders, and Casca, who was standing behind his chair, stabbed him in the neck. The first blow was struck, and the whole pack fell upon their noble victim. Cassius stabbed him in the face, and Marcus Brutus in the groin. Caesar made no further resistance; but, wrapping his tunic over his head and the lower part of his body, he fell at the base of Pompey's[12] statue, which was drenched with the martyr's blood.

All: *(with shock and disgust)* **They murdered the Great Caesar!**

R9: Great tumult and commotion followed; and, in their alarm, most of the Senators fled. It was two days before the Senate met, the conspirators meanwhile having taken refuge in the Capitol. Public sentiment was against them. Many of Caesar's old soldiers were in the city, and many more were flocking there from all directions. The funeral oration of Mark Antony over the remains produced a deep impression upon the crowd. They became so excited when the speaker removed the dead man's toga, and disclosed his wounds, that, instead of allowing the body to be carried to the Campus Martius for burial, they raised a funeral pyre in the Forum, and there burned it. The crowd then dispersed in troops, broke into and destroyed the houses of the conspirators. Brutus and Cassius fled from the city for their lives, followed by the other murderers.

All: *(relieved, then dejectedly)* **They are gone, but so is he.** *(trailing off)* **Hail, Caesar.**

Notes: Roman references and help with pronunciations of proper names:

1. *Gauls refers to the people of the area that is now France.*
2. *The "ph" in Pharnaces is pronounced /f/.*
3. *Juba is a Roman term for a northern part of Africa (roughly Algeria).*
4. *A Pontifex is a senior Roman official.*
5. *Corinth was a city in Greece.*
6. *Carthage was a city on the coast of northern Africa.*
7. *Ostia was an ancient city in Italy.*
8. *The Adriatic and Tyrrhenian Seas were arms of the Mediterranean Sea off the coast of Italy.*
9. *The Apennines refers to the mountain chain extending through Italy.*
10. *Mars was the Roman god of War.*
11. *The Tarpeian Rock was an important site to ancient Romans, which no longer exists.*
12. *Pompey was Caesar's mortal enemy, whom he had defeated in many battlefronts. This is not to be confused with Pompeii, the city.*

Name_____

Analyzing "Hail, Caesar!"

Directions: After listening to and reading "Hail, Caesar!" think about not just what you read, but how it was presented. Then complete the activities and questions below.

Part 1—Breaking Up: The text was originally written in running paragraphs, without the interjections of "Hail, Caesar!" and the other added responses. Read the selection again, this time just as paragraphs, without those additions.

1. Does the way in which the text is presented make a difference? _____

2. Which way did you like better and why? _____

_____

_____

3. Do you think that breaking the text up into parts and adding the responses made it easier and more interesting? Or did it take away the flow and make it distracting?

_____

4. If you were going to present the orginal material to students your age, in what format or layout would you present it (in two columns, like a magaine, etc.)? Why?

_____

_____

5. What did you like about this selection? _____

6. What did you dislike? _____

Part 2—Got Notes?: You no doubt noticed the little numbers next to some words in the text.

1. What were they doing there? _____

2. Did you find them helpful while reading, or just distracting? _____

3. Did you stop and look at the notes while you were reading, or did you read them at the end? Why? _____

_____

4. What do you usually do when you come across a term you don't understand?

_____

_____

_____

"The Coliseum" by Edgar Allan Poe

Baltimore Saturday Visiter, October 26, 1833

Objective

√ Students will participate in a "line-a-child" choral reading activity to practice and perform reading a poem fluently, with emphasis on natural flow.

Preparation

√ Make copies of *Reading Verse: "The Coliseum"* (page 138), *Using Synonyms to Simplify* (page 139), and *"Chunking" for Fluency* (page 140) for each student.

√ For optional use, copy *"The Coliseum" by Edgar Allen Poe* (page 137) for students and/or the audience.

Fluency Suggestions and Activities

To help students analyze the text and read with comprehension and fluency, present the historical background and preteach the vocabulary on the following page before starting the fluency activity.

1. Distribute copies of *Reading Verse: "The Coliseum"* (page 138). Tell students that the stanzas at the top of the page are two out of six that make up the entire poem. (Poe's writing is challenging, therefore students are being asked to handle only two of the stanzas.) Ask students to follow along as you read the stanzas aloud. For the first read through, read the poem line by line, pausing slightly at the end of each line. Ask students if it was easy to understand. You will likely observe many puzzled looks.

2. Next read aloud the middle section of the page, which explains a trick for reading verse—chunking. Tell students that chunking means grouping parts of text into phrases that contain complete ideas. Have students look at the "chunked" rewrite of the stanzas at the bottom of the page, where they have been separated into ideas rather than lines. For the second reading, direct students to listen as you read the chunks. Ask them if their comprehension improved. Finally, for the third reading, have students look back up at the poem written in lines. Have students follow along as you read the poem again, but this time in chunks.

3. Ask for volunteers or assign reading parts by chunks rather than by lines or stanzas. Have the selected students highlight their assigned chunks. Direct students to practice reading their parts using the chunks at the bottom. Then have them underline or highlight their chunk—no more and no less—in the stanzas at the top. Tell them to practice again reading from the poem while chunking the ideas.

4. Let students invite parents or other guests to the presentation of the poem. Explain that it will be done in Reading Relay form. This means everyone must be alert and ready to read their chunks when it is their turn. For practice, supply a small object to pass to the next person as a signal to read—just like a baton in a relay race.

"The Coliseum" by Edgar Allan Poe (cont.)

History Connection

The Colosseum (also known as the Coliseum) is Rome's most famous and still-standing wonder. Its construction began under Emperor Vespasian in A.D. 72 and was completed by his son, Titus, in the 80s. The Colosseum was huge. The base took up the equivalent of six acres and could hold the whole population of a town—as many as 50,000 people—much like our football stadiums now. It was used for entertainment, which at that time was primarily gladiatorial combat. The citizens would sometimes spend the whole day there watching sports, which usually involved fighting to the death. The emperor had his own entrance and his own private box seat. The building was designed to handle crowds efficiently. With many exits, the entire audience could empty the building in a matter of minutes. The Colosseum was in continual use until A.D. 217, when it was damaged by fire after being struck by lightning.

Far from Rome in time and distance—the late 1800s in Baltimore, Maryland—a writer, literary critic, and accomplished poet named Edgar Allan Poe wrote a poem about his impressions of the ruins of the Roman Colosseum. Rather than a description of the building, Poe's words capture the feeling of what it once was and is now. One thing to note: Poe includes a line referring to the ivory couch on which Caesar sat, but this was how he was imagining the past, not how it really was, because the Colosseum was built after Julius Caesar's death in 44 B.C.

Vocabulary Connection

Reading in verse can be challenging in itself, but even more so when there are unfamiliar terms. It is helpful to skim the piece first to identify possible words that may cause confusion. For the two verses selected for this activity, 17 words have been identified as potentially troublesome. One approach to reducing the confusion is to simplify these words with synonyms. Give students *Using Synonyms to Simplify* (page 139). Here students will see the terms highlighted in the context of the verse and then choose appropriate synonyms for the selected words. You may want to complete this page as a class before reading the poem aloud.

Answer Key (page 139): 1. old 2. shrine 3. noble 4. thought 5. display 6. journey 7. stories 8. you 9. changed 10. your 11. magnificence 12. watch 13. shadowy 14. grass 15. weed 16. sat 17. snake

Extension Ideas

- Invite students to write a poem or description of the Coliseum, or of another place that elicits a feeling of awe for them.
- Challenge your advanced readers to check out some of Edgar Allan Poe's other poetry, such as his classics "The Raven" or "The Bells."

Name_____

"The Coliseum" by Edgar Allan Poe

As it appeared in the *Baltimore Saturday Visiter,* October 26, 1833

Lone ampitheatre! Grey Coliseum!
Type of the antique Rome! Rich reliquary
Of lofty contemplation left to Time
By buried centuries of pomp and power!
At length, at length—after so many days
Of weary pilgrimage, and burning thirst,
(Thirst for the springs of love [lore] that in thee lie,)
I kneel, an altered, and an humble man,
Amid thy shadows, and so drink within
My very soul thy grandeur, gloom, and glory.

Vastness! and Age! and Memories of Eld!
Silence and Desolation! and dim Night!
Gaunt vestibules! and phantom-peopled aisles!
I feel ye now: I feel ye in your strength!
O spells more sure then [than] e'er Judean king
Taught in the gardens of Gethsemane!
O charms more potent than the rapt Chaldee
Ever drew down from out the quiet stars!

Here, where a hero fell, a column falls:
Here, where the mimic eagle glared in gold,
A midnight vigil holds the swarthy bat:
Here, where the dames of Rome their yellow hair
Wav'd to the wind, now wave the reed and thistle:
Here, where on ivory couch the Caesar sate,
On bed of moss lies gloating the foul adder:

Here, where on golden throne the monarch loll'd,
Glides spectre-like unto his marble home,
Lit by the wan light of the horned moon,
The swift and silent lizard of the stones.

These crumbling walls; these tottering arcades;
These mouldering plinths; these sad, and blacken'd
shafts;
These vague entablatures; this broken frieze;
These shattered cornices; this wreck; this ruin;
These stones, alas!—these grey stones—are they all;
All of the great and the colossal left
By the corrosive hours to Fate and me?

"Not all,"—the echoes answer me; "not all:
Prophetic sounds, and loud, arise forever
From us, and from all ruin, unto the wise,
As in old days from Memnon to the sun.
We rule the hearts of mightiest men:—we rule
With a despotic sway all giant minds.
We are not desolate—we pallid stones;
Not all our power is gone; not all our Fame;
Not all the magic of our high renown;
Not all the wonder that encircles us;
Not all the mysteries that in us lie;
Not all the memories that hang upon,
And cling around about us now and ever,
And clothe us in a robe of more than glory."

Name_____

Reading Verse: "The Coliseum"

Selected stanzas from Edgar Allan Poe's "The Coliseum"

(Stanza 1)
Lone ampitheatre! Grey Coliseum!
Type of the antique Rome! Rich reliquary
Of lofty contemplation left to Time
By buried centuries of pomp and power!
At length, at length—after so many days
Of weary pilgrimage, and burning thirst,
(Thirst for the springs of love [lore] that in
thee lie,)
I kneel, an altered, and an humble man,
Amid thy shadows, and so drink within
My very soul thy grandeur, gloom, and glory.

(Stanza 3)
Here, where a hero fell, a column falls:
Here, where the mimic eagle glared in gold,
A midnight vigil holds the swarthy bat:
Here, where the dames of Rome their yellow
hair
Wav'd to the wind, now wave the reed and
thistle:
Here, where on ivory couch the Caesar sate,
On bed of moss lies gloating the foul adder. . .
        —*Edgar Allan Poe, 1833*

The trick to reading verse is to ignore the individual line breaks and instead read the poem in meaningful chunks that sound natural. Here are the two verses rewritten in natural chunks. Try reading the verses this way to see how they make more sense. Your teacher will assign individual students chunks to practice and then perform later in a Reading Relay. This is like relay tag, only with reading! If you are assigned a chunk (C1–C7), highlight your part below.

C1: Lone ampitheatre!

C2: Grey Coliseum!

C3: Type of the antique Rome!

C4: Rich reliquary of lofty contemplation left to Time by buried centuries of pomp and power!

C3: At length, at length—after so many days of weary pilgrimage, and burning thirst, (thirst for the springs of lore that in thee lie,) I kneel—an altered and an humble man—amid thy shadows, and so drink within my very soul thy grandeur, gloom, and glory.

C4: Here, where a hero fell, a column falls.

C5: Here, where the mimic eagle glared in gold, a midnight vigil holds the swarthy bat.

C6: Here, where the dames of Rome their yellow hair wav'd to the wind, now wave the reed and thistle.

C7: Here, where on ivory couch the Caesar sate on bed of moss, lies gloating the foul adder.

Name_____

Using Synonyms to Simplify

Synonyms are words that mean the same or almost the same thing. When you come across a term you don't quite understand, you can try using a thesaurus. A thesaurus is like a dictionary, except that it lists synonyms for words instead of definitions. You can try replacing each unfamiliar word with a simpler synonym to see if it makes better sense.

Directions: Here's a chance to practice. Below are two verses from the poem "The Coliseum" by Edgar Allan Poe. Seventeen words have been bolded in the poem and listed in the numbered column. The words in the box are simpler synonyms for the terms. Find each term's synonym and write it on the line.

Synonyms		
changed	shrine	weed
display	thought	sat
journey	noble	you
stories	shadowy	your
watch	snake	old
grass	magnificence	

1. antique: _____

2. reliquary: _____

3. lofty: _____

4. contemplation: _____

5. pomp: _____

6. pilgrimage: _____

7. lore: _____

8. thee: _____

9. altered: _____

10. thy: _____

11. grandeur: _____

12. vigil: _____

13. swarthy: _____

14. reed: _____

15. thistle: _____

16. sate: _____

17. adder: _____

Lone ampitheatre! Grey Coliseum!
Type of the **antique** Rome! Rich **reliquary**
Of **lofty contemplation** left to Time
By buried centuries of **pomp** and power!
At length, at length—after so many days
Of weary **pilgrimage**, and burning thirst,
(Thirst for the springs of **lore** that in **thee** lie,)
I kneel, an **altered**, and an humble man,
Amid **thy** shadows, and so drink within
My very soul thy **grandeur**, gloom, and glory. . .

Here, where a hero fell, a column falls:
Here, where the mimic eagle glared in gold,
A midnight **vigil** holds the **swarthy** bat:
Here, where the dames of Rome their yellow hair
Wav'd to the wind, now wave the **reed** and **thistle**:
Here, where on ivory couch the Caesar **sate**,
On bed of moss lies gloating the foul **adder**. . .

Name_____

"Chunking" for Fluency

Below is a very short excerpt from William Shakespeare's play "Julius Caesar," written in the late 1500s. Brutus, who was one of Caesar's murderers, is about to be visited by the Ghost of Caesar. Brutus hears someone playing soft music, and although tired, Brutus does not want to go to sleep. He decides to try to read a book to ward off slumber.

Part 1: Below is the text exactly as written by Shakespeare. It is difficult to read and understand line by line. Test your skill at using chunking to help you read fluently. Draw a dividing line (/) after each complete thought, regardless of where the end of the line falls. Then go back and read it again, using your chunks to guide you.

> **BRUTUS:** This is a sleepy tune. O murtherous slumber,
> Layest thou thy leaden mace upon my boy
> That plays thee music? Gentle knave, good night.
> I will not do thee so much wrong to wake thee.
> If thou dost nod, thou break'st thy instrument;
> I'll take it from thee; and, good boy, good night.
> Let me see, let me see; is not the leaf turn'd down
> Where I left reading? Here it is, I think.
>
> *Enter the Ghost of Caesar.*
>
> How ill this taper burns! Ha, who comes here?
> I think it is the weakness of mine eyes
> That shapes this monstrous apparition.
> It comes upon me. Art thou anything?
> Art thou some god, some angel, or some devil
> That makest my blood cold and my hair to stare?
> Speak to me what thou art.

Part 2: After you have marked your divisions and reread Brutus's words, turn this page upside down to see the answers and check how well you did. If you made mistakes, correct them, and then try again to read the passage using the chunks.

Suggested placement of dividing marks: This is a sleepy tune./O murtherous slumber, Layest thou thy leaden mace upon my boy that plays thee music?/Gentle knave good night./I will not do thee so much wrong to wake thee./If thou dost not, thou break'st thy instrument;/I'll take it from thee; and, good boy, good night./Let me see;/is not the leaf turn'd down where I left reading?/Here it is, I think./ How ill this taper burns!/Ha, who comes here?/I think it is the weakness of mine eyes That shapes the monstrous apparition./It comes upon me./Art thou anything?/Art thou some god, some angel, or some devil That makest my blood cold and my hair to stare?/Speak to me what thou art.

The Last Day of Pompeii

Excerpts from *The Last Days of Pompeii* by Edward Bulwer-Lytton (1803–1873)

Objective

√ Students will enhance comprehension and fluency by participating in an oral reading presentation in reader's theater format.

Preparation

√ Copy *"The Last Day of Pompeii" A Tale for Reader's Theater* (pages 144–149) and *Using Similes and Metaphors to Paint a Picture with Words* (page 150) for each student.

√ For optional use, supply a collection of ordinary materials, so students can experiment with producing Foley (sound) effects to accompany the reading.

Fluency Suggestions and Activities

To help students analyze the text and read with comprehension and fluency, present the historical background and preteach the vocabulary on the following page before starting the fluency activity.

1. Distribute copies of *"The Last Day of Pompeii" A Tale for Reader's Theater* (pages 144–149). Ask students to follow along as you read the tale aloud with appropriate expression and fluency. Follow by asking students to tell what the story is about, including its setting, characters, problem, and solution. Remind students that the story is fiction, but the eruption of Mt. Vesuvius and the destruction of Pompeii is historical fact. Explain that the script is comprised of excerpts from a novel, which have been edited, woven together, and rewritten as a script to perform as reader's theater.

2. This story is filled with similes and metaphors that make the descriptions especially vivid. Distribute copies of *Using Similes and Metaphors to Paint a Picture with Words* (page 150), which highlights ten examples from the script. To enhance comprehension and focus on these literary elements, you may want to complete this page as a class before rereading the script. Answer Key (page 150): 1. metaphor 2. metaphor 3. metaphor 4. simile 5. simile 6. simile 7. metaphor 8. metaphor 9. simile 10. simile

3. The script has parts for two narrators and up to 23 individual speaking parts. If you have more than 25 students, have those without speaking parts be "Foley artists." Explain that a Foley artist creates sound effects for productions. Ask students to suggest what kinds of sound effects would be appropriate to include in this reading and how they might be simulated using ordinary objects. For example, the sound of people running through the ash-covered streets might be made by a felt board eraser.

4. Assign everyone a role—either a speaking part or that of a Foley artist. As the students with speaking parts rehearse, have your Foley artists experiment with making sound effects.

5. Allow plenty of practice time for students to prepare for the reader's theater presentation. Have them read and reread their parts alone and as a group. Have the Foley artists demonstrate what they plan to do and at what points in the script. Include them in the whole-group practices.

6. Since this presentation involves every student in the class, a perfect venue for the performance would be back-to-school night or a PTA meeting. You could also perform at a school assembly. Whatever you choose, be sure to coach the students about keeping in mind the size of the room and audience with regard to the level of their voices and projection. If possible, hold a final rehearsal in the performance venue.

The Last Day of Pompeii (cont.)

History Connection

In the first century, Pompeii was a flourishing city at the base of Mt. Vesuvius on the west side of Italy. Pompeii and the surrounding area was home to 10,000–20,000 people when, in the year A.D. 79, Mt. Vesuvius violently erupted and buried the area in thick layers of ash. The people and buildings lay under the rubble just as they were that day in August until they were discovered more than 1,500 years later.

The Last Days of Pompeii, a fictional book written in 1834, is set in Pompeii just prior to the eruption of the volcano. The characters and action are inventions, but they are made more believable and engaging by intertwining them with the facts of history. This type of story is called historical fiction—a made-up story that takes place in the context of a real situation, time, or event in history. A more modern example of this type of storytelling is the movie *Titanic*.

Vocabulary Connection

Discuss unfamiliar vocabulary encountered in the text. Begin with these and then add any others you feel need to be reviewed or introduced. Discuss the words' meanings and how they are used specifically in the context of the material.

- **wrath**—anger
- **torrent**—a fast and powerful rush of liquid; a violent flow or outpouring
- **ominous**—threatening
- **Isis**—goddess of fertility and motherhood
- **scoria**—loose rubble, porous rock, or solidified lava from a volcano
- **pitchy**—sticky, tar-like
- **prodigal**—producing large amounts
- **abyss**—endless space
- **save**—except
- **primal**—basic, primary
- **nether**—located in the lower position or under
- **quelled**—brought to an end; suppressed

The Last Day of Pompeii *(cont.)*

Extension Ideas

- The tale students read in this lesson is a woven-together compilation of excerpts from the novel, *The Last Days of Pompeii* (one of the most widely read books of all time). Although this work has some challenging vocabulary, it is a well-written, fast-paced story that will motivate students to read. It has all the classic elements—hero, villain, love triangle, murder, mystery, plus plenty of action described in accurate historical context (including descriptions of gladiator contests and conflicts between different national and ideological groups—Romans, Greeks, Egyptians, and Early Christians). Best of all, you or your students can find the complete, printable book online at Project Gutenberg. You will want to preview it before recommending to students to read independently. Another idea is to read it aloud to your class one chapter at a time. This way, you can skip or paraphrase any part you wish.

- Separate fact from fiction by having students read an eyewitness account of what happened at Pompeii. This is recorded in the form of letters from Pliny the Younger to his friend Tacitus. Pliny the Elder,* his uncle, died in the event, and he describes in great detail what he saw, heard, and felt that day. Interestingly, he describes the earthquakes, the eruption column (modern estimates put this at more than 20 miles high), and even the retreating of the sea (tsunami). Although it may be difficult for many students to read independently, it may be worth attempting with shared or paired reading. This text is also available online ((*The Letters of Pliny the Younger,* VI.16).

*Both Plinys were writer/historians. Pliny the Elder contributed to the second lesson in this book, "A Description of Mesopotamia."

Name_____

"The Last Day of Pompeii" A Tale for Reader's Theater

Excerpted from *The Last Days of Pompeii* by Edward Bulwer-Lytton (1803–1873)
Condensed and edited for reader's theater

Narrator 1 : *The date is August 24, A.D. 79. The place is a Roman amphitheater in the city of Pompeii. This is the story of the eruption of Mt. Vesuvius, but told as the backdrop of a personal drama. As we join the story, a Greek man who has been accused of being a criminal has been sent into the area to decide his fate. There, a lion purposely kept near starvation is to be his opponent. As was customary at the time, the crowd anticipated seeing how the man would either conquer the lion or, as more commonly occurred, be devoured by it.*

Narrator 2: *But, when the famished lion entered the area, it surprisingly took no interest in the Athenian! It just paced around, agitated, and then on its own, retreated back into its cage! The crowd was astonished. Many felt that this was a sign from the gods that the man was innocent. We now enter into the story as Glaucus, the accused Athenian, seizes this moment of good fortune.*

R1: Glaucus stretched his hand on high; over his lofty brow and royal features there came an expression of unutterable solemnity and command.

R2: 'Behold!' he shouted with a voice of thunder, which stilled the roar of the crowd; 'Behold how the gods protect the guiltless! The fires of the avenging Orcus burst forth against the false witness of my accusers!'

R3: The eyes of the crowd beheld, with ineffable dismay, a vast vapor shooting from the summit of Vesuvius, in the form of a gigantic pine-tree; the trunk, blackness—the branches, fire!—a fire that shifted and wavered in its hues with every moment, now fiercely luminous, now of a dull and dying red, that again blazed terrifically forth with intolerable glare!

R4: There was a dead, heart-sunken silence—through which there suddenly broke the roar of the lion, which was echoed back from within the building by the sharper and fiercer yells of its fellow-beasts. Animals have keener senses than men. These roaring lions were dread seers—wild prophets of the wrath to come!

R5: Then there arose on high the universal shrieks of women; the men stared at each other, but were speechless. At that moment they felt the earth shake beneath their feet; the walls of the theatre tremble, and, beyond in the distance, they heard the crash of falling roofs. An instant more and a mountain-cloud seemed to roll towards them, dark and rapid, like a torrent. At the same time, it cast forth from its bosom a shower of ashes mixed with vast fragments of burning stone! Over the crushing vines—over the desolate streets—over the amphitheatre itself—far and wide—with many a mighty splash in the agitated sea—fell that awful shower!

"The Last Day of Pompeii"
A Tale for Reader's Theater (cont.)

R6: The crowd, who a moment before were enveloped in deciding the fate of Glaucus, no longer thought about justice; safety for themselves was now their sole thought. Each turned to run—each dashing, pressing, crushing, against the other. Trampling recklessly over the fallen—amidst groans, and oaths, and prayers, and sudden shrieks—the enormous crowd vomited itself forth through the numerous passages.

Narrator 1: *Earthquakes were common in this area and the people took them in their stride.*

Narrator 2: *Some, anticipating this as the coming of a larger-than-usual earthquake, hastened to their homes to load themselves with their more costly goods, and escape while it was yet time; others, dreading the showers of ashes that now fell fast, torrent upon torrent over the streets, rushed under the roofs of the nearest houses or temples or sheds—shelter of any kind—for protection from the terrors of the open air.*

Narrator 1: But darker, and larger, and mightier, spread the cloud above them. Suddenly, though it was only noon, the darkness rushed in and ghastly Night took over the midday. Now people realized this was not an oncoming thunderstorm or momentary tremor of the earth, but something far more ominous.

R7: Gods!—how the darkness gathers! Ho, ho!—by yon mountain, what sudden blazes of lightning!'—How they dart and quiver! Hades is loosed on earth! Oh, Jupiter! What sound is that?—the hissing of fiery water! What! Does the cloud give rain as well as flame! Ha!—what! shrieks? Look forth!. . .

R8: Amidst the other horrors, the mighty mountain now cast up columns of boiling water. Blended and kneaded with the half-burning ashes, the streams fell like seething mud over the streets in frequent intervals. As the priests of Isis cowered around the altars on which they had vainly sought to kindle fires and pour incense, one of the fiercest of those deadly torrents—mingled with immense fragments of scoria—poured its rage. Over the bended forms of the priests it dashed. Their cries had been of death—then their silence of eternity! The ashes—the pitchy streams—sprinkled the altars, covered the pavement, and half concealed the quivering corpses of the priests!. . .

R9: Meanwhile, the streets were already thinned; the crowd had hastened to disperse itself under shelter; the ashes began to fill up the lower parts of the town; but here and there, you heard the steps of fugitives, or saw their pale and haggard faces by the blue glare of the lightning, or the more unsteady glare of torches, by which they endeavored to steer their steps. But ever and on and on, the boiling flow, or the strangling ashes, mysterious and gusty winds, rising and dying in a breath, extinguished these wandering lights, and with them the last living hope of those who bore them. . .

"The Last Day of Pompeii"
A Tale for Reader's Theater *(cont.)*

R10:   The air was now still for a few minutes: the lamp from the gate streamed out far and clear. The fugitives hurried on—they reached the gate—they passed by the Roman sentry. The lightning flashed over his livid face and polished helmet, but his stern features were composed even in their awe! He remained erect and motionless at his post. That hour itself had not animated the machine of the ruthless majesty of Rome into the reasoning and self-acting man. There he stood, amidst the crashing elements: he had not received permission to desert his station and escape. . .

R11:   The cloud, which had scattered so deep a murkiness over the day, had now settled into a solid and impenetrable mass. It resembled less the thickest gloom of a night in the open air than the close and blind darkness of some narrow room. But in proportion to the gathering blackness, the lightning around Vesuvius increased in its vivid and scorching glare. Nor was their horrible beauty confined to the usual hues of fire; no rainbow ever rivaled their varying and prodigal dyes. Colors as brightly blue as the most azure depth of a southern sky, a livid and snakelike green, darting restlessly to and fro as the folds of an enormous serpent, and a lurid and intolerable crimson, gushing forth through the columns of smoke, far and wide, and lighting up the whole city from arch to arch—then all suddenly dying into a sickly paleness, like the ghost of their own life!

R12:   In the pauses between the showers, you heard the rumbling of the earth beneath, and the groaning waves of the tortured sea; or, lower still, an audible grinding and hissing murmur of the escaping gases through the chasms of the distant mountain. Sometimes the cloud appeared to break from its solid mass, and, by the lightning, to assume quaint and vast mimicries of human or of monster shapes, striding across the gloom, hurtling one upon the other, and vanishing swiftly into the turbulent abyss of shade; so that, to the eyes and fancies of the frightened wanderers, the unsubstantial vapors were as the bodily forms of gigantic foes—the agents of terror and of death.

R13:   The ashes in many places were already knee-deep; and the boiling showers which came from the steaming breath of the volcano forced their way into the houses, bearing with them a strong and suffocating vapor. In some places, immense fragments of rock, hurled upon the house roofs, bore down along the streets masses of confused ruin, which yet more and more, with every hour, obstructed the way; and, as the day advanced, the motion of the earth was more sensibly felt—the footing seemed to slide and creep—neither chariot or litter could be kept steady, even on the most level ground.

"The Last Day of Pompeii" A Tale for Reader's Theater (cont.)

R14:   Sometimes the larger stones, striking against each other as they fell, broke into countless fragments, emitting sparks of fire, which caught whatever was combustible within their reach. Along the plains beyond the city the darkness was now terribly interrupted—for several houses and even vineyards, had been set into flames, and at various intervals the fires rose suddenly and fiercely against the solid gloom. To add to this partial relief from the darkness, the citizens had endeavored to place rows of torches; but these rarely continued long; the showers and the winds extinguished them.

R15:   The ocean had retreated rapidly from the shore where an utter darkness lay over it, and upon its groaning and tossing waves the storm of cinders and rock fell without the protection which the streets and roofs afforded to the land. Frequently, by the momentary light of the torches, parties of fugitives encountered each other, some hurrying towards the sea, others fleeing from the sea back to the land. As these groups met, they did not speak. For the intermittent lights revealed to each the deathlike faces of the other, all hurrying to seek refuge beneath the nearest shelter.

Narrator 2:   *Never had there been such a situation. It was as if the whole of civilization was breaking up. So many trying to escape to safety, only to find others doing the same. It seemed inescapable. If, in the darkness, wife was separated from husband, or parent from child, vain was the hope of reunion. Each hurried blindly and confusedly on—to somewhere, anywhere driven only by the instinct for self-preservation. Nothing in all the various and complicated machinery of social life was left save the primal law of self-preservation!*

R16:   Through this awful scene Glaucus wade his way, with two companions—Ione, and Nydia, the blind girl. Suddenly, a rush of hundreds, in their path to the sea, swept by them. Nydia was torn from the side of Glaucus, who, with Ione, was borne rapidly onward; and when the crowd (whose forms they saw not, so thick was the gloom) were gone, Nydia was still separated from their side. Glaucus shouted her name. No answer came.

R17:   They retraced their steps—in vain: they could not discover her—it was evident she had been swept along some opposite direction by the human current. Their friend, their preserver, was lost! And hitherto Nydia had been their guide. Her blindness rendered the scene familiar to her alone. Accustomed, through a perpetual night, to thread the windings of the city, she had led them unerringly towards the sea-shore, by which they had resolved to hazard an escape. Now, which way should they go? They found themselves in a maze without a clue. Wearied, despondent, bewildered, they pressed, with the ashes falling upon their heads and the fragmentary stones dashing up in sparks before their feet.

"The Last Day of Pompeii"
A Tale for Reader's Theater *(cont.)*

R18:   Suddenly everything was lit with an intense and lurid glow. Bright and gigantic through the darkness, which closed around it like the walls of hell, the mountain shone—a pile of fire! Its summit seemed torn in half; or rather, above its surface there seemed to rise two monster shapes, each confronting each, as Demons contending for a world. These were of one deep blood-red hue of fire, which lit up the whole atmosphere far and wide; but, below, the nether part of the mountain was still dark and shrouded, except in three places, adown which flowed, serpentine and irregular, rivers of the molten lava. Darkly red through the profound gloom of their banks, they flowed slowly on, as towards the devoted city.

Narrator 1:   *As Glaucus and Ione pressed on amid the ever-increasing peril, something stopped Glaucus in his tracks. A figure from his past, which now seemed so distant, appeared right in front of him. There stood Glaucus's mortal enemy, Arbaces, who thinking there was nothing to lose, posed to strike Glaucus down.*

R19:   Arbaces advanced one step—and it was his last on earth! The ground shook beneath him with a convulsion that jerked all around upon its surface. A simultaneous crash resounded through the city, as down toppled many a roof and pillar!—the lightning, as if caught by the metal, lingered an instant on the Imperial Statue—then shivered bronze and column! Down fell the ruin, echoing along the street, and splitting the solid pavement where it crashed!

R20:   The sound—the shock, stunned the Athenian for several moments. When he recovered, the light still illuminated the scene—the earth still slid and trembled beneath! Ione lay senseless on the ground; but he saw her not yet—his eyes were fixed upon a ghastly face that seemed to emerge, without limbs or trunk, from the huge fragments of the shattered column—a face of unutterable pain, agony, and despair! The eyes shut and opened rapidly, as if sense were not yet fled; the lips quivered and grinned—then sudden stillness and darkness fell over the features, yet retaining that aspect of horror never to be forgotten! . . .

R21:   Glaucus turned in gratitude but in awe, caught Ione once more in his arms, and fled along the street that was still intensely luminous. But suddenly a duller shade fell over the air. Instinctively he turned to the mountain, and beheld! One of the two gigantic crests, into which the summit had been divided, rocked and wavered to and fro; and then, with a sound, the mightiness of which no language can describe, it fell from its burning base, and rushed, an avalanche of fire, down the sides of the mountain! At the same instant gushed forth a volume of blackest smoke—rolling on, over air, sea, and earth.

"The Last Day of Pompeii"
A Tale for Reader's Theater (cont.)

R22: Another—and another—and another shower of ashes, far more profuse than before, scattered fresh desolation along the streets. Darkness once more wrapped them as a veil; and Glaucus, his bold heart at last quelled and despairing, sank beneath the cover of an arch, and, clasping Ione to his side— resigned himself to die.

Narrator 2: *The day ended, but not the world, and the morning of the next day arrived.*

R23: Meekly, softly, beautifully, dawned at last the light over the trembling deep! The winds were sinking into rest and the foam died from the glowing azure of that delicious sea. Around the east, thin mists caught gradually the rosy hues that heralded the morning; light was about to resume her reign. Yet, still, dark and massive in the distance, lay the broken fragments of the destroying cloud, from which red streaks, burning dimmer and dimmer, betrayed the yet rolling fires of the mountain. The white walls and gleaming columns that had adorned the lovely coasts were no more. Sullen and dull were the shores crested by the cities of Herculaneum and Pompeii. Century after century shall the mighty Mother stretch forth her azure arms, and know them not—moaning round the sepulchers of the Lost!

Narrator 1: *On August 24, A.D. 79, Mt. Vesuvius erupted and buried the thriving city of Pompeii and neighboring towns and communities. Pompeii itself was buried under about 10 feet (3 meters) of tephra (material ejected from a volcano, such as ash, dust, and boulders). The town of Herculaneum, which was closer to the mountain but less populated, was buried under 75 feet of material deposited by pyroclastic surges (toxic, fast-moving "avalanche" of super-hot material from an eruption). The population of the area is estimated to have been 10,000–20,000. Many, but not all of the people died. Some did escape. But what of Glaucus?*

Narrator 2: *The descriptions of Mt. Vesuvius's eruption, including the different phases of its activity, is consistent with what actually occurred. However, the narrative— meaning the characters and plot, including the fate of Glaucus—are fiction. Making an historical event or setting the backdrop of a story can make it seem more real. Or, creating an entertaining tale around true events can make learning about history more fun. This tale was a little of both!*

Name_____

Using Similes and Metaphors to Paint a Picture with Words

The story you read, "The Last Day of Pompeii," paints a vivid picture of what it might have been like to be in Pompeii when Mt. Vesuvius erupted. Rather than just telling you that the sky was red or the volcano erupted, the author uses many similes and metaphors to enrich the description. Similes and metaphors are comparisons of one thing to another.

A simile is a comparison using *like* or *as*.

Example: Solid rock **melted like butter**.

A metaphor is a direct comparison.

Example: A **blanket of smoke** smothered the town.

Directions: Below are some excerpts from the story. Each uses a simile or metaphor to describe something. In parentheses after each excerpt is a reference to where the complete quote appears in the story. Go back and reread the paragraph in which it appears. Then, on each line, write if the bold section is a simile or a metaphor.

_____ 1. "Behold!" he shouted with a **voice of thunder**. (R2)

_____ 2. . . . in the form of . . . tree; **the trunk, blackness—the branches, fire**! (R3)

_____ 3. . . . lions were dread seers—**wild prophets** of the wrath to come! (R4)

_____ 4. Colors . . . darting . . . to and fro **as the folds of an enormous serpent** . . . (R11)

_____ 5. Colors . . . suddenly dying . . . **like the ghost of their own life**! (R11)

_____ 6. . . . vapors were **as the bodily forms of gigantic foes** . . . (R12)

_____ 7. Nothing in the . . . **complicated machinery of social life** was left . . . (N2)

_____ 8. . . . she had been swept along in some opposite direction **by the human current**. (R17)

_____ 9. . . . darkness, which closed around it **like the walls of hell,** . . . (R18)

_____ 10. Darkness once more **wrapped them as a veil**; . . . (R22)

Ibn Battuta's Travels to Mali

Objective

√ Students will participate in an interview-style radio reading as readers or listeners to improve fluency and comprehension.

Preparation

√ Ask students to have their copies of the world map (pages 188–189) from previous lessons.

√ Copy *An Interview with Ibn Battuta* (pages 153–154) for selected student readers.

√ Copy *Inferring from Ibn's Words* (page 155) for each student.

Fluency Suggestions and Activities

To help students analyze the text and read with comprehension and fluency, present the historical background and preteach the vocabulary on the following page before starting the fluency activity.

1. Assist students in finding on their maps key places related to this lesson: Mecca, the Sahara Desert, Mali, and the Niger River.

2. Select two competent readers to prepare for a radio reading presentation of *An Interview with Ibn Battuta* (pages 153–154). While the other students are working independently, take these students aside to preview the activity. Explain that one is to be the Interviewer and the other, Ibn Battuta, as if they were on the radio as host and guest. The interviewer will give the audience the background introduction and ask the questions. The other student will read the answers in Ibn Buttuta's own words, which were written in a travel journal as he toured Asia and Africa from 1325 to 1354. Direct the pair to practice together, reading and rehearsing, until they can each perform their reading fluently.

3. In the meantime, prepare the rest of the students for listening to the performance of the radio reading. Review the vocabulary they will hear and discuss the historical information given in the History Connection section on the following page.

4. When the student readers are ready, set aside about 30 minutes for the presentation and follow up. Create a "studio set" for the performance. For example, you could have the students seated in chairs with a table between them.

5. Instruct the rest of the class to listen very carefully to the presentation. Tell them that, following the radio reading, they will answer specific questions about what they heard.

6. After the performance, distribute copies of *Inferring from Ibn's Words* (page 155). Usually, students are asked questions about what they have read to check comprehension. This page checks comprehension and critical thinking skills of the material they have heard. You may or may not want to have students take notes. This will allow you to observe strengths and weaknesses of skills in a different learning style (auditory vs. visual).

Ibn Battuta's Travels to Mali (cont.)

History Connection

In the early thirteenth century, Mali was a kingdom located on the western side of Africa. The kingdom grew into an important empire after 1235, when under Sundiata the kingdom expanded and held control of the Niger River. This not only gave Mali a transportation route, but also fertile lands on the river banks. Mali had great resources in gold and salt, and through heavy taxation of goods going both in and out, the kingdom grew wealthy and prospered. The success of Mali also depended upon strong leadership and the allegiance of the people. This began with Sundiata and continued through several subsequent kings. Most of these kings were Muslim, and some made the *haj*, or pilgimage to Mecca, which was required under Islamic law. The most famous ruler of Mali was Mansa Musa, who ruled with the authority of a king, yet gave some power locally to keep the kingdom united. In 1324, Mansa Musa made the pilgrimage with much fanfare and earned himself fame by giving away large amounts of money and gifts.

This lesson is drawn from the writings of a Moroccan Muslim, Ibn Battuta, who journeyed throughout the Muslim world between 1325 and 1354. In 1352, he set out from the west side of the Sahara to travel to Mali and back. Here we learn about some of his personal observations.

Vocabulary Connection

Discuss unfamiliar vocabulary encountered in the text. Begin with these and then add any others you feel need to be reviewed or introduced. Discuss the words' meanings and how they are used specifically in the context of the material.

- **forage**—food for animals
- **Massufa**—a specific Muslim tribe based in Africa
- **Koran**—the holy book of Islam, the word of Allah—God of the Islamic faith
- **Muslim**—follower of Islam
- **reprehensible**—highly unacceptable
- **cannibals**—humans who eat the flesh of their own kind
- **quid** (also **cadi**)—a minor judge in a Muslim community where Islamic law is followed
- **heathen**—a negative term used to describe a "nonbeliever" in one God

Extension Idea

- In the 1300s, Ibn Battuta, the kingdom of Mali, and much of northern Africa followed the Islam faith. Today there are more than a billion Muslims in the world. Divide your class into study groups to find out more about the followers of Islam—their religion, their sub-sects, their culture, their customs, and their distribution throughout the world. Then hold a presentation and conversation hour in which students discuss and learn about the topics.

Name_____

An Interview with Ibn Battuta

Note: The script integrates fictional text and original source material from Ibn Battuta's writings (in quotes).

Host: *Welcome, listeners. My name is _____ and I am the host of "Eyewitness Travelers," a radio show in which we talk to people who have visited exotic places. Today's guest is renowned traveler Ibn Battuta, who, between the years of 1325 and 1354, traveled extensively through Asia and Africa. His book, A Gift to Those Who Contemplate the Wonders of Cities and the Marvels of Travelling will be available in marketplaces soon. However, today we will concentrate on asking him about his experiences journeying to Mali and back. Ibn, a devoted Muslim, has agreed to share with us some of his experiences on his trip across the Sahara to Mali and back. We're sure to find out some fascinating facts about northern Africa—a place shrouded in mystery. Welcome to "Eyewitness Travelers," Mr. Battuta.*

Ibn: Thank you. Glad to be here. You can call me Ibn.

Host: *Okay, Ibn. Tell us, what was it was like to cross the Sahara and how long did it take?*

Ibn: Well, I began my trip "at Sijilmasa [at the edge of the desert]. I bought camels and four months' supply of forage for them. On February 13, 1352, I set out with a caravan. We reached the town of Iwalatan [Walata] after a journey of two months to a day. After staying there for a while, I went on to Mali, which is reached in 24 days from Iwalatan if the traveler pushes on rapidly."

Host: *Wow. That must have been grueling. How did you survive?*

Ibn: "At that time we used to go ahead of the caravan, and when we found a place suitable for pasturage we would graze our beasts. We went on doing this until one of our party was lost in the desert; after that I neither went ahead nor lagged behind. We passed a caravan on the way and they told us that some of their party had become separated from them. We found one of them dead under a shrub, of the sort that grows in the sand. The water was only about a mile away from him." Once we reached Iwalatan and were ready to go on to Mali, "I hired a guide from the Massufa."

Host: *On the way to Mali, did you see anything particularly strange or unknown to you?*

Ibn: Indeed! "There are many trees [baobabs], and these trees are of great age and girth; a whole caravan may shelter in the shade of one of them. There are trees which have neither branches nor leaves, yet the shade cast by their trunks is sufficient to shelter a man. Some of these trees are rotted in the interior and the rain-water collects in them, so that they serve as wells and the people drink of the water inside them. In others there are bees and honey, which is collected by the people. I was surprised to find inside one tree, by which I passed, a man, a weaver, who had set up his loom in it and was actually weaving."

Host: *What about at the river itself? We know about crocodiles in the Nile. Are they also in the Niger?*

An Interview with Ibn Battuta *(cont.)*

Ibn: Oh, yes. "I saw a crocodile in the [Niger River] close to the bank; it looked just like a small boat. One day I went down to the river to satisfy a need, and lo, one of the blacks came and stood between me and the river. I was amazed at such lack of manners and decency on his part, and spoke of it to someone or other. [That person] answered, 'His purpose in doing that was solely to protect you from the crocodile, by placing himself between you and it.'"

Another time "we came to a wide channel which flows out to the [Niger] and can only be crossed in boats. The place is infested with mosquitoes, and no one can pass that way except by night. We reached the channel three or four hours after nightfall on a moonlit night. On reaching it I saw 16 beasts with enormous bodies, and marveled at them, taking them to be elephants, of which there are many in that country. Afterwards I saw that they had gone into the river, so I said to Abu Bakr, 'What kind of animals are these?' He replied, 'They are hippopotami which have come out to pasture ashore.'"

Host: *When you reached the kingdom of Mali, did you have the chance to meet the current king?*

Ibn: "The sultan of Mali is Mansa Sulayman, 'mansa' meaning [in Mandingo] 'sultan,' and Sulayman being his proper name. He is a miserly king, not a man from whom one might hope for a rich present." After attending a ceremony, a gift from the sultan was delivered to my room. "I stood up thinking that it consisted of robes of honor and money, and lo!, it was three cakes of bread, a piece of beef fried in native oil, and a calabash of sour curds. When I saw this I burst out laughing!"

Host: *Ah, so you thought the king was a bit stingy. How about the people of Mali? What of them?*

Ibn: "The negroes possess some admirable qualities. They are seldom unjust, and have a greater abhorrence of injustice than any other people. . . There is complete security in their country. Neither traveler nor inhabitant in it has anything to fear from robbers or men of violence. . . Another of their good qualities is their habit of wearing clean white garments on Fridays. Even if a man has nothing but an old worn shirt, he washes it and cleans it, and wears it to the Friday service. Yet another is their zeal for learning the Koran by heart." However, "Among their bad qualities are. . .women go about without a stitch of clothing on them. . . Then there is their custom of putting dust and ashes on their heads, as a mark of respect, and the reprehensible practice among many of them is the eating of carrion, dogs, and "beasts of burden."

Host: *One last question, Mr. Battuta—Ibn. . . There are rumors that the natives in that part of the world are cannibals. Is this true, or are people letting their imaginations run away with them?*

Ibn: A quick story will answer your question. "We halted near this channel at a large village, which had as governor a negro, a pilgrim, and man of fine character named Farba Magha. He was one of the negroes who made the pilgrimage in the company of Sultan Mansa Musa. Farba Magha told me that when Mansa Musa came to this channel, he had with him a qadi, a white man. This qadi attempted to make away with four thousand mithqals and the sultan, on learning of it, was enraged at him and exiled him to the country of the heathen cannibals. He [the qadi] lived among them for four years, at the end of which the sultan sent him back to his own country. The reason why the heathens did not eat him was that he was white, for they say that the white is indigestible because he is not 'ripe,' whereas the black man is 'ripe' in their opinion."

Host: *Amazing! Thank you sir, for being our guest and sharing your eyewitness accounts of Africa.*

Name_____

Inferring from Ibn's Words

You have listened to a mock interview with Ibn Battuta, who traveled extensively between 1335 and 1364 and described his trip to Mali and back. The answers to the questions below were not directly stated in the story, but try to figure them out from the information given.

1. We live in the twenty-first century. In what century did Ibn visit Mali?

    _____

2. What river in Mali is equivalent in importance to the Nile River in Egypt?

    _____

3. Did Ibn Battuta visit Mali before or after the reign of Mansa Mansu?

    _____

4. Ibn describes trees of great age and girth. What does he mean by *girth*?

    _____

5. Had Ibn seen an elephant before? _____ Had he seen a hippopotamus? _____
    How can you tell? _____

6. Was Mansa Mansu a follower of the Islam faith? _____ How do you know?

    _____

7. Was the current sultan of Mali, Mansu Sulayman, a Muslim?

    _____

8. Why might have Ibn expected a more lavish gift from Sulayman?

    _____

9. What does *service* mean in the phrase "he wears it to the Friday service"?

    _____

10. Ibn mentions meeting a man who made the pilgrimage with Mansa Mansu. What does "the pilgrimage" refer to?

    _____

11. When the host asks Ibn about cannibalism, does he or she expect Ibn to confirm or deny the rumors? Why do you think so? _____

    _____

I Was Taken from My Village and Sold!

Objective

√ Students will use repeated readings with feedback on accuracy, pace, and expression to focus on increasing fluency skills.

Preparation

√ Copy *I Was Taken from My Village and Sold!* (pages 158–159) and *Repeated Reading Response Form* (page 160) for each student.

√ For optional use, make a transparency of *I Was Taken from My Village and Sold!* (pages 158–159).

Fluency Suggestions and Activities

To help students analyze the text and read with comprehension and fluency, present the historical background and preteach the vocabulary on the following page before starting the fluency activity.

1. Have students return to the maps on which they located Mali. Point out that this true story of an African man who was kidnapped and sold into slavery. The story begins in Benin, a country in West Africa, south of Mali (in the "crook" where the coast of Africa turns from east-west to north-south). Point out its location on the world map or a globe.

2. Display a transparency of *I Was Taken from My Village and Sold!* (pages 158–159), or distribute copies to students. Preteach any vocabulary you feel might be troublesome or unfamiliar. Highlight these on the transparency. Next ask students to follow along as you model fluent reading of the text. Afterwards point out your use of three specific skills: accuracy (reading the words correctly), pacing (reading at a good rate for listeners to follow and understand), and expression (reading smoothly with good phrasing and with appropriate feeling).

3. If you haven't yet done so, give students copies of *I Was Taken from My Village and Sold!* Explain that they are to practice reading the passages with fluency by doing repeated readings with feedback. You can direct students to practice in class with a peer or at home with a parent or other adult. Tell them that they are to focus on accuracy, pacing, and expression. Distribute copies of the *Repeated Reading Response Form* (page 160). Direct students to use this form as they read aloud the first or second time, and then again for the final reading. Instruct them to have the same person be the listener both times and to complete the feedback both after the practice reading and the final reading. If you are having students do this at home, require that both the reader and listener sign the sheet to acknowledge that they have participated as directed. Collect the signed sheets.

Option: You could also use this page for an oral reading assessment after the students have practiced. After the listener does the practice rating, listen to the student for his or her final reading, and fill out the second part of the form as an evaluation. To modify the reading for ELLs or struggling students, reduce the amount they are required to read.

I Was Taken from My Village and Sold! (cont.)

History Connection

It is 1754—more than a hundred years before the Civil War in the United States. A young boy is playing near his home in a small village of Africa, when suddenly, strange men appear and carry him off. He is frightened but helpless. His only comfort is that he clings to his sister, who was taken with him. Soon the strangers take her away, too. Thirty years later this small boy is a grown man with a story to tell. He is not writing for fame or fortune—only to tell anyone who happens to read his words what it was like to be taken from his village and sold into slavery. Few slaves ever learned to read or write, so little is recorded of their experiences, feelings, and observations. However, this man, Olaudah Equiano, was eventually freed and ended up in England, where he wrote an account of his life. It is a touching narrative that gives us the opportunity to see life through the eyes of a slave who immigrated to the New World—not by choice, but by force.

Vocabulary Connection

Discuss unfamiliar vocabulary encountered in the text. Begin with these and then add any others you feel need to be reviewed or introduced. Discuss the words' meanings and how they are used specifically in the context of the material.

- **vale**—valley
- **theatre (theater)**—a place where significant events take place, such as battles
- **apprehend**—become aware of
- **booty**—money or valuables stolen or seized
- **procured**—acquired; obtained
- **prevails**—wins
- **vanquished**—defeated
- **ebony**—black with a hint of brown or olive (from the dark wood of the ebony tree)
- **haughty**—behaving with arrogance or purposely putting down others
- **exultation**—a feeling of triumph or delight

Extension Idea

- In the last two paragraphs, Olaudah expresses his feelings and hopes about the future of slavery. This is especially poignant because it was written in the 1780s when the United States was just being formed. Ask your students to discuss this passage with a partner and then write a paragraph giving their personal responses to it.

Name_____

I Was Taken from My Village and Sold!

Excerpts from *The Interesting Narrative of the Life of Olaudah Equiano, or Gustavus Vassa, the African*
by Olaudah Equiano, 1789

Introduction: *Olaudah Equiano was born in 1745 in Benin, Africa. Before he was kidnapped and sold into slavery, he knew nothing of things outside his home in the village of Eboe. He had never seen a white man, nor did he know that there was an ocean, let alone lands across it. Here he describes his native land, tells how and why people were taken, and shares his insightful commentary on slavery itself. Text in brackets has been edited for spelling or clarity.*

That part of Africa . . . to which the trade for slaves is carried on, extends along the coast above 3,400 miles, from the Senegal to Angola, and includes a variety of kingdoms. Of these the most considerable is the kingdom of [Benin], both as to extent and wealth, the richness and cultivation of the soil, the power of its king, and the number and warlike disposition of the inhabitants. It is situated nearly under the line, and extends along the coast about 170 miles, but runs back into the interior part of Africa to a distance [that up to this time] I believe unexplored by any traveler . . . This kingdom is divided into many provinces or districts: in one of the most remote and fertile of which, called Eboe, I was born, in the year 1745, in a charming fruitful vale, named Effaka. The distance of this province from the capital of Benin and the sea coast must be very considerable; for I had never heard of white men or Europeans, nor of the sea . . .

Our [plowing is done on] a large plain, or common, some hours walk from our dwellings, and all the neighbors [go there together]. They use no beasts of husbandry; and their only instruments are hoes, axes, shovels, and beaks, or pointed iron to dig with . . . This common is often the theatre of war; and therefore when our people go out to till their land, they not only go in a [group], but generally take their arms with them for fear of a surprise; and when they apprehend an invasion they guard the [paths] to their dwellings by driving sticks into the ground, which are so sharp at one end as to pierce the foot, and are generally [dipped] in poison.

From what I can recollect of these battles, they appear to have been [eruptions] of one little state or district on the other, to obtain prisoners or booty. Perhaps they were incited to this by those traders who brought the European goods . . . amongst us. Such a mode of obtaining slaves in Africa is common; and I believe more are procured this way, and by kidnapping, than any other. When a trader wants slaves, he applies to a chief for them, and tempts him with his wares. It is not extraordinary, if on this occasion [the chief] yields to the temptation with as little firmness, and accepts the price of his fellow creatures' liberty with as little reluctance as the enlightened merchant. Accordingly he [attacks] his neighbors, and a desperate battle ensues. If he prevails and takes prisoners, he gratifies his [greed] by selling them; but, if his party be vanquished, and he falls into the hands of the enemy, he is put to death: for, as he has been known to [cause] their quarrels, it is thought dangerous to let him survive, and no ransom can save him. . .

I Was Taken from My Village and Sold! *(cont.)*

These instances, and a great many more which might be [offered in evidence], while they [show] how the complexions of the same persons vary in different climates, [it is hoped they] may tend also to remove the prejudice that some conceive against the natives of Africa on account of their color. Surely the minds of the Spaniards did not change with their complexions! Are there not causes enough to which the apparent inferiority of an African may be ascribed, without limiting the goodness of God, and supposing he [stamped all of us in] his own image, [purposely making some] "carved in ebony."

Might [inferiority] not naturally be ascribed to their situation? When they come among Europeans, they are ignorant of their language, religion, manners, and customs. Are any pains taken to teach them these? Are they treated as men? Does not slavery itself depress the mind, and extinguish all its fire and every noble sentiment? But, above all, what advantages do not a refined people possess over those who are rude and uncultivated. Let the polished and haughty European recollect that his ancestors were once, like the Africans, uncivilized, and even barbarous. Did Nature make them inferior to their sons? And should they too have been made slaves? Every rational mind answers, No. Let such reflections as these melt the pride of their superiority into sympathy for the wants and miseries of their brethren, and compel them to acknowledge, that understanding is not confined to feature or color. If, when they look round the world, they feel exultation, let it be tempered with benevolence to others, and gratitude to God, "who hath made of one blood all nations of men for to dwell on all the face of the earth; and whose wisdom is not our wisdom, neither are our ways."

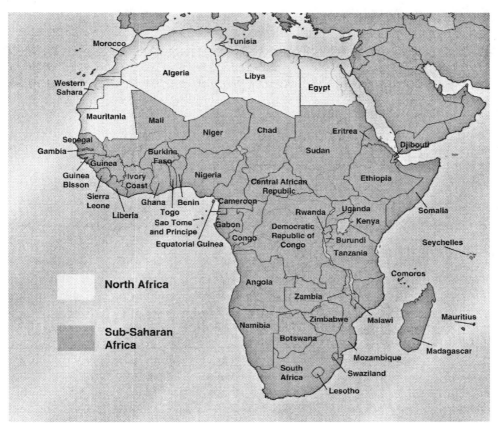

Name_____

Repeated Reading Response Form

Adapted from Dr. Timothy Rasinski's *The Fluent Reader*, Scholastic Professional Books, page 92

Listener: _____

Passage read: _____

1. Accuracy *(reading the words correctly)*

Practice Reading:	1	2	3	4	5
	Outstanding		Good		Fair

Final Reading:	1	2	3	4	5
	Outstanding		Good		Fair

2. Pacing *(reading at a good rate for listener to follow and understand)*

Practice Reading:	1	2	3	4	5
	Outstanding		Good		Fair

Final Reading:	1	2	3	4	5
	Outstanding		Good		Fair

3. Expression *(reading smoothly with good phrasing and with appropriate feeling)*

Practice Reading:	1	2	3	4	5
	Outstanding		Good		Fair

Final Reading:	1	2	3	4	5
	Outstanding		Good		Fair

Comments by the listener: _____

_____

_____

Comments by the reader: _____

_____

The Magic Flyswatter:
A Hero Tale of the Congo

Retold by Aaron Shepard, from the Mwindo epic

Objective

√ Students will work in cooperative learning groups to rewrite and perform a story in reader's theater format.

Preparation

√ Copy *The Magic Flyswatter: A Hero Tale of the Congo* (pages 163–166) for each student.

√ Make a copy of *Planning Our Rewrite for Reader's Theater* (pages 167–168) for each group.

Fluency Suggestions and Activities

To help students analyze the text and read with comprehension and fluency, present the historical background and preteach the vocabulary on the following page before doing the fluency activity.

1. Distribute copies of *The Magic Flyswatter: A Hero Tale of the Congo* (pages 163–166). Point out that it contains a preface, which tells some background information about the story. Preview the preface by reading it aloud as students follow along. Be sure to take a few moments to go over the pronunciations provided by the author. Have students practice saying the names aloud. Show students the location of the Congo on the west side of Africa.

2. Next ask students to follow along as you model a dramatic reading of the story. Ask students to look at the form in which the story is written (running narrative). Explain that they are going to work in cooperative groups to rewrite the story as a reader's theater script and perform it for the class. Assign each student to a group, and choose group facilitators. Give that student the *Planning Our Rewrite for Reader's Theater* (pages 167–168). Tell students to meet in their groups and work together to plan, rewrite, and practice their reader's theater scripts under the direction of the group facilitator. Explain that they can use the ideas and suggestions on the worksheet to plan their script.

3. Explain to students that storytellers are highly regarded in African tribal cultures. They are both teachers and entertainers. It is traditional to sit on the ground in front of the storyteller with complete attention and respect. At each group's performance, listeners will simulate this by sitting on the floor and listening intently to the storytellers. (If possible, sit with them on the floor among the other listeners.)

4. Give students time to work on their productions, and set a performance date. For best results and evaluation of their abilities to work together and produce the project, make the performance the first time you listen directly to their presentation. You can assess students on the ability to work together and the product itself, or simply just observe and enjoy the performances.

The Magic Flyswatter:
A Hero Tale of the Congo *(cont.)*

History Connection

Note: The following is additional information provided by the author.

Mwindo—The Nyanga do not seem to claim Mwindo as a historical figure, and there is no reason to believe he was one. The name itself has no remembered meaning, but it is now commonly given to a son born after many daughters.

Shemwindo—The name means "father of Mwindo"—so, of course, it could not really have been his name when the story starts!

bride-price—In most of Africa, and in many other cultures worldwide, it is the custom for a groom and his family to send a substantial wedding gift to the family of the bride. This is basically the reverse form of a dowry, a custom that is common elsewhere. Names for the gift include "wooing present," "bride-price," and "bride-wealth." Where this is practiced, the birth of many sons can impoverish a family, while the birth of many daughters can enrich it.

conga—This is a flyswatter with a scepter-like handle of wood. The swatter attached at the top can be leaves, an antelope tail, or, as in this story, the tail of a Cape buffalo. A conga is included in the regalia of a chief, and so it signifies here the destiny of Mwindo, who will become chief after his father.

Vocabulary Connection

With the exception of the proper names, the vocabulary used in this retelling should present no difficulties. During your first reading, ask students to mark any words they are not sure of. Review these at the end of the reading.

Extension Idea

- Throughout the fluency lessons in this book, students have been asked to tackle a wide variety of writing. Many of these have been challenging due to the nature of the primary sources. Translations were often done by scholars, making the vocabulary and syntax difficult for today's readers. Although fluency skills have been the focus, to cultivate fluency, it is just as important that reading is perceived as valuable and enjoyable. Aaron Shepard's retellings and original stories are perfect for oral presentation and fostering enjoyment of reading. Mr. Shepard has made a number of his narratives and reader's theater scripts available online for teachers to download and use at no cost. They are labeled with age-level ranges and categorized by culture or concept, making them a fun way for students to increase their multicultural awareness while enjoying the stories.

  Mr. Shepard gave his permission to include his retelling of the old Mwindo epic in this book. Extend your students' fluency and promote enjoyment of reading by sharing additional tales by Aaron Shepard. Visit his website, **www.aaronshep.com** to find more stories and books for all reading levels.

Name_____

The Magic Flyswatter: A Hero Tale of the Congo

Adapted with permission of Aaron Shepard. Please visit www.aaronshep.com.

About the Story: The Mwindo epic comes from the Nyanga, one of the Bantu-speaking peoples that live in the mountainous rainforests east of the Congo (for a while called Zaire). In the 1950s, when the epic was collected, the Nyanga numbered about 27,000. Traditionally, they are governed by chiefs, each one ruling over several villages.

The Nyanga themselves have no written version of the Mwindo epic, so it has never reached a standardized form. Of the four versions transcribed and published by outsiders, no two are even nearly the same—and no doubt there are many other distinct versions.

The epic is performed as simple entertainment by amateur bards. The bards' performance includes song and dance, accompanied by drummers and other musicians. Only a portion of the epic is performed at a time, as a complete performance would take too long. This retelling itself includes only a part of Mwindo's adventures.

How to say the names: conga ~ KOHNG-gah; Iyangura ~ EE-yong-GOO-rah; Mwindo ~ MWEE-'n-do; Shemwindo ~ shay-MWEE-'n-do; Tubondo ~ too-BOH-'n-do

These pronunciations are only approximate. To be more accurate, say all vowels as in Spanish or Italian. The letter *o*, for example, is pronounced halfway between a long and short *o*. The letter *e* is pronounced halfway between a short *e* and a long *a*.

"The Magic Flyswatter"

The storyteller stands beside the fire, swaying, dancing, miming, singing, reciting. With one hand he shakes a gourd rattle, with the other he swings a *conga*—a flyswatter made with a buffalo tail on a wooden handle. Anklet bells tinkle as he moves. Three young men beat a wooden drum with sticks.

Listening to him is a crowd of men, women, and children. They sing along at a song's refrain, they repeat whole lines of the story when he pauses to see if they're paying attention. They encourage him with little shouts, whoops, claps. Food and drink are passed around.

A Nyanga village hears once more the tale of its favorite hero—Mwindo, the one born walking, the one born talking . . .

In the village of Tubondo lived a great chief. His name was Shemwindo.

One day he called together his seven wives and his counselors and all his people. He told them, "When a daughter marries, her family is paid a bride-price. But when a son marries, it is his family that pays it. So, all my children must be daughters."

The people were astonished. But they said nothing, for they were afraid of him.

Soon all the chief's seven wives had children. Six children arrived on the same day. They were all daughters. But the child of his favorite wife did not arrive.

The Magic Flyswatter:
A Hero Tale of the Congo (cont.)

The child that did not arrive was Mwindo. He was not ready to arrive.

At last he told himself, "I am ready." He jumped down and ran around his mother's room. In his hand was a conga flyswatter, with a handle of wood and a swatter of buffalo tail. His mother cried out. *"Aieeeeeee! What kind of child is this?"*

The baby sang and danced and waved his conga.

> *I am Mwindo,*
> *the one born walking,*
> *the one born talking.*
> *My father does not want me.*
> *But what can he do against me?*

Shemwindo heard the noise. He went to the house of his favorite wife. He saw the boy and was full of rage. "What is this? Did I not say 'no sons'?"

He thrust his spear in the floor. Mwindo waved his conga. The spear flew to Mwindo's hand. He broke it in two.

Shemwindo cried out. *"Aieeeeeee! What kind of child is this?"*

Mwindo sang and danced and waved his conga.

> *I am Mwindo,*
> *the one born walking,*
> *the one born talking.*
> *O my father, you do not want me.*
> *But what can you do against me?*

The chief rushed out. He called his counselors. "My favorite wife has given birth to a son. I do not want him. I will float him down the river. Make a drum and put him in."

The counselors said nothing. They cut a piece of log and hollowed it. They prepared two antelope hides. They placed the baby inside. They laced and pegged the hides.

The chief took the drum to the river. He threw it far out. He looked to see it float downstream.

The drum did not float downstream. It floated just where it was. The chief heard a song.

> *I am Mwindo,*
> *the one born walking,*
> *the one born talking.*
> *O my father, you do not want me.*
> *O my father, you send me downriver.*
> *But Mwindo will not go downriver.*
> *Mwindo will go upriver.*
> *Mwindo goes where he wants to go.*

The drum floated upstream. Shemwindo cried out. *"Aieeeeeee! What kind of child is this?"* Then he said, "But now he's gone." He returned to the village.

Mwindo went upstream. He was going to his father's sister, Aunt Iyangura. He came near her village. He floated his drum to the bank.

The serving girls of Iyangura came to draw water. They saw the drum and heard a song.

The Magic Flyswatter: A Hero Tale of the Congo *(cont.)*

> *I am Mwindo,*
> *the one born walking,*
> *the one born talking.*
> *My father does not want me.*
> *But Aunt Iyangura will want me.*

The girls rushed to tell Iyangura. She came running. With a knife, she slashed open the drum. There was the baby with his conga. Iyangura was astonished. He shone like the rising sun.

Iyangura said, "What a fine boy is Mwindo! How could my brother reject him? Iyangura will not reject him!" She picked him up and carried him to her house. She cared for him.

Mwindo grew up. A day went by, a week, a month, and he was grown. Then he said, "O my aunt, thank you for caring for me. Now I go to fight my father."

His aunt said, "What is this talk? Your father's village is huge. He has many men to fight for him. You cannot fight your father."

But Mwindo sang and danced and waved his conga.

> *I am Mwindo,*
> *the one born walking,*
> *the one born talking.*
> *My father does not want me.*
> *My father tried to get rid of me.*
> *But now he must fight me.*

His aunt said, "All right, then. But I will go with you."

Mwindo and his aunt started off. Iyangura brought her servants and the musicians and drummers of her village. They all sang and danced as they went.

They danced to the village of Tubondo. Mwindo danced ahead through the gate. He had no weapon.

The chief said, "Who is this strange fellow? What should we do with him?"

Mwindo sang and danced and waved his conga.

> *I am Mwindo,*
> *the one born walking,*
> *the one born talking.*
> *O my father, you do not want me.*
> *O my father, you tried to get rid of me.*
> *But now you must fight me.*
> *What can you do against me?*

The men of Tubondo shot their arrows. Mwindo waved his conga. All the arrows fell short. Shemwindo trembled. "O men of Tubondo, throw your spears!"

The men of Tubondo threw their spears. Mwindo waved his conga. All the spears fell short. Shemwindo shook. "O men of Tubondo, shoot your arrows!"

Shemwindo quaked. "O men of Tubondo, throw yourselves at him!"

The men threw themselves at him. Mwindo waved his conga. All the men fell down.

Shemwindo cried out. *"Aieeeeeee!* What kind of man is this?"

The Magic Flyswatter:
A Hero Tale of the Congo *(cont.)*

Mwindo sang and danced and waved his conga.

> *I am Mwindo,*
> *the one born walking,*
> *the one born talking.*
> *O my father, still you do not want me.*
> *O my father, now you try to kill me.*
> *But what can you do against me?*

All the men of Tubondo got up. They said, "What a great man is Mwindo! What can anyone do against you?"

Mwindo stopped dancing. He looked around. "Where is my father?"

Iyangura came up. "O Mwindo, your father ran out the other gate."

Mwindo ran from the village. He saw his father. His father ran fast. Mwindo ran faster. Mwindo caught his father. They fell to the ground.

Shemwindo trembled and shook and quaked. He said, "Will you kill me?"

Mwindo said, "No, I will not kill you."

"Will you hurt me?"

"No, I will not hurt you."

"Will you take what is mine?"

"No, I will not take what is yours."

"Then what do you want with me?"

Mwindo said, "A father cannot be a father without a son, and a son cannot be a son without a father. You must be my father so I can be your son."

Shemwindo was astonished. "What a wise young man is Mwindo! What a mistake to reject him! No more will Shemwindo reject him. I will be your father, and you will be my son."

Mwindo sang and danced and waved his conga.

> *I am Mwindo,*
> *the one born walking,*
> *the one born talking.*
> *O my father, you did not want me.*
> *O my father, you tried to get rid of me.*
> *Then you tried to kill me.*
> *Then you ran from me.*
> *But the son caught his father.*
> *The father faced his son.*
> *Now Shemwindo has a son!*
> *Now Mwindo has a father!*

Mwindo and his father returned to the village. Everyone was happy to see them—Iyangura, the counselors, the seven wives of the chief, all the people of Tubondo.

Shemwindo told them, "This I have learned: A man must not value only a daughter or only a son. Each is a blessing of its own. What a wonderful son is Mwindo!"

Planning Our Rewrite for Reader's Theater

You have been given the task of working together as a group to rewrite and perform the narrative "The Magic Flyswatter: A Hero Tale of the Congo" as reader's theater. You can use this page as a guide for planning how you will do this.

Group # _____ Date of our performance: _____

Names of group members: _____

_____

_____

1. **Make sure everyone understands the concept of Reader's Theater.** Reader's theater is written as a script, like a play, but there are important differences. Although you practice for the performance, you do not memorize your lines. You may have simple props, but there are no costumes, sets, or action. The script may have a few parts, many parts, and even parts read by all participants together.

2. **Plan how many parts there will be and who will perform each part.** Reread the narrative version of the story. Keep track of how many different characters speak in addition to the narrator or storyteller. List the different parts and decide together who will take each part. If there are not enough individual parts, have two or more read a part together. For example, several students can read Mwindo's refrain, which occurs just after the repeated line, *"Mwindo sang and danced and waved his conga."* You might even have more than one narrator. Perhaps one person could read just that line every time it occurs. Also, keep in mind that if there is a part said by more than one person, such as the Tubondo men, it should be read by more than one person. Each student may have more than one speaking part.

3. **Decide how you will make your presentation interesting and enjoyable for the audience.** Since costumes and action are not part of reader's theater, think about ways to engage your listeners. For example, do you want to use any simple props? If so, what? Do you want audience participation? Perhaps you could have them repeat something you read, such as the part of Mwindo's repetition of *"I am Mwindo, the one born walking, the one born talking."* Another idea is to have the characters read their parts in special voices. For example, the part of Shimwindo could be read in a purposely deep and heavy voice, while the part of Mwindo's mother as she says, *"Aieeeeeee!"* could be shrill. You could have the reader change the tone of voice along with the mood of the character. Perhaps Shemwindo's voice is deep and loud when he is being threatening, but softer and higher when he is scared.

Planning Our Rewrite
for Reader's Theater *(cont.)*

4. **Figure out how you will do the actual rewriting in script form.** Perhaps you will share this task, with each person doing a portion, or perhaps someone will want to do it all. Will you do it on a computer or will it be handwritten? How will you reproduce copies for your whole group? (Perhaps your teacher will help with this.)

5. **Practice, practice, practice!** Use the time you are given to practice reading your script together. Make sure that you are all reading your parts fluently. If there are things that don't work the way you planned, now is the time to make changes. Be sure that everyone is aware of any changes you make so that the final presentation goes smoothly. Finally, have fun!

The Mystery of the Mayas

Excerpts from *The Myths of Mexico and Peru* by Lewis Spence, 1913

Objective

√ Students will demonstrate oral reading fluency in an instructional presentation.

Preparation

√ Ask students to have their copies of the world map (pages 188–189) for each student.

√ Copy *The Mystery of the Mayas* (pages 171–173) for selected student readers.

√ Make available a computer with internet access, preferably with *PowerPoint*®. (If *PowerPoint* is not available, provide a tape recorder.)

√ For the optional Side Trip, copy *The Mayan Numeral System* (page 174) for each student.

Fluency Suggestions and Activities

Note: This lesson is a bit different from all the others in approach and participation.

1. Ask students to locate Mexico on their maps. Point out the Yucatan peninsula as the location of the Mayan civilization, which flourished in A.D. 250–900.

2. Explain to students that they will learn about the Mayas from lessons prepared by guest teachers—their classmates. These student teachers will create a presentation of the material, and the rest of the class will listen and answer questions about it in writing.

3. Even though not everyone will be reading the text, to help students comprehend what they will hear, present the historical background and preteach the vocabulary on the following page.

4. Choose a few pairs of students to prepare audio-visual lessons (ideally as a *PowerPoint* presentation with photos, illustrations, and text) that teach about the Mayas using *The Mystery of the Mayas* (pages 171–173). Students then practice reading the information and assemble coordinating slides. When they have polished their presentations, they can record the reading in *PowerPoint* for use at a center. Or, have the groups show the presentations as they read the narration live. If *PowerPoint* is unavailable, have students print their visual materials, create a picture booklet, and tape record the accompanying text.

5. Require the rest of the students to listen and answer questions as a follow up to the lesson. Have your student teachers add their own questions to the end of the presentation, or provide the questions yourself. Following are some suggestions (answers in italics):

   • Despite the achievements of the Mayas, why might have Europeans considered them uncivilized? *(Human sacrifice was considered barbaric, and therefore Europeans may have discounted their "civilized" achievements.)*

   • Why do many Mayan cities have Nahua names, which suggest Aztec origin? *(The Spanish were guided by Nahua, who applied their own designated names to the cities.)*

   • For what preventable reason are Mayan native manuscripts so few in number? *(They were purposely destroyed.)*

   • Why were Egyptian hieroglyphics decipherable, whereas the Mayan's remain mysterious? *(The Rosetta Stone supplied clues for the Egyptian hieroglyphics.)*

   • What kind of structure was as El Castillo? *(a pyramid-temple)*

The Mystery of the Mayas *(cont.)*

History Connection

In 1913, a book called *The Myths of Mexico and Peru* presented a comprehensive look at the native peoples of Mexico. Its author, Lewis Spence, attempted to demystify the people who populated Mexico before the conquest by the Spanish. To his credit, Mr. Spence remained unbiased in his descriptions and sometimes even gave concrete evidence that contradicts the generalization of native peoples of the Americas as "uncivilized" or "barbarian."

With only a few changes of wording for clarification or updating of terms, excerpts from Lewis Spence's book appear here as he wrote them.

Vocabulary Connection

Discuss unfamiliar vocabulary encountered in the text. Begin with these and then add any others you feel need to be reviewed or introduced. Discuss the words' meanings and how they are used specifically in the context of the source.

- **evinced**—revealed; showed clearly
- **appellations**—labels; tags; designations
- **ordained**—formally commanded
- **wholesale**—done on a large scale or in bulk without regard to individual items
- **bibliophiles**—people who love books or are collectors of books or manuscripts
- **Americanists**—specialists in the languages and cultures of Native Americans
- **demotic**—the late form of the Egyptian language (related to Greek); simplified hieroglyphics
- **elucidation**—a clarifying explanation; a bringing to light or understanding

Extension Ideas

- Chichen Itza is arguably the most famous of the Mayan ruins. Challenge students to compare the pyramid structures of the Mayas and other early western civilizations to those of the Egyptians.
- **Side Trip:** The Mayas are credited with a very simple, but extremely important idea—the concept of zero. Let students speculate about what it might be like without zero, and how it has impacted the development of all societies since. Next distribute copies of *The Mayan Numeral System* (page 174). Introduce the chart and read the background information. Then challenge students to write a few basic addition and subtraction facts "in Mayan" (using the Mayan number symbols in place of our numerals). Tell students that the problems cannot have an answer greater than 19. Have them leave the answers blank, and then when they have created ten problems, exchange papers with a partner to solve them (in Mayan symbols, of course). Have students check their partner's answers.

Name _____

The Mystery of the Mayas

Excerpts from *The Myths of Mexico and Peru* by Lewis Spence, 1913

Early Civilization in Mexico

The first civilized American people with whom the discoverers came into contact were those of the Nahua or ancient Mexican race. We use the term "civilized" advisedly, for although several authorities of standing have refused to regard the Mexicans as a people who had achieved such a state of culture as would entitle them to be classed among civilized communities, there is no doubt that they had advanced nearly as far as it was possible for them to proceed when their environment and the nature of the circumstances which handicapped them are taken into consideration. In architecture they had evolved a type of building, solid yet wonderfully graceful, which, if not so massive as the Egyptian and Assyrian, was yet more highly decorative. Their artistic outlook as expressed in their painting and pottery was more versatile and less conventional than that of the ancient people of the Orient, their social system was of a more advanced type, and a less rigorous attitude was evinced by the ruling caste toward the subject classes. Yet, on the other hand, the picture is darkened by the terrible if picturesque rites which attended their religious ceremonies, and the dread shadow of human sacrifice which eternally overhung their teeming populations. Nevertheless, the standard of morality was high, justice was even-handed, the forms of government were comparatively mild, and but for the fanaticism which demanded such troops of victims, we might justly compare the civilization of ancient Mexico with that of the peoples of old China or India, if the literary activity of the Oriental states be discounted.

Maya History

[Writings about this highly interesting people] as exist in English are few, and their value doubtful. For the earlier history of the people of Maya stock we depend almost wholly upon tradition and architectural remains. The net result of the evidence wrung from these is that the Maya civilization was one and homogeneous, and that all the separate states must have at one period passed through a uniform condition of culture, . . . and that this is sufficient ground for the belief that all were at one time beneath the sway of one central power. For the later history we possess the writings of the Spanish fathers, but not in such profusion as in the case of [the rest of] Mexico. In fact the trustworthy original authors who deal with Maya history can almost be counted on the fingers of one hand. We are further confused in perusing these, and, indeed, throughout the study of Maya history, by discovering that many of the sites of Maya cities are designated by Nahua names. This is due to the fact that the Spanish conquerors were guided in their conquest of the Maya territories by Nahua, who naturally applied Nahuatlac designations to those sites of which the Spaniards asked the names. These appellations clung to the places in question; hence the confusion, and the blundering theories which would read in these place-names relics of Aztec conquest.

The Mystery of the Mayas *(cont.)*

Native Manuscripts

The *pinturas*, or native manuscripts, which remain to us are but few in number. Priestly fanaticism, which ordained their wholesale destruction, and the still more potent passage of time have so reduced them that each separate example is known to bibliophiles and Americanists the world over. In such as still exist we can observe great fullness of detail, representing for the most part festivals, sacrifices, tributes, and natural phenomena, such as eclipses and floods, and the death and accession of monarchs. These events, and the supernatural beings who were supposed to control them, were depicted in brilliant colors, executed by means of a brush of feathers.

The Riddle of Ancient Mayan Writing

What may possibly be the most valuable sources of Mayan history are, alas! sealed to us at present. We allude to the native Mayan manuscripts and inscriptions, the writing of which cannot be deciphered by present-day scholars. Some of the old Spanish friars who lived in the times which directly succeeded the settlement of the country by the white man were able to read and even to write this script, but unfortunately they regarded it either as an invention of the Father of Evil or, as it was a native system, as a thing of no value. In a few generations all knowledge of how to decipher it was totally lost, and it remains to the modern world almost as a sealed book, although science has lavished all its wonderful machinery of logic and deduction upon it, and men of unquestioned ability have dedicated their lives to the problem of unraveling what must be regarded as one of the greatest and most mysterious riddles of which mankind ever attempted the solution.

The romance of the discovery of the key to the Egyptian hieroglyphic system of writing is well known. For centuries the symbols displayed upon the temples and monuments of the Nile country were so many meaningless pictures and signs to the learned folk of Europe, until the discovery of the Rosetta stone a hundred years ago made their elucidation possible. This stone bore the same inscription in Greek, demotic, and hieroglyphics, and so the discovery of the "alphabet" of the hidden script became a comparatively easy task. But Central America has no Rosetta stone, nor is it possible that such an aid to research can ever be found. Indeed, such "keys" as have been discovered or brought forward by scientists have proved for the most part unavailing.

The Mystery of the Mayas (cont.)

Chichen-Itza

At Chichen-Itza, in Yucatan, the chief wonder is the gigantic pyramid-temple known as El Castillo. It is reached by a steep flight of steps, and from it the vast ruins of Chichen radiate in a circular manner. To the east is the market-place, to the north a mighty temple, and a tennis-court, perhaps the best example of its kind in Yucatan, whilst to the west stand the Nunnery and the Chichan-Chob, or prison. Concerning Chichen-Itza, Cogolludo tells the following story:

"A king of Chichen called Canek fell desperately in love with a young princess, who, whether she did not return his affection or whether she was compelled to obey a parental mandate, married a more powerful Yucatec cacique. The discarded lover, unable to bear his loss, and moved by love and despair, armed his dependents and suddenly fell upon his successful rival. Then the gaiety of the feast was exchanged for the din of war, and amidst the confusion the Chichen prince disappeared, carrying off the beautiful bride. But conscious that his power was less than his rival's, and fearing his vengeance, he fled the country with most of his vassals."

It is a historical fact that the inhabitants of Chichen abandoned their city, but whether for the reason given in this story or not cannot be discovered.

Pam Burley/Shutterstock, Inc.

Name_____

The Mayan Numeral System

Excerpts from *The Myths of Mexico and Peru* by Lewis Spence, 1913

The Maya numeral system was on a very much higher basis than that of many civilized peoples, being, for example more practical and more fully evolved than that of ancient Rome. This system employed four signs altogether, the point for unity, a horizontal stroke for the number 5, and two signs for 20 and 0. Yet

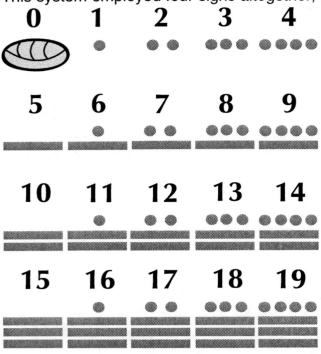

from these simple elements, the Maya produced a method of computation which is perhaps as ingenious as anything which has ever been accomplished in the history of mathematics. In the Maya arithmetical system, as in ours, it is the position of the sign that gives it its value. The figures were placed in a vertical line, and one of them was employed as a decimal multiplier. The lowest figure of the column had the arithmetical value which it represented. The figures which appeared in the second, fourth, and each following place had 20 times the value of the preceding figures, while figures in the third place had 18 times the value of those in the second place. This system admits of computation up to millions, and is one of the surest signs of Maya [as an advanced and civilized] culture.

How Is Your Mayan Math?

Try This! Use a sheet of blank paper. On it, write ten basic addition and subtraction facts for a classmate to solve. The basic facts are those you had to memorize when you were first learning to add and subtract. Remember 2 + 3, 9 − 5, and 7 + 7? Easy, right? But instead of using the numbers 0 through 19, you are going to write the problems using the Mayan symbols. When you have drawn ten basic facts, trade papers with a partner and solve each other's problems. The answers should be in Mayan numerals, of course! When you are finished, trade back and check your partner's work.

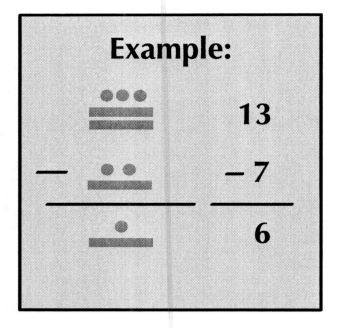

The Incas of Peru

Excerpts from *The Myths of Mexico and Peru* by Lewis Spence, 1913

Objective

√ Students will participate in an oral reading of a text, using a tape recorder to practice and evaluate their fluency.

Preparation

√ Ask students to have their copies of the world map (pages 188–189) from previous lessons.

√ Have two or more tape recorders available.

√ Copy *The Incas of Peru* (pages 178–179) for each student.

Fluency Suggestions and Activities

To help students analyze the text and read with comprehension and fluency, present the historical background and preteach the vocabulary on the following pages before starting the fluency activity.

1. Have students first locate South America on their maps, and then the Andes mountain range and Peru. Explain to students that the Incan Empire was centered in what is now Peru from 1438 to 1533. Over that period, the Incas used conquest and peaceful assimilation to incorporate into their empire a large portion of western South America. The Incan Empire was short-lived. By 1533, Atahualpa, the last Incan emperor, was killed on the orders of the conquistador Francisco Pizarro, marking the beginning of Spanish rule.

2. After sharing the background in the History Connection section, distribute copies of *The Incas of Peru* (pages 178–179). Ask students to follow along as you model reading the text fluently. Take a few moments to discuss the content and ask questions that will let you know how well students understood the passage.

3. Read the first paragraph as if a robot were reciting it. Ask a volunteer to reread the first paragraph in a more fluid manner. Remind students that fluent reading involves reading the words accurately, but also with appropriate expression and flow. Ask different volunteers to read the remaining paragraphs.

4. Divide the class in half. Explain that the class will have an oral reading competition. Each group is to prepare a fluent reading of the text, and you will record their performances. There are 14 paragraphs, so each group will have to divide up the reading accordingly. (Some may have more than one part, or a part can be read in unison by more than one student.) Let students practice with a tape recorder, if possible. Then record their final reading as their performance.

5. Play both recordings to the group. Then tell students that the competition was not against the other group, but against themselves! Have them listen to their own reading and then fill out the evaluation of their own individual performance (bottom of page 179).

The Incas of Peru (cont.)

History Connection

Of all the major peoples who inhabited the Americas before the arrival of the Europeans, the Incas are probably the least familiar to us. There are similarities between these native peoples, who lived in the area of what is now Peru in South America, and those who lived in what is now Mexico. However, there are distinctive differences as well. As stated in the previous lesson about the Mayas, in 1913 a book called *The Myths of Mexico and Peru* presented a comprehensive look at the native peoples of Mexico. Its author, Lewis Spence, attempted to demystify much of the speculation about the nature of these people.

The fluency lesson focuses on one aspect of Incan life—the customs surrounding the end of life. For this, Lewis Spence relies on the description given by an earlier writer, Joseph Skinner (1805). Spence introduces the quote with this preface: "A quaint account of the methods of the medicine men of the Indians of the Peruvian Andes probably illustrates the manner in which the superstitions of a barbarian people evolve into a more stately ritual." This suggests at least, that Skinner's account may or may not be entirely without embellishment.

With only a few changes of wording for clarification or updating of terms, the excerpts from Lewis Spence's book appear as he wrote them. Keep in mind that this was written almost 100 years ago. You may either have to explain Spence's reference to surveillance in Russia or omit that sentence (in italics) as you read the information to students.

An Absolute Theocracy: The empire of Peru was the most absolute theocracy the world has ever seen. The Incas were the direct representative of the sun upon earth, the head of a socio-religious edifice, intricate and highly organized. This colossal bureaucracy had ramifications into the very homes of the people. The Incas were represented in the provinces by governors of the blood-royal. Officials were placed above ten thousand families, a thousand families, and even ten families, upon the principle that the rays of the sun enter everywhere, and that therefore the light of the Incas must penetrate to every corner of the empire. There was no such thing as personal freedom. Every man, woman, and child was numbered, branded, and under surveillance as much as were the llamas in the royal herds. Individual effort or enterprise was unheard of. Some writers have stated that a system of state socialism was obtained in Peru. *If so, then state surveillance in Central Russia might also be branded as socialism.* A man's life was planned for him by the authorities from the age of five years, and even the woman whom he was to marry was selected for him by the Government officials. The age at which the people should marry was fixed at not earlier than twenty-four years for a man and eighteen for a woman. Colored ribbons worn round the head indicated the place of a person's birth or the province to which he belonged.

The Incas of Peru (cont.)

History Connection (cont.)

The Character of Incan Civilization: Apart from the treatment which they meted out to the subject races under their sway, the rule of the Incan monarchs was enlightened and contained the elements of high civilization. It is scarcely clear whether the Incan race arrived in the country at such a date as would have permitted them to profit by adopting the arts and sciences of the Andean people who preceded them. But it may be affirmed that their arrival considerably post-dated the fall of the megalithic empire of the Andeans, so that in reality their civilization was of their own manufacture. As architects they were by no means the inferiors of the prehistoric race. Their massive art and engineering skills—with which they pushed long, straight tunnels through vast mountains and bridged seemingly impassable gorges—still excite the wonder of modern experts. They also made long, straight roads after the most improved macadamized* model. Their temples and palaces were adorned with gold and silver images and ornaments; sumptuous baths supplied with hot and cold water by means of pipes laid in the earth were to be found in the mansions of the nobility, and much luxury and real comfort prevailed.

*See Vocabulary Connection below.

Vocabulary Connection

Discuss unfamiliar vocabulary encountered in the text. Begin with these and then add any others you feel need to be reviewed or introduced. Discuss the words' meanings and how they are used specifically in the context of the source.

- ***macadamized**—paved with stone mixed with tar or asphalt in compressed layers
- *agorero* (Spanish)—a person who prophesies, or fortune-teller
- **falsetto**—artificially high voice
- **quadrupeds**—four-footed animals (Latin: *quad*-four; *ped*-foot)
- **effected**—done; carried out
- **expelled**—pushed or driven out by force
- *masato* (Spanish)—a fermented drink
- **exequies**—funeral rites or ceremonies

Extension Idea

- Challenge students to compare and contrast the Mayas and Incas. After students have done some research, have them create a Venn diagram or write a short compare-and-contrast essay based on their work. There are many resources available on the web, including the entire text of *The Myths of Mexico and Peru*, by Lewis Spence (excerpted in the lessons on the Mayas and the Aztecs as well as this one on the Incas).

Name _____

The Incas of Peru

Excerpts from *The Myths of Mexico and Peru* by Lewis Spence, 1913

Inca Life, Death, and the Medicine Man

"It cannot be denied that the *mohanes* [priests] have, by practice and tradition, acquired a knowledge of many plants and poisons, with which they effect surprising cures on the one hand, and do much mischief on the other, but the mania of ascribing the whole to a preternatural virtue occasions them to blend with their practice a thousand charms and superstitions.

The most customary method of cure is to place two hammocks close to each other, either in the dwelling, or in the open air: in one of them the patient lies extended, and in the other the *mohane*, or *agorero*. The latter, in contact with the sick man, begins by rocking himself, and then proceeds, by a strain in falsetto, to call on the birds, quadrupeds, and fishes to give health to the patient.

From time to time he rises on his seat, and makes a thousand extravagant gestures over the sick man, to whom he applies his powders and herbs, or sucks the wounded or diseased parts. If the malady augments, the *agorero*, having been joined by many of the people, chants a short hymn, addressed to the soul of the patient, with this burden: 'Thou must not go, thou must not go.'

In repeating this he is joined by the people, until at length a terrible clamor is raised, and augmented in proportion as the sick man becomes still fainter and fainter, to the end that it may reach his ears.

When all the charms are unavailing, and death approaches, the *mohane* leaps from his hammock, and betakes himself to flight, amid the multitude of sticks, stones, and clods of earth which are showered on him.

Successively all those who belong to the nation assemble, and, dividing themselves into bands, each of them (if he who is in his last agonies is a warrior) approaches him, saying: 'Whither goest thou? Why dost thou leave us? With whom shall we proceed to the aucas [the enemies]?'

They then relate to him the heroic deeds he has performed, the number of those he has slain, and the pleasures he leaves behind him. This is practiced in different tones while some raise the voice, it is lowered by others and the poor sick man is obliged to support these importunities without a murmur, until the first symptoms of approaching dissolution manifest themselves.

Then it is that he is surrounded by a multitude of females, some of whom forcibly close the mouth and eyes, others envelop him in the hammock, oppressing him with the whole of their weight, and causing him to expire before his time, and others, lastly, run to extinguish the candle, and dissipate the smoke, that the soul, not being able to perceive the hole through which it may escape, may remain entangled in the structure of the roof. That this may be speedily effected, and to prevent its return to the interior of the dwelling, they surround the entrances with filth, by the stench of which it may be expelled.

The Incas of Peru *(cont.)*

As soon as the dying man is suffocated by the closing of the mouth, nostrils, etc., and wrapped up in the covering of his bed, the most circumspect, whether male or female, takes him in the arms in the best manner possible, and gives a *gentle* shriek, which echoes to the bitter lamentations of the immediate relatives, and to the cries of a thousand old women collected for the occasion.

As long as this dismal howl subsists, the latter are subjected to a constant fatigue, raising the palm of the hand to wipe away the tears, and lowering it to dry it on the ground. The result of this alternate action is, that a circle of earth, which gives them a most hideous appearance, is collected about the eyelids and brows, and they do not wash themselves until the mourning is over.

These first clamors conclude by several good pots of *masato*, to assuage the thirst of sorrow, and the company next proceed to make a great clatter among the utensils of the deceased: some break the kettles, and others the earthen pots, while others, again, burn the apparel, to the end that his memory may be the sooner forgotten.

If the defunct has been a *cacique*, or powerful warrior, his exequies are performed after the manner of the Romans: they last for many days, all the people weeping in concert for a considerable space of time, at daybreak, at noon, in the evening, and at midnight.

When the appointed hour arrives, the mournful music begins in front of the house of the wife and relatives, the heroic deeds of the deceased being chanted to the sound of instruments. All the inhabitants of the vicinity unite in chorus from within their houses, some chirping like birds, others howling like tigers, and the greater part of them chattering like monkeys, or croaking like frogs.

They constantly leave off by having recourse to the *masato*, and by the destruction of whatever the deceased may have left behind him, the burning of his dwelling being that which concludes the ceremonies. Among some of the Peruvian Indians, the nearest relatives cut off their hair as a token of their grief. . . ."

Follow-up Directions: Listen to the performance of Inca Life, Death, and the Medicine Man. Then evaluate it by filling out the rating scale below. Circle your rating for the group in blue and your rating of your own performance in red.

  1. Accuracy *(reading the words correctly)*

1	2	3	4	5
Awesome. . . . . .Good . . . . Needs Work				

  2. Pacing *(reading at a good rate for listeners to follow and understand)*

1	2	3	4	5
Awesome. . . . . .Good . . . . Needs Work				

  3. Expression *(reading smoothly, with good phrasing, and with appropriate feeling)*

1	2	3	4	5
Awesome. . . . . .Good . . . . Needs Work				

Sacred Songs of the Aztecs

Excerpts from *Rig Veda Americanus* by Daniel G. Brinton, 1890

Objective

√ Students will participate in a cooperative choral reading activity and independent reading extension activities to increase fluency and comprehension.

Preparation

√ Ask students to have their copies of the world map (pages 188–189) from previous lessons.

√ Copy for the student readers *Sacred Songs of the Aztecs* (pages 182–183) and as needed *Who Were the Aztecs?* (pages 184–185)

√ For the optional Side Trips, copy *Legends of the Foundation of Mexico* (page 186) and *Before and After the Conquest* (page 187) for each student.

Fluency Suggestions and Activities

To help students analyze the text and read with comprehension and fluency, present the historical background and preteach the vocabulary on the following page before starting the fluency activity.

Note: The core fluency activity of this lesson is oral reading of the sacred songs, however, several related reading activities are provided to use at your option—each based on different primary sources. *Who Were the Aztecs?* (pages 184–185) includes additional excerpts from Lewis Spence's book *The Myths of Mexico and Peru*. This would be useful as a prereading activity before studying the sacred songs.

1. Ask students to locate central Mexico on their maps. Explain that this was the area of the Aztec empire in the 1500s, before the arrival of the Spanish.

2. Choose how you want to use and perform the sources. On pages 182–183 are two separate hymns, or sacred songs, of the Aztecs. The first is divided into ten reading parts, intended to be used for line-a-child reading or group choral reading. The second hymn is also divided into separate parts, but with blanks for you to label the parts. For example, you may want to have it read by two voices or use the cumulative reading approach (see page 18).

3. Regardless of which method you choose to have students participate in oral reading, begin by modeling fluent reading and sharing the author's notes at the bottom of the page. Then allow students to practice several times before performing their final reading. Remind students to show appropriate expression in their voices to convey the intended emotion of the lines.

4. If possible, coordinate your students' performances with a multicultural event at your school. If you like, add to your presentation by asking student volunteers to read the supplementary material on the Aztecs included in this lesson.

Sacred Songs of the Aztecs *(cont.)*

History Connection

The Aztecs thrived in central Mexico from the fourteenth to the sixteenth century. They called themselves Mexicas, pronounced *Meshica* in accordance with the Spanish spelling practiced at that time. The Republic of Mexico and its capital, Mexico City, derive their names from the word *Mexica*. The capital of the Aztec empire was Tenochtitlan, built on raised islets in Lake Texcoco (Tezcuco). Mexico City, the capital of the country of Mexico today, is built on the ruins of Tenochtitlan (Tezcuco).

Moctezuma II (also Montezuma) was the ruler of the Aztecs from 1502 to 1520, when the Spanish conquest of Mexico began. Spanish conquistador Hernán Cortés arrived in Tenochtitlan on November 8, 1519.

At the time of his arrival, it is believed that the city of Tenochtitlan was one of the largest in the world. Common estimates put the population between 60,000 and 130,000 people. Because of a prophecy and a number of events that occurred seemingly to confirm it, Montezuma may have believed Cortés to be the returning god Quetzalcoatl, and welcomed him with great honor. The Spanish not only conquered the Mexicas with weapons, but also brought diseases, such as smallpox, that took the lives of large numbers of the people.

Vocabulary Connection

Begin with the notes by the author, which explain a bit of background that helps with reading and understanding the hymns. Then discuss any additional unfamiliar vocabulary encountered in the notes or hymns. Begin with these and then add any others you feel need to be introduced.

- **pantheon**—the group of all the deities (gods) of a specific religion
- **terrestrial**—having to do with or belonging to the Earth or land
- **doctrine**—rules, principles, or ideas taught as absolute truth
- **maguey**—a variety of tropical plant cultivated in Mexico and other tropical regions
- **liberality**—generosity; largeness in size or amount; broad-mindedness

Extension Ideas

- **Side Trip, Part 1:** Extend learning and opportunities to read for meaning by sharing *Legends of the Foundation of Mexico* (page 186) with students. Here they read expository text written in 1913 that tells the stories of how the symbols of the eagle, cactus, and serpent on the flag of Mexico may have come to be. There is also a vocabulary activity that challenges students to use context clues first to try to determine word meanings.
- **Side Trip, Part 2:** *Before and After the Conquest* (page 187) offers students two primary sources—a quote by an explorer in 1840 and a 1585 illustration of a meeting between the Aztecs and the Spanish. Students begin with the facts and then read and react (orally or in writing) to an observer's words. The challenge is to make the connection between the two in a leap of cause-and-effect reasoning.

Name _____

Sacred Songs of the Aztecs

"Hymn III" from *Rig Veda Americanus*, with notes by Daniel G. Brinton, 1890

The Hymn of Tlaloc

R1:   In Mexico the god appears; thy banner is unfolded in all directions, and no one weeps.

R2:   I, the god, have returned again, I have turned again to the place of abundance of blood-sacrifices; there when the day grows old, I am beheld as a god.

R3:   Thy work is that of a noble magician; truly thou hast made thyself to be of our flesh; thou hast made thyself, and who dare affront thee?

R4:   Truly he who affronts me does not find himself well with me; my fathers took by the head the tigers and the serpents.

R5:   In Tlalocan, in the verdant house, they play at ball, they cast the reeds.

R6:   Go forth, go forth to where the clouds are spread abundantly, where the thick mist makes the cloudy house of Tlaloc.

R7:   There with strong voice I rise up and cry aloud.

R8:   Go ye forth to seek me, seek for the words which I have said, as I rise, a terrible one, and cry aloud.

R9:   After four years they shall go forth, not to be known, not to be numbered, they shall descend to the beautiful house, to unite together and know the doctrine.

R10: Go forth, go forth to where the clouds are spread abundantly, where the thick mist makes the cloudy house of Tlaloc.

Notes

The god Tlaloc shared with Huitzilopochtli the highest place in the Mexican pantheon. He was the deity who presided over the waters, the rains, the thunder, and the lightning. The annual festival in his honor took place about the time of corn-planting, and was intended to secure his favor for this all-important crop. His name is derived from *tlalli*, earth. Tlalocan, referred to in #5, "the place of Tlaloc," was the name of a mountain east of Tenochtitlan, where the festival of the god was celebrated, but it also had a mythical meaning, equivalent to "the earthly Paradise," the abode of happy souls.

In #6 and #10, . . . "house of mist," [refers to] the home of the rain god, which was represented at the annual festival by four small buildings near the water's edge, carefully disposed to face the four cardinal points of the compass.

In #10, . . . "after four years" appears to refer to the souls of the departed brave ones, who, according to Aztec mythology, passed to the heaven for four years and after that returned to the terrestrial Paradise, the palace of Tlaloc.

Sacred Songs of the Aztecs (cont.)

Hymn to the Mother of the Gods

_____ Hail to our mother, who caused the yellow flowers to blossom, who scattered the seeds of the maguey, as she came forth from Paradise.

_____ Hail to our mother, who poured forth flowers in abundance, who scattered the seeds of the maguey, as she came forth from Paradise.

_____ Hail to our mother, who caused the yellow flowers to blossom, she who scattered the seeds of the maguey, as she came forth from Paradise.

_____ Hail to our mother, who poured forth white flowers in abundance, who scattered the seeds of the maguey, as she came forth from Paradise.

_____ Hail to the goddess who shines in the thorn bush like a bright butterfly.

_____ Ho! She is our mother, goddess of the earth, she supplies food in the desert to the wild beasts, and causes them to live.

_____ Thus, thus, you see her to be an ever-fresh model of liberality toward all flesh.

_____ And as you see the goddess of the earth do to the wild beasts, so also does she toward the green herbs and the fishes.

Notes

The goddess to whom this hymn is devoted was called Teleoinan, the Mother of the Gods, Toçi, our Mother (maternal ancestor), and also by another name which signified "the Heart of the Earth," the latter being bestowed upon her because she was believed to be the cause of earthquakes. Her general functions were those of a genius of fertility, extending both to the vegetable and the animal world. Thus, she was the patroness of the native midwives and of women in childbirth. Her chief temple at Tepeyacac was one of the most renowned in ancient Mexico.

In #1, the reference to Paradise (Tamoanchan) is synonymous with Xochitlycacan, "the place where the flowers are lifted." It was the mystical Paradise of the Aztecs, the Home of the Gods, and the happy realm of departed souls. It was believed that the gods were born there, which explains the introduction of the word into this hymn.

Name _____

Who Were the Aztecs?

Directions: Read the general information below about the Aztecs, which comes from *The Myths of Mexico and Peru*, written in 1913 by Lewis Spence. This will not only help prepare you for oral reading about the Aztecs, but also give you some background about the people. Remember, the object of reading is not just to be able to say the words, but to understand, learn, and enjoy. When you finish each section, check your understanding by answering the questions that follow.

The Earliest Mexicans

The earliest Mexicans are known as the Nahua (Those who live by Rule), a title adopted by them to distinguish them from those tribes who still roamed in an unsettled condition over the contiguous plains of New Mexico and the more northerly tracts. Much controversy has raged around the question regarding the original home of the Nahua, but their migration legends consistently point to a northern origin. In Nahua tradition the name of the locality where the people began their wanderings is called Aztlan (The Place of Reeds), but this place-name is of little or no value as a guide to any given region, though probably every spot between the Bering Strait and Mexico has been identified with it by zealous antiquarians. Other names discovered in the migration legends are Tlapallan (The Country of Bright Colors) and Chicomoztoc (The Seven Caves), and these may perhaps be identified with New Mexico or Arizona.

1. The Nahua migrated from a more northern region than the area that is now Mexico. Is this statement a fact, an opinion, or speculation (a guess): _____

2. Why is it so difficult to pinpoint the location from which the Nahua began their wanderings?

_____

Legends of Mexican Migration

All early writers on the history of Mexico agree that the Toltecs were the first of the several swarms of Nahua who streamed upon the Mexican plateau in ever-widening waves. Ixtlilxochitl, a native chronicler who flourished shortly after the Spanish conquest of Mexico, gives two separate accounts of the early Toltec migrations, the first of which goes back to the period of their arrival in the fabled land of Tlapallan, alluded to above. In this account Tlapallan is described as a region near the sea, which the Toltecs reached by voyaging southward, skirting the coasts of California. It is not outside the bounds of possibility that the early swarms of Nahua immigrants made their way to Mexico by sea, but it is much more probable that their migrations took place by land, following the level country at the base of the Rocky Mountains.

3. Was Ixtlilxochitl a person, place, or thing? _____

4. Does the author think the Toltecs more likely arrived by land or by sea?

_____

Who Were the Aztecs? *(cont.)*

The Nahua Peoples

The Nahua peoples included all those tribes speaking the Nahuatlatolli (Nahua tongue), and occupied a sphere extending from the southern borders of New Mexico to the Isthmus of Tehuantepec on the south, or very much within the limits of the modern Republic of Mexico. But this people must not be regarded as of one homogeneous origin. There are circumstances which justify the assumption that on their entrance to the Mexican valley they consisted of a number of tribes loosely united, presenting in their general organization a close resemblance to some of the composite tribes of modern American Indians.

5. To what does the author compare the organization of the Nahua? _____

6. Were the Nahua a single, united group of people? _____

The Aztecs

The Aztecâ, or Aztecs, were a nomad tribe of doubtful origin, but probably of Nahua blood. Wandering over the Mexican plateau for generations, they at last settled in the marshlands near the Lake of Tezcuco. The name Aztecâ means "Crane People." They founded the town of Tenochtitlan, or Mexico, and for a while paid tribute to the Tecpanecs. But later they became the most powerful allies of that people, whom they finally surpassed entirely in power and splendor.

7. What does the word *blood* mean as it is used here? _____

8. Does the author tell us that the Aztecs conquered the Tecpanecs? _____

The Aztec Character

The features of the Aztecs as represented in the various Mexican paintings are typically Indian, and argue a northern origin. The people were, and are, of average height, and the skin is of a dark brown hue. The Mexican is grave, taciturn, and melancholic, with a deeply rooted love of the mysterious, slow to anger, yet almost inhuman in the violence of his passions when aroused. He is usually gifted with a logical mind, quickness of apprehension, and an ability to regard the subtle side of things with great nicety. Patient and imitative, the ancient Mexican excelled in those arts which demanded such qualities in their execution. He had a real affection for the beautiful in nature and a passion for flowers, but the Aztec music lacked gaiety, and the national amusements were too often of a gloomy and ferocious character. The women are more vivacious than the men, but were in the days before the conquest very subservient to the wills of their husbands.

9. In this paragraph does the author mainly use fact or opinion for his description?

_____

10. Does the author have more positive or negative impressions of the people?

_____

11. What does *taciturn* mean? _____ *melancholic*? _____

Name _____

Legends of the Foundation of Mexico

Directions: Read the information below, which comes from *The Myths of Mexico and Peru*, written in 1913 by Lewis Spence. Then look at the five words below. If you already know their meanings, write a word that means the same thing or a phrase that tells what each word means in simple terms. If you don't know what a word means, look it up in a dictionary.

At the period of the conquest of Mexico by Cortés, the city presented an imposing appearance. Led to its neighborhood by Huitzilopochtli, a traditional chief afterwards deified as the god of war, there are several legends which account for the choice of its site by the Mexicans. The most popular of these relates how the nomadic Nahua beheld perched upon a cactus plant an eagle of great size and majesty, grasping in its talons a huge serpent, and spreading its wings to catch the rays of the rising sun. The soothsayers or medicine-men of the tribe, reading a good omen in the spectacle, advised the leaders of the people to settle on the spot, and, hearkening to the voice of what they considered divine authority, they proceeded to drive piles into the marshy ground, and thus laid the foundation of the great city of Mexico.

Daniel Gilbey/Shutterstock, Inc.

An elaboration of this legend tells how the Aztecs had about the year 1325 sought refuge upon the western shore of the Lake of Tezcuco, in an island among the marshes on which they found a stone on which forty years before one of their priests had sacrificed a prince of the name of Copal, whom they had made prisoner. A nopal plant [cactus] had sprung from an earth-filled crevice in this rude altar, and upon this the royal eagle alluded to in the former account had alighted, grasping the serpent in his talons. Beholding in this a good omen, and urged by a supernatural impulse which he could not explain, a priest of high rank dived into a pool close at hand, where he found himself face to face with Tlaloc, the god of waters. After an interview with the deity the priest obtained permission from him to found a city on the site, from the humble beginnings of which arose the metropolis of Mexico-Tenochtitlan.

1. imposing: _____

2. nomadic: _____

3. talons: _____

4. hearkening: _____

5. crevice: _____

Mislik/Shutterstock, Inc.

Name _____

Before and After the Conquest

In 1519 Hernán Cortés sailed from Cuba, landed in Mexico, and made his way to the Aztec capital. There he met Montezuma, the Aztec ruler, who, based on a prophecy, may have mistakenly thought that the strange white men were gods. He welcomed them with open arms and lavish gifts. The white men saw many things that would bring them riches back in Spain. Going back on their word as "friends," they slaughtered unarmed people and eventually conquered Mexico.

Read the following quote, and be prepared to offer your thoughts and feelings about it.

> **"We sat down on the very edge of the wall, and strove in vain to penetrate the mystery by which we were surrounded. Who were the people that built this city? In the ruined cities of Egypt, even in the long-lost Petra, the stranger knows the story of the people whose vestiges are around him. America, say historians, was peopled by savages; but savages never reared these structures, savages never carved these stones. We asked the Indians who made them, and their dull answer was 'Quien sabe?'—'Who knows?'"**
>
> —John Lloyd Stephens, explorer and travel-writer,
> recounting his explorations in Central America, 1840

World Map

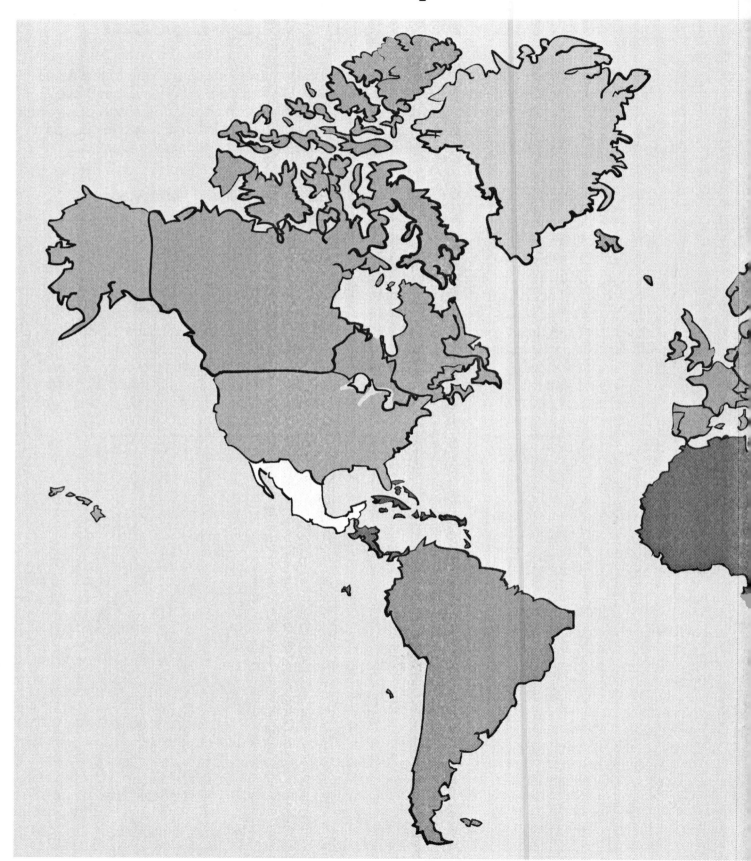

World Map (cont.)

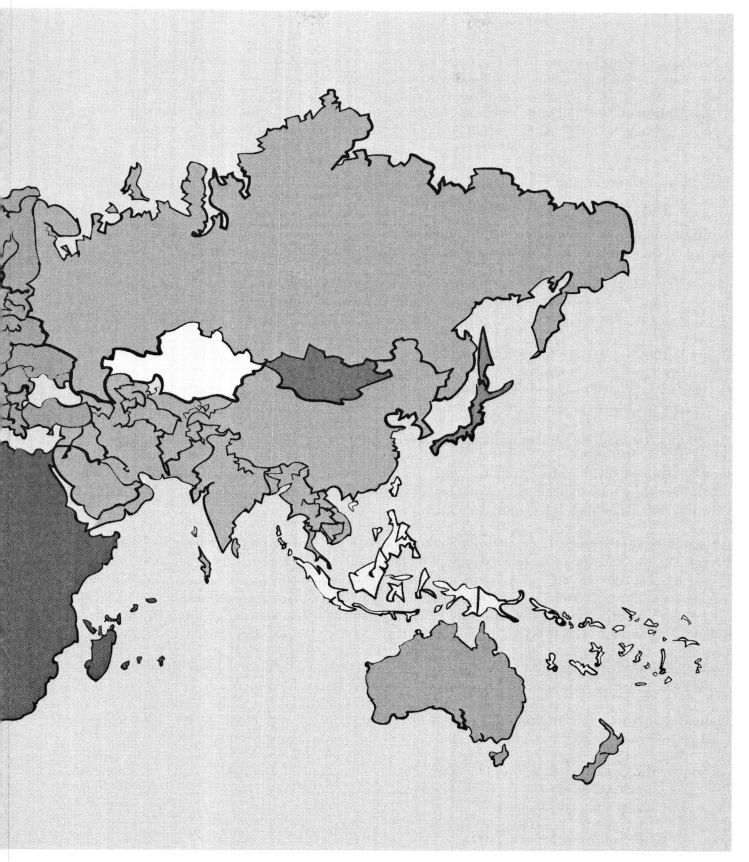

Notes

The following are notes from the author to provide information about the primary sources used in this book.

A Sumerian Poem: Excerpts from *The Ludlul Bêl Nimeqi.* George A. Barton, *Archaeology and The Bible,* 3rd ed. Philadelphia: American Sunday School, 1920.*

A Description of Mesopotamia: Excerpts from *Pliny the Elder, The Natural History, Book VI.* John Bostock, M.D., F.R.S. H.T. Riley, Esq., B.A. London: Taylor and Francis, Red Lion Court, Fleet Street, 1855.

The Code of Hammurabi: Excerpts from *Hammurabi's Code of Laws.* Translated by L.W. (Leonard William) King, 1869–1919. T & T Clark, January, 1903.

Ten Babylonian Proverbs: Excerpts from *Babylonian Proverbs from the Library of Ashurbanipal.* George A. Barton, *Archaeology and The Bible,* 3rd ed. Philadelphia: American Sunday School, 1920.*

The Shipwrecked Sailor: Excerpts from *The Shipwrecked Sailor.* Eva March Tappan, ed., *The World's Story: A History of the World in Story, Song and Art,* Vol. 3: *Egypt, Africa, and Arabi,* translated by W. K. Flinders Petrie. Boston: Houghton Mifflin, 1914.***

Hymn to the Nile: Hymn from *The Library of Original Sources, Vol. I: The Ancient World.* Oliver J. Thatcher, ed. Milwaukee: University Research Extension Co., 1907.**; "The History of Plumbing—Egypt" article printed in *Plumbing and Mechanical Magazine,* July, 1989. (Jim Olsztynski, Editorial Director; **www.PMmag.com**) Used with permission.

Herodotus' Description of Mummification: Excerpt from Herodotus's *The Histories.* 440 B.C.

Exodus from Egypt: Excerpts from the *Old Testament: Book of Exodus Revised Standard Version.* Provided in the public domain by Exploring Ancient World Cultures (EAWC) Internet Index; "Go Down Moses" from Shell Education, Book 8187.

Ancient Greek Olympics: Excerpts from Strabo's *The Geography of Strabo.* Strabo. ed. H. L. Jones. Cambridge, Mass.: Harvard University Press; London: William Heinemann, Ltd. 1924.; Excerpts from Pausanias's *Description of Greece.* Translated by W.H.S. Jones, Litt.D., and H.A. Ormerod, M.A., in 4 Volumes. Cambridge, MA: Harvard University Press; London, William Heinemann Ltd., 1918.; Single quote from Diodorus Siculus from *Historical Library,* 9.14.1. English Translation by C. H. Oldfather. Vol. 4–8. Cambridge, Mass.: Harvard University Press; London: William Heinemann, Ltd. 1989.

Aesop's Fables: Selected fables by Aesop, 620–563 B.C. Translated by George Fyler Townsend, 1814–1900. Provided in the public domain by Project Gutenberg.

Plato and Socrates: Excerpt from Plato's *Phaedrus* (360 B.C.). Translated by Benjamin Jowett. Distributed by the Greek Online Library with GNU Free Documentation License.

Alexander the Great: Excerpt from Plutarch's *Parallel Lives: Life of Alexander.* Loeb Classical Library, 1919; Excerpt from *The Odyssey.* Translated by Alexander Pope (1688–1744). Provided in the Public Domain by Project Gutenberg

Notes (cont.)

Arrian's Description of India: Excerpts from Sections XI and XII in Book 7 of Arrian's *Indica*. Extracted from *Megasthanese (Anabasis Alexandri: Book VII).**; Single quote from Swami Vivkananda, India, given in a speech on September 11, 1893.

One Law There Is: Excerpt from King Bhartrihari's poem *"One Law There Is."* Eva March Tappan, ed., *The World's Story: A History of the World in Story, Song and Art,* Vol. 2: *India, Persia, Mesopotamia, and Palestine.* Boston: Houghton Mifflin, 1914.***

Buddha and His Teachings: Background information about the Eightfold Path and selected sayings from the *Dhammapada* provided by **www.spaceandmotion.com**. Used under the site's GNU Free Documentation License.

Tales from Ancient India: Selected tales from Eva March Tappan, ed., *The World's Story: A History of the World in Story, Song and Art,* Vol. 2: *India, Persia, Mesopotamia, and Palestine.* Boston: Houghton Mifflin, 1914.***

San Zi Jing (Three Character Classic): Excerpts from the *San Zi Jing* (Sanzijiang) collection. Translated by Herbert Giles, 1910; Excerpts from *The Chinese Classics, Vol. 1.* Translated by James Legge, 1861.

Marco Polo's City of Heaven: (A.D. 1300) Excerpts from *The Book of Ser Marco Polo the Venetian concerning the Kingdoms and Marvels of the East,* Vol 2. Translated and edited by Henry Yule, 3rd ed. revised by Henri Cordier. London: John Murray, 1903.

An Old Chinese Poem: Anonymous poem. Translated by Arthur Whaley, 1919; Story "When I When to School in China" from *The World's Story: A History of the World in Story, Song, and Art,* Volume 1: *China, Japan, and the Islands of the Pacific.* Eva March Tappan, ed. Boston: Houghton Mifflin, 1914.***; Chinese characters from *Zhendic*, a Chinese (trad.)-Pinyin-English dictionary based on CEDICT (Chinese-English Dictionary Project).

Julius Caesar!: Excerpts from *Ancient Rome: From the earliest times down to 476.* Robert Franklin Pennell, 1890. Provided in the public domain by Project Gutenberg.

"The Coliseum" by Edgar Allan Poe: From *Edgar Allan Poe's Complete Poetical Works.* Edgar Allan Poe, 1839. Provided in the public domain by Project Gutenberg.

The Last Day of Pompeii: Excerpts from *Last Days of Pompeii.* Edward Bulwer Lytton, 1910. Provided in the public domain by Project Gutenberg. Also referenced: *The Letters of Pliny the Younger* (A.D. 62?–113), specifically VI.16. Provided in the public domain by Project Gutenberg.

Notes *(cont.)*

Ibn Battuta's Travels to Mali: Selected quotes from *Ibn Battuta, Travels in Asia and Africa 1325–1354.* Translated and edited by H. A. R. Gibb. London: Broadway House, 1929. Provided by the Medieval Sourcebook, **www.fordham.edu/halsal/source.**

I Was Taken from My Village and Sold!: Excerpts from *The Interesting Narrative of the Life of Olaudah Equiano, or Gustavus Vassa, the African*, Vol. 1. London, 1789. Provided in the public domain by Hanover Historical Texts Project.

The Magic Flyswatter: A Hero Tale of the Congo: A retelling of the Mwindo epic by Aaron Shepard. Printed in Cricket magazine, February, 2003. Copyright © 1999, 2003 by Aaron Shepard. Used with permission by the author. Please visit **www.aaronshep.com.**

The Mystery of the Mayas; The Inca of Peru: From *The Myths of Mexico and Peru.* Lewis Spence, 1913. Provided in the public domain by Internet Sacred Texts Archives **http://sacred-texts.com.**

Sacred Songs of the Aztecs: From *Rig Veda Americanus.* Daniel G. Brinton, 1890. Provided in the public domain by Internet Sacred Texts Archives.

Before and After the Conquest: Quote from John Lloyd Stephens, explorer and travel-writer, recounting his explorations in Central America, 1840. Provided in the public domain by Project Gutenberg.

* Portions of original materials were drawn from the *Internet History Sourcebook Projects*, which is "a collection of public domain and copy-permitted texts." **www.fordham.edu.** Care was taken to use only texts with copyright dates before 1923.

**Original scanned by Prof. J.S. Arkenberg, Cal State Fullerton.

***Prof.Arkenberg modernized the text, but without assigning a new copyright.

Additional reference material from Wikipedia, the online encyclopedia. The Wikipedia and Gutenberg Projects are under GNU Free Documentation License.